D1564654

The Outraged Conscience

The Outraged Conscience:
Seekers of Justice
for Nazi War Criminals in America

Rochelle G. Saidel

State University of New York Press
ALBANY

Published by
State University of New York Press, Albany

© 1984 State University of New York

Printed in the United States of America

For information, address State University of New York
Press, State University Plaza, Albany, N.Y., 12246

Library of Congress Cataloging in Publication Data

Saidel, Rochelle G.
    The outraged conscience.

    Includes bibliographical references.
    1. Holocaust survivors—United States—Biography.
2. Jews—United States—Biography. 3. War criminals—
Germany. I. Title.
E184.J5S28 1984   940.53'15'03924073   84–15
ISBN 0–87395–897–7
ISBN 0–87395–898–5 (pbk.)

10 9 8 7 6 5 4 3 2 1

To my parents, Florence and Joseph Saidel, and my children, Esther and Daniel Wolk—my links to seekers of justice in past and future generations.

"Let justice well up as waters, and righteousness as a mighty stream."

Book of Amos, 5:24

Contents

Acknowledgments _____

Without the cooperation of many people and the special help of a few, this book could not have been written. I am grateful to all of the seekers of justice, their families, and their colleagues who took the time to share with me knowledge, insights, and in some cases, photographs. Their names appear throughout the book, and I thank them collectively here.

Because three of the justice seekers were no longer living when I wrote about them, I am especially indebted to their family members who provided me with background: Lena Gray, mother of James Gray; Brenda Kaplowitz, widow of Seymour Kaplowitz; and Lani Yampol Gershon, granddaughter of Rabbi S. Burr Yampol.

Dr. Ezekiel Barber of Union, N.J., Norman Brickman of Albany, N.Y., and Carl and Helen Seidel of Skokie, Ill. graciously funded the expenses incurred, with donations to either the State University of New York Research Foundation or the Greater Albany Jewish Federation.

Some of the interviews in this book were originally conducted for articles I wrote (bylined Rochelle Saidel-Wolk) beginning in 1978 for the Jewish Telegraphic Agency. Murray Zuckoff, editor of JTA, has always encouraged my writing on this subject.

Dr. Robert Mandel, former editor of State University of New York Press, provided the opportunity for me to begin this book, and other editors at SUNY Press guided me during the final stages. The American Jewish Committee library was an important resource.

Throughout my writing, my father, Joseph Saidel, provided reassurance and skillful editorial advice. Charles R. Allen, Jr. first advanced the concept behind this book.

I would like to express my appreciation to all of the above-mentioned for their generous assistance and support. Special thanks to my two children, Esther and Daniel Wolk, who have shared their mother with the worst kind of "sibling rival"—the writing of a book.

To any seekers of justice whose activities I may have inadvertently omitted, I apologize. While I am deeply grateful to those whose help I have acknowledged here, I alone am responsible for any errors of omission or commission.

Rochelle G. Saidel
Albany, New York
April, 1984

Preface _____

While my own activities have exposed and sought justice for Nazi war criminals now living in Europe and Latin America, a small number of commendable individuals has been seeking justice for the Nazi war criminals who escaped to live comfortable lives in the United States.

This book documents the efforts of these noble individuals, who have dedicated themselves to the pursuit of justice. Some of their names are already well known, but, without this book, the work of others might never have been recognized. Each in his or her own way, these people have been devoted to the cause of purging Nazi evil doers from our midst.

I feel a special kinship with the people in this book, and with its author. Especially since the United States admitted utilizing and protecting Klaus Barbie, a notorious Nazi war criminal whom I have pursued for years in South America, I know that we are allies working together on a global issue.

We can only have a moral victory if there is a loud, persistent cry against injustice. By telling the stories of the criers, "The Outraged Conscience" makes this cry a little louder, a little more persistent.

Beate Klarsfeld
Paris, France
April, 1984

Introduction

The matter of Nazi war criminals in America first came home to me when the deportation hearing of accused Nazi war criminal Vilis A. Hazners began in Albany, N.Y. in February, 1977. I assumed naively that the government's case against him would be won in a few days.

I sat in the courtroom ten months later, when eyewitnesses from Israel (formerly from Riga, Latvia), detailed Hazners' participation in Nazi murder. I spoke with the witnesses and discussed their background and feelings with them.

About then I became shockingly aware of the lack of interest of most of the organized Jewish community. Many of the thirty-six seats in the courtroom were often empty. Few Jewish professionals or leaders, national or local, showed up for what I considered an historic event.

In 1977, I was sure that Hazners' hearing would end quickly, and he would be immediately deported. Hazners and hundreds of other accused and admitted Nazi war criminals are still living freely in the United States, and today I am no longer so naive.

Part of the Hazners hearing took place in 1978, just before the Jewish holiday of Purim. While baking traditional *Hamantashen* cookies with my son, Daniel, then age seven, I tried to explain the Hazners hearing to him: "These *Hamantashen* are to remind us of Haman, who wanted to kill all of the Jews of Persia a long time ago," I said. "But men like Hazners are worse than Haman, because people say that they really did kill millions of Jews when I was a little girl."

"We should be baking *Haznerstashen*, instead of *Hamantashen*," my perceptive son replied. He's right: not to bake figurative "Haznerstashen" degrades the memory of the Six Million, and Hitler's other victims.

1

But as the bureaucracy of justice moves ever so slowly, the issue of Nazi war criminals in America is low priority, almost forgotten. Virtually no massive, vigorous campaign to protest the presence here of these alleged murderers has been forthcoming from the government, nor from veteran or Jewish groups.

The only dedicated effort to bring Nazi war criminals and collaborators to justice has come from less than three dozen individuals, acting out of a sense of moral outrage. Although they share a deep sense of morality, each has different reasons for total commitment to the issue. They are not "Nazi hunters" in the cloak-and-dagger connotation. They are mainly well-educated professionals who pursue the issue from their own vantage points.

Other than their determination to right this situation, most of them have little in common: ages range from mid-30s to mid-80s. Not all are Jewish. Some are survivors of the Holocaust; some are native-born Americans. Some are men; some, women. Some deal with the issue as part of their profession; others' professions are unrelated.

At the Hazners hearing and since, I met most of these unusual people who have made the issue of Nazi war criminals in America a major part of their lives. Their stories, and why each of them has become involved with this issue, are part of modern American history.

One

Background

Soon after World War II, Nazi war criminals and collaborators began to make their way to the United States. Few of the implicated individuals were of German origin. The great majority came from Eastern Europe and the Soviet Union, where most of the crimes of the Holocaust were committed by Nazi Germany and its collaborators.

Estimates vary as to the number of war criminals and collaborators living in the U.S. Nazi hunter Simon Wiesenthal has claimed that more than 3,000 war criminals have found haven here. The U.S. Justice Department Office of Special Investigations (OSI), charged with investigating and prosecuting alleged Nazi war criminals living here, is processing over 400 cases, but estimates that more than a third of the persons may be dead. As of this writing, less than forty cases have been brought to court by the OSI.

As early as 1949, the German-language newspaper *Aufbau*, published in New York City, listed thirty-eight names that originated with Wiesenthal. Charles R. Allen, Jr.'s *Nazi War Criminals Among Us* (1963) was the first work to seek out and document charges against sixteen accused Nazi war criminals and collaborators. Allen later found evidence that possibly twenty-two more might have then been in the United States. By the mid-1960s, the unofficial estimate matched his thirty-eight. In the late 1960s, the World Jewish Congress compiled its listing of fifty-nine, many derived from Allen's writings.

From the first reports to the carefully checked and computerized current listings, the incontestable fact remains: hundreds of Nazi war criminals and collaborators entered the United States. Many still live here. Accused Latvian war criminal Vilis Hazners lives in a hamlet in northeastern New York State. Large cities such as New York, Philadelphia, Baltimore, Cleveland, Chicago and Los Angeles have been sites for trials. There have been proceedings in Florida, Michigan, California and Connecticut. Other alleged Nazi war criminals, not yet prosecuted, live throughout the United States. Some have been (or still are) at prestigious universities, colleges and corporations.

They are accused of crimes between 1939 and 1945 ranging from individual to mass murders; from acts of persecution to high-level responsibility for the institutionalization of concentration and death camps; from carrying out experiments on humans to top-level implementation of the Nazi genocide program. Most of them were low-level operators: concentration and death camp guards and guard supervisors, members of execution and punitive squads in collaborator armies, *Gestapo* agents and informers. Some, however, were at high levels: in the secret police, diplomacy, the military, or the *SS (Schutzstaffel)*. Many were leaders of the treasonous Fifth Columns of their native lands: the Iron Guard or Green Shirts in Rumania, the Arrow/Cross in Hungary, the Iron Wolf in Lithuania, the Thunder-Cross in Latvia, the Black Shirts in Italy, and the Ustashi in Yugoslavia.

Some Nazi war criminals came to the U.S. under the Displaced Persons Act of 1948–1951, slipping in with legitimate displaced persons. In some cases, they were secretly requested by various agencies of the government, including the State Department, the Central Intelligence Agency, the Federal Bureau of Investigation, Voice of America, Radio Free Europe and Radio Liberty. They were used for Cold War activities. Simon Wiesenthal told me, "The Cold War had no winners. The only winners were the Nazi war criminals. For twelve years we had a closed season for these crimes, and during that time they escaped from Europe to South America, Arab countries, Spain, and the United States. Only after the Eichmann trial in 1961 did a new search begin." [1]

The author interviews Nazi hunter Simon Wiesenthal on WTEN-television (ABC affiliate, Albany, N.Y.), November, 1978.

Some 1,558 German and Austrian scientists were brought to the United States through a Pentagon–State Department–Intelligence operation called Project Paperclip.[2] Most had been, minimally, members of the Nazi party, and some had been in the *SS*. Of the OSI's pending cases, at least twenty-one are implicated in United States government utilization. At least 156 alleged Nazi war criminals have been utilized by United States intelligence agencies over the past thirty-five years, according to Charles R. Allen, Jr. No single war criminal or collaborator was ever barred at his or her American port of entry because of war crimes or collaboration.

The United States government knew about the entry of these Nazi war criminals and collaborators from the beginning. Those that were brought in knowingly (and covertly) by various intelligence agencies were used as "contract agents" and "consultants." But from 1948 to 1978, these government agencies flatly denied utilization of war criminals.

The expulsion of Nazi war criminal Klaus Barbie from Bolivia to France in February, 1983 brought with it provable charges he was utilized and abetted by United States government intelligence. Known as "the Butcher of Lyons," from 1942 to 1944 Barbie headed the *Gestapo* in Lyons, France. He is accused of involvement in the murder of some 11,000 people, including the torture and death of French Resistance leader Jean Moulin.

In a 216-page report prepared by Allan A. Ryan, Jr., then a special assistant in the Criminal Division of the Justice Department (on leave from his OSI directorship), the United States government officially admitted for the first time that it had used and protected from prosecution by an ally a known Nazi war criminal. The report, submitted by Ryan to Attorney General William French Smith on August 9, 1983 (but not made public until August 16), detailed Barbie's employment by the U.S. Army Counter-Intelligence Corps (CIC) in Germany from 1947 to 1951, when he was assisted in escaping to South America.

Although Barbie did not live in the United States, in 1983 his case exploded into headlines the entire question of government intelligence utilization and harboring of Nazi war criminals. Some of these alleged Nazi war criminals and collaborators have been living in the United States for over thirty-five years.

In April, 1983, Hans Lipschis, an admitted former *SS* corporal at the Auschwitz-Birkenau death camp complex, was the first Nazi war criminal ever deported for concealing his crimes. A West German citizen and permanent resident here, Lipschis was scheduled to leave the U.S. for West Germany on April 21. On that date, his attorney informed OSI Acting Director Neal Sher that Lipschis had departed for West Germany a week earlier. Ironically, this first deportation was accomplished quickly. "It's a source of great satisfaction that we were able to complete this case within only ten months from the time of filing," Eli Rosenbaum, one of three OSI prosecutors of Lipschis, told me.[3]

In contrast to Lipschis, the presence here of Andrija Artukovic, Minister of the Interior of Nazi-occupied Croatia, was known as early as 1948. Yugoslavia formally requested his extradition in 1951; he is still living here freely. Early allegations were published in the 1950s and 1960s by several journalists such as Drew Pearson, Walter Winchell, and Milton

Friedman of the Jewish Telegraphic Agency (JTA), as well as by three congressmen in the *Congressional Record*.

In the mid-1970s, Rep. Joshua Eilberg (D-Pa.) and Rep. Elizabeth Holtzman (D-N.Y.) of the House Judiciary Subcommittee on Immigration succeeded in putting the issue on the congressional agenda. At about the same time, a former concentration camp guard supervisor, Hermine Braunsteiner Ryan, was extradited to West Germany for trial. Circumstances surrounding her case and others led Immigration and Naturalization Service (INS) attorney Vincent Schiano and investigator Anthony DeVito to leave the INS, accusing the agency of years of cover-ups on Nazi war criminal cases.

Beginning in 1973, a series of task forces and prosecution units was set up first in the INS, and then in the Criminal Division of the Justice Department. Prodded by Eilberg- and Holtzman-led forces, INS set up a Special Litigation Unit (SLU) in 1977, headed by attorney Martin Mendelsohn. By 1979, there was widespread dissatisfaction with both the INS and SLU because of their lack of progress with the Nazi war criminal cases. Rep. Holtzman, by then chairperson of the Judiciary Subcommittee on Immigration, used her influence to transfer the SLU to the Criminal Division of the Justice Department, where it became the OSI.

In January, 1977, Congress requested an investigation to determine whether U.S. government agencies had obstructed investigations and prosecutions of alleged Nazi war criminals. On May 15, 1978, the General Accounting Office (GAO), the investigative arm of the House of Representatives, reported it found no evidence of a "widespread conspiracy" within the government to cover up Nazi war criminal cases. The FBI and CIA did admit officially for the first time, however, that they had "utilized" Nazi war criminals and collaborators. On July 19–21, 1978, the House Subcommittee on Immigration held hearings on the GAO findings.

The OSI was launched in 1979; its budget was eventually $2.3 million. Former Nuremberg prosecutor Walter Rockler was OSI's first director. On April 1, 1980, Deputy Director Allan A. Ryan, Jr. succeeded Rockler. With a staff of forty-seven that included eighteen lawyers, three investigators and six historians, OSI's 1981–1982 budget was $2.6 million. Staff size and budget for fiscal year 1984 were about the same.

On February 6, 1981, Rep. Hamilton Fish, Jr. (R-N.Y.) and Rep. William Lehman (D-Fla.) were joined by over 100 members of the House in signing a letter to President Ronald Reagan, urging him to give the OSI his full public endorsement. In April, 1981, Sen. Christopher Dodd (D-Conn.) and eleven other senators sent an additional letter to the president, urging him not to cut the OSI's budget for the 1982 fiscal year. The senators also recommended that Attorney General William French Smith "take a personal interest" in the OSI.

According to former OSI Director Ryan, "If we file an airtight case against a naturalized American citizen tomorrow and there are no judicial delays, it would still take eight years to complete a case." [4] Ryan took leave as director in the spring and summer of 1983 to prepare the Barbie report. Upon its completion, he resigned from the agency. Neal Sher served as OSI's acting director during Ryan's special Barbie assignment and afterward.

Over the past thirty-five years, the subject of Nazi war criminals has seemed to surface and make headlines intermittently, then fade away until someone or something again draws national attention.

In May, 1982, a segment called "Nazi Connection" on CBS-TV's "60 Minutes" triggered a public outcry by journalists, legislators and others. Mike Wallace interviewed a former OSI staff attorney, John Loftus, who claimed that U.S. intelligence agencies had used accused Nazi war criminals smuggled in for that purpose. Expressing shock and dismay, Wallace said on the air: "I mean, the fact of the matter is that this has gone on for thirty-five years and nobody, until this moment, has had the desire to tell the story!" [5]

But Wallace's assessment of the situation was not accurate. A small but vigorous group of individuals, each in his or her own way, has been shouting the story—some of them for over twenty years. They have shouted against the indifference of the government and of Jewish organizations and leaders, against the proven cover-ups and ineptitude of government agencies, against too little progress that has come too late.[6]

Two _____

The Rabbi's Masquerade

In desperation, Rabbi Paul Silton put on a Nazi SS uniform in November, 1979 and strode through the dining room of the Concord Hotel to prove a point. His masquerade culminated two years of frustration with the Jewish community's failure to actively protest against Nazi war criminals living freely in America.

A Conservative rabbi, he was at the hotel to attend the National Biennial Convention of United Synagogue of America, the national organization for Conservative synagogues. After convention leaders refused to place the issue of Nazi war criminals on the program, Rabbi Silton decided on his startling attire to create grassroots interest.

As the then 36-year-old rabbi walked among the 2,000 delegates assembled for dinner, few people realized he was actually a rabbi. Some delegates, mistaking him for a neo-Nazi, went pale with shock or fear.

Although Rabbi Silton was in good shape, he is only five feet, seven inches tall. He could have easily been overpowered by a larger man or a group effort. No one, however, confronted him or tried to throw him out. Most delegates continued eating the Concord's plentiful ethnic delicacies. Maybe they hoped the "SS officer" would disappear, if they pretended he didn't exist.

Rabbi Silton said later that their behavior reminded him of the attitudes of most American Jews and Jewish organizations regarding real SS officers and other Nazi war criminals and

Rabbi Paul Silton wearing Nazi uniform at United Synagogue Convention, November, 1979, at the Concord Hotel. (photo by author)

collaborators living in America. For nearly thirty years, most Jews had completely avoided the question, as had the United States government. Jewish leaders and organizations didn't seem to care that some of the murderers of six million Jews and millions of other victims were living in the U.S. freely. When some of these organizations finally put the subject on their agendas in the late 1970s, most did little more than pay lip service to the government's fledgling and belated efforts.

"If we continue to pretend these real Nazis don't exist, they will indeed disappear," Rabbi Silton said of this attitude. "They'll die of old age, peacefully in their beds. As famous Nazi hunter Simon Wiesenthal has said of the situation, 'We will reach a biological solution.' "

But Rabbi Silton wasn't looking for a biological solution. He wanted action, and he wanted justice. He was sure that the organized Jewish community in America would agree with him, as soon as he told them the facts. He would merely say, "There are hundreds of Nazi war criminals living here—Simon Wiesenthal says there may even be thousands." And organized American Jewry would say, "We can't stand for such a situation. We've got to get on the bandwagon, educate people about this scandal, and pressure our government for justice." Rabbi Silton was wrong. They said nothing.

He decided to work first within his own organization, United Synagogue. Through phone calls, correspondence and trips to the national office in New York City, he requested United Synagogue to include among convention speakers one of several well-known experts on the subject of Nazi war criminals in America. He naively assumed his suggestion would be warmly welcomed. Leaders encouraged him at the beginning, but shortly before plans were finalized, they denied his request.

When he discovered that the national convention's organizers had not put the issue on the program, Rabbi Silton arranged as a sidelight of the convention a regional meeting on the subject. (Many of United Synagogue's regions hold special receptions or workshops for their convention delegates.) Metropolitan Region (New York City and suburbs) and Empire (upstate New York and western Massachusetts—Rabbi Silton's region) agreed to cooperate with him and host a workshop on Nazi war criminals. Costumed to dramatize the issue, the rabbi was in the dining room passing out factsheets and invitations to this regional meeting.

At the workshop, Rabbi Silton explained to about 100 people that for many months he had been asking leadership of United Synagogue to place the issue on the convention's agenda. "The fact is that I've begged, implored, made trips to New York," he said. "I asked that Nazi war criminals in America be one of the major issues discussed at this convention. Promises were made and broken. In the end, I was turned down."

It isn't prudent or rational for anyone to wear an *SS* uniform in a room filled with 2,000 Jews. It is even less so if that person is a rabbi (who at the time needed to earn a living for himself, his wife, five children and a hungry collie), and if those Jews are the synagogue leaders who control his future employment opportunities. But Rabbi Silton is often imprudent and irrational when justice and morality are at stake.

His unorthodox—and potentially dangerous—stunt had been seething within him for two years. In the fall of 1977, he had discovered two startling facts that were to haunt both his waking and sleeping hours: (1) there are Nazi war criminals in America; and (2) with few exceptions, no one in America really cares.

Rabbi Silton's active involvement with the issue of Nazi war criminals began in October, 1977, when he read in the Albany *Times-Union* that the deportation hearing of alleged Nazi war criminal Vilis Hazners was going to begin in Albany, N. Y. on October 25. Rabbi Silton had been educational director of Temple Israel in Albany since 1974.

"When I first read the announcement of the trial of a war criminal here, I said, 'This is ridiculous,' " Rabbi Silton recalled to me. "I never knew there were war criminals in this country. The article protruded out of the paper at me. I was especially interested to read that witnesses from Israel would be at the hearing. I wanted to meet these people, and I followed up on the article." Rabbi Silton soon became totally engrossed with the hearing, the visiting Israeli witnesses, and the lack of interest in the Jewish community.

Although he doesn't remember reading about the Hazners hearing before October, 1977, proceedings started on January 28, 1977. That day Hazners, then 71, was served with a show-cause order by the U.S. Immigration and Naturalization Service (INS). He was subject to deportation under the anti-war crimes provision of the 1953 Refugee Relief Act, if he "had personally advocated or assisted in the persecution of any person or groups of persons because of race, religion or national origin." The order cited Hazners for six specific actions while he was an officer in the Nazi-sponsored Latvian Legion and police commissioner in the Abrene district of Latvia.

According to the show-cause order, Hazners participated, in or about 1941, "In the selection of a group of Jews, in the location known as the Dwinsk (Latvia) Ghetto, for execution at the location known as the Pogulanka Woods"; committed "assaults upon a group of Jews . . . at a police station located in Riga, Latvia"; and took part in "collecting a group of Jews in Riga, Latvia, and detaining them at the Big Synagogue

(Choral Synagogue) on Gogol Street, Riga, Latvia, after which the said synagogue was set afire and the detained Jews burned to death therein." [1]

Hazners, a permanent resident alien living in the Washington County town of Dresden, N. Y., about eighty miles north of Albany, came to the United States from West Germany in August, 1956 as a displaced person. He and his wife, Elza, lived in retirement on their 200-acre farm from 1972.

Accusations against him appeared in two books, *Daugavas Vanagi: Who Are They?* and *Political Refugees Unmasked*, official Latvian publications. His name was cited in connection with actions of the Latvian Legion, Latvian police authorities, and the *Perkonkrust*, the fascist Thunder-Cross organization. The books also contain several photos of a military officer who is identified as Hazners. One of the photos shows this officer in the company of high Nazi officials, reviewing the troops of the Latvian Legion. [2]

Dr. Gertrude Schneider, a survivor of the Riga Ghetto and Stutthof extermination camp who now lives in New Jersey, obtained these publications when she visited Latvia in 1971. A naturalized United States citizen, she was born in Austria and deported to Latvia by the Nazis at the beginning of World War II. A scholar of Latvian history and faculty member at the Graduate Center of City University of New York, Dr. Schneider has written a book on her life in the Riga Ghetto. [3] In a January 14, 1981 interview with me at her City University office, she discussed her involvement with the question of Nazi war criminals.

During her 1971 trip, Dr. Schneider was in Riga doing research on her doctoral dissertation, and she met with the Latvian Minister of Culture as part of her work. Since their meeting had nothing to do with war criminals, she was quite shocked when the minister said, "You know, you have lots of Nazis in your country."

"I beg your pardon!" Dr. Schneider exclaimed. She was totally uninformed about the situation. She knew there were big war criminals, like Dr. Josef Mengele, in South America. But like most Americans in 1971, she had never heard there were Nazi war criminals living in the U.S.

The minister said that he had documentation proving the truth of his allegations, and that many of the Nazis living in America had been tried in Latvia *in absentia*. He mentioned Vilis Hazners, among others, as a person who allegedly committed Nazi atrocities and who now lived in the U.S. Dr. Schneider asked the minister for his documentation, and brought back with her the trial records of Hazners and Boleslavs Maikovskis of Mineola, New York.

Dr. Schneider called the Anti-Defamation League of B'nai B'rith (ADL) when she returned to New York, and told an official there that she had brought back the documents. He admitted freely that ADL knew about the presence here of Nazi war criminals. "We know all about that," he said. Dr. Schneider then asked, "Well, what are you doing about it? " His response was, "What can we do? "

The ADL official told her that the subject was very complicated, and that she didn't understand. He said the U.S. could only act on Nazi war criminals if they came into the country on false pretenses. Dr. Schneider replied that war criminals would not have been allowed into the country if they had admitted their *SS* activities. Therefore, they had all entered under false pretenses. The ADL official replied, "Don't be so logical."

Hazners' name was well-known to United States immigration authorities before he entered the country in 1956, according to Simon Wiesenthal. In 1978, Wiesenthal told me that he published Hazners' name in 1949 on a list of fifty war criminals from the Baltic countries. "We were searching in some displaced persons camps in Germany, because these people in 1944 escaped with the Germans," he said. "I sent this list to a German-language American newspaper, *Aufbau*, and they sent it to the immigration authorities."

Hazners admitted in court that he had been a major in the Latvian Legion, fighting on the Nazi side against the Russians. He claimed, however, that the Legion was a nationalist group fighting for Latvia, and never committed war crimes. The case against him began with a brief hearing in an Albany federal courtroom on February 14, 1977 (see Chapter 1).

Dr. Schneider does not agree with Hazners' description of the Latvian Legion. According to her, "The Latvian Legion officers were so anti-Semitic it was unbelievable." She told me over thirty years later, "To this day, their behavior is an enigma to me. They should have been on our [the Jewish victims'] side. They were enslaved by the Nazis themselves. But they went out of their way to gain favor with the Nazis.

"The German Nazis were following the policy of their government. But Latvia was an occupied country, overrun by the Nazis. We can add collaboration with the enemy to the other crimes of Latvian Legion officers," she said. As an example of "unbelievable anti-Semitism," Dr. Schneider recalled an incident of severe mistreatment of Jews by the Latvian guards around the Riga Ghetto. "These Latvians were so brutal to the Jews that the German commander actually had to intervene to stop them. A German Nazi had to protect the Jews from them! " she exclaimed.

At a party shortly after she returned from her trip to Latvia, Dr. Schneider was introduced to Chris Borgen of CBS-TV News, Channel 2, in New York City. On impulse, she said, "Have I got a hot story for you! " and told him about the documents the Latvian Minister of Culture had given her.

Because of her chance meeting with Borgen, she was interviewed on the Channel 2 News, and eventually gave the documents to CBS Channel 2 News in New York. On January 13, 1975, she again appeared on Channel 2, on a half-hour program called "Shadows Behind the Golden Door." And on November 14, 1976, she discussed Nazi war criminals in America on the television program "60 Minutes." She also spoke on the issue with Bill Boggs on the "Midday Live" show of January 17, 1977.

As a result of her media exposure, Dr. Schneider became known as an "expert" on the subject. She explained that this is probably because she is more detached, articulate and educated than most other survivors. She served as a consultant to the U.S. Department of State on procedural matters concerning alleged Nazi war criminals who had emigrated from Latvia to America, and also advised Justice Department units responsible for their prosecution.

About two years after Dr. Schneider's 1971 trip to Latvia, Rep. Joshua Eilberg (D-Pa.), then Chairman of the House Judiciary Subcommittee on Immigration, was investigating why the INS had never deported any of the more than 100 alleged Nazi war criminals then believed to be living in the United States. His efforts, and those of subcommittee member (and his successor in 1978–80) Rep. Elizabeth Holtzman (D-N.Y.), brought about the creation in 1973 of an INS New York district task force—with only one investigator.

Through this task force, INS began in 1974–1977 to prepare twelve denaturalization and deportation cases for hearings. In August, 1977, the task force was replaced by a Special Litigation Unit (SLU), headed by attorney Martin Mendelsohn in Washington, D. C., and specifically created by the Justice Department to investigate and prosecute suspected Nazi war criminals living here. The Hazners case, initiated by the New York task force, was one of the first cases transferred to the SLU for hearings. Preliminary investigatory procedures must have been at least adequate, because the SLU, aided by the Israeli government, produced eight witnesses against Hazners and brought them to Albany.

When the Hazners hearing reconvened on October 25, 1977 with the witnesses from Israel, Rabbi Silton singlehandedly took on the responsibility of making the witnesses comfortable in the Albany Jewish community. He arranged home hospitality for their meals, brought them to Jewish schools and to his synagogue for Saturday morning services. His *mitzvah* (good deed) of hospitality served two purposes: the witnesses, reliving nightmares as they testified, felt the support of the community; and the community heard from eyewitnesses that Hitler's victims were real people and not just statistics.

SLU attorneys William Strasser and Ralph Smith represented the government at the hearing. Unit Chief Mendelsohn was also in the courtroom for the opening days. Smith, who was supposed to be chief counsel for the case, was hospitalized during the proceedings, and Strasser took over. Because of the shift to the SLU in the middle of the case, Smith's illness, and other problems, the Hazners case was handled poorly by the fledgling unit.

Deportation hearings continued intermittently until May 18, 1979. On February 27, 1980, the immigration judge terminated the proceedings, concluding that the government's evidence was insufficient to prove the defendant's deportability.

The Office of Special Investigations (OSI), which superseded SLU, appealed this decision to the Board of Immigration Appeals (BIA) on March 5, 1980, and an oral argument before the BIA was held on September 4, 1980. On July 15, 1981, the BIA dismissed OSI's appeal and motion to reopen, holding that the record did not contain clear, convincing and unequivocal evidence of Hazners' deportability. Since that date, official OSI digests of cases in litigation have stated, "Various possible courses of action are now under consideration by OSI." But there has been no action.

Sitting in the Albany courtroom in October and November, 1977, Rabbi Silton learned in detail from the witnesses about the inhuman harshness of life in the Riga Ghetto. He also learned that, with few exceptions, members of the Jewish community were not in the courtroom to offer their moral support to the witnesses.

The rabbi learned another lesson sitting in that courtroom, a lesson that a handful of others had known for some time: the issue of Nazi war criminals living in America was neither new nor easily rectified.

Three _____

In The Beginning

As early as 1948, twenty-nine years before the Hazners hearing in Albany, N. Y. brought the situation to Rabbi Silton's attention, information on the issue of Nazi war criminals in America was available. Charges were first made that year against Andrija Artukovic, the Minister of the Interior of Nazi-occupied Croatia; in 1951, Yugoslavia formally requested his extradition. He is accused of direct responsibility for the genocide of more than 600,000 persons, including 78,000 Jews. (The Justice Department was still seeking his deportation as of this writing.)

Most accused Nazi war criminals now living in the United States came here in the late 1940s and early 1950s. Of the cases that have been brought to court by the Justice Department's Office of Special Investigations, the earliest arrival date is for Bronius Kaminskas in May, 1947. He is accused of participating in the shooting of some 200 Jews in Lithuania and the selection of some 400 Jews for execution. (His case has been adjourned indefinitely because of his poor health.)

The most thorough early research on the subject was done by Charles R. Allen, Jr. for *Jewish Currents* magazine. His articles were published first in 1963 in several issues of that periodical, and later that year reprinted as *Nazi War Criminals Among Us* (see Chapters 5, 6). Substantiated accusations were published in the 1950s and early 1960s by several journalists, including Drew Pearson, Walter Winchell, and Milton Friedman, a freelance writer and also then chief of the Washington

Charles R. Allen, Jr., leading expert on Nazi war criminals in America, whose writings on the subject first appeared in 1963.

office of the Jewish Telegraphic Agency (JTA, an international wire service and publisher of a daily news bulletin).

In the March 1, 1952 issue of *The Nation,* Friedman wrote an article entitled "The Nazis Come In". (Although they did not meet until 30 years later, Charles R. Allen, Jr. was, at the time, assistant editor of the magazine.) Friedman's article, only four paragraphs long, named some of the alleged Nazi war criminals who had entered the United States and explained how they were able to do so:

> Nazis and others with bona fide fascist records are experiencing little difficulty with the United States visa regulations which are keeping from our shores so many distinguished democrats. It is true that there is a paper barrier against fascists. An amendment to the Internal Security Act of 1950 bars all present or former members of "totalitarian" parties except those who were coerced into joining or were not more than sixteen when they enrolled. But the ninth proviso, third section,

of the Immigration Act of 1917, which gives discretionary power to the Attorney General to admit "otherwise inadmissible aliens applying for temporary admission," makes the barrier very fragile indeed. Moreover, the Central Intelligence Agency is empowered by Congress to import annually 100 aliens who possess strategic skills. It is not required to divulge their identity.

The ninth proviso and the C. I. A. are affording avenues of admission to some interesting people. Dr. Walter P. Schreiber, former commanding officer of the Department of Medical Science of Hitler's Supreme Command, to whom some unflattering references were made at the Nurnberg *[sic]* war-crimes trials, recently arrived to join the faculty of the United States Army Air Force School of Aviation Medicine at Randolph Field, Texas. Dr. Otto Reuleaux and about fifty other Germans were granted visas to attend an international meeting of industrialists held in New York in connection with a convention of the National Association of Manufacturers. Dr. Reuleaux held the Nazi title of Defense Economy Director and is on the original 1945 War Department list of those who participated in and benefitted from the Hitler Regime. Some of his colleagues who accompanied him to New York were also Nazi Party members and beneficiaries of the regime.

Dr. Andrija Artukovic, war-time Minister of Justice of the Nazi puppet government of Croatia, traveling under an assumed name, entered the United States as a visitor on July 16, 1948. His signature is recorded on anti-Semitic decrees, and he is charged with zealously implementing Hitler's extermination program. His temporary visa was extended three times. To escape extradition, Dr. Artukovic has applied for status as a "refugee from communism." Another Balkan collaborator cleared by the immigration service is Viorel Trifa, who participated in the pro-Nazi revolt in Bucharest in 1941 as a leader of the Iron Guard and also played a role in anti-Semitic activities.

Although the Displaced Persons Act expired last December 31, the official machinery has been kept functioning to admit 54,774 additional *Volkdeutsche [sic]* from Eastern Europe. Many of these people, according to Rabbi Irving Miller, ex-president of the American Jewish Congress, "volunteered for service with the execution squads which gassed and otherwise exterminated six million Jews and millions of other faiths." When Congress amended the D. P. act in 1950 it provided especially

for immigration visas for General Wladyslaw Anders's Polish
Corps. Among those who joined Anders's group after the war
were such personalities as Roch Mankowski, commander of the
Nazi concentration camp at Krems; Father I. Nahajewski, chap-
lain of Hitler's Ukrainian S. S. division, which murdered thousands of civilians; Dr. Wladyslaw Dering, named on the international list of war criminals for surgical experiments on living
human beings at Auschwitz; Henryk Gutman, commander of
camps in Austria. Approximately 11,000 visas were issued to
Anders's men, who were welcomed under the Statue of Liberty
as part of the "huddled masses yearning to breathe free." [1]

In the early 1960s, Friedman also wrote articles on Nazi
war criminals in America for his weekly column, which ran
in some local weekly Jewish newspapers. For example, in the
June 21, 1960 *Jewish Floridian,* Friedman quotes Artukovic as
bragging that he outdid the Nazis in the speed and efficiency
with which he solved "the Jewish problem." According to
Friedman, Artukovic said, "I acted against the Jews at once.
I was not like the Germans who procrastinated matters with
the Jews for years."

Although Friedman was from 1949 to 1970 the Washington
correspondent for JTA, in the 1960s his articles on Nazi war
criminals were conspicuously absent from the pages of the
daily news bulletins of that wire service which publishes news
of Jewish interest. Considering JTA's readership and the nature of the subject, the scarcity of information there by Friedman or others seems puzzling.

On June 23, 1960, the *JTA Daily News Bulletin* printed the
following, which bore a New York dateline but no byline:

> The Anti-Defamation League of B'nai B'rith asked Attorney
> General William P. Rogers today to order the expulsion from
> this country of Ferdinand Durcansky, one-time foreign minister
> of the Nazi puppet State of Slovakia.
> Arnold Forster, general counsel of the ADL, asked the
> Attorney General to initiate deportation proceedings against
> Durcansky on the grounds that his record as a Nazi collaborator
> and war criminal made him an "excludable alien" under the
> immigration laws. He pointed out that Durcansky was accused
> of responsibility for the first anti-Jewish laws in the puppet

State of Slovakia which "resulted in the disappearance of 68,000 Jews of whom 60,000 are estimated to have been killed." [2]

On December 11, 1963, another article appeared, again with no byline. Datelined Philadelphia and headlined "Moscow Charges Two Americans with Aiding Nazis to Kill Jews," the JTA item said:

> Two Philadelphia residents refused comment today on charges by the Soviet press that they helped to liquidate a Jewish ghetto while serving in the German police during the Nazi occupation of the Ukraine.
>
> The charge was made in the trade union newspaper, Trud, which called yesterday for the prosecution of Serhij Kowalczuk, 44, and his brother Mykola, 37. The newspaper charged that the brothers took part in liquidating the Jewish ghetto in Lyumboml, their home town, and in seizing the property of the 5,000 Jews in the ghetto.
>
> Trud asserted that the brothers fled from the Ukraine with the retreating German forces in 1944 when the Russians retook the area. The Soviet paper said that residents in Lyumboml had identified Serhij as the man who transported Jews to an execution site and confiscated their property. The brothers, Trud added, had started a correspondence recently with their parents, who live in Kremenets, in the Ukraine, and have been sending them gift parcels.[3]

These small articles were the only significant exceptions to JTA's silence on the question during the early 1960s.

Asked twenty-two years later (in a telephone interview on November 1, 1982) why JTA printed the first item, Forster understandably did not remember the details. He told me, however, that the ADL made a practice of "calling for the deportation of all of the *mamserim*" [bastards] whose names came up. Forster claims press releases were issued every time the ADL learned of the presence of a Nazi war criminal. They were sent to JTA, "which may not have printed them," he said. The index of press releases filed under "Nazi War Criminals" in the ADL library at the organization's New York City headquarters begins with June, 1974. The index of press releases on all subjects, arranged in chronological order, goes back to 1971. This index revealed that no ADL press release was issued on Nazi war criminals in America from 1971 through May, 1974. The JTA article about ADL cited above is evidence there was at least one earlier release, but further documentation is unavailable.

When Friedman was asked why JTA seemed to ignore the topic of Nazi war criminals at that time, he told me in a February 15, 1982 telephone conversation: "The Jewish organizations never wanted to pick up on it. In some instances they wanted to suppress the information. My articles were not in JTA because JTA would not print them. [Then editor Boris] Smolar censored them, along with some Jewish organizations. It wasn't really a conspiracy, just a lot of fear. And taking their instructions from the Israelis, making deals to get reparations."

Friedman cites the McCarthyism of that time as one of the reasons the organized Jewish community suppressed the issue of Nazi war criminals in America in the 1950s and 1960s. "When I wrote my first story about Artukovic in *The Nation*, Jewish organizations said I shouldn't have done so because Yugoslavia was a Communist country," he said. "The 1952 McCarran-Walter Act allowed Jews to come into America above quotas, but also let in *Volksdeutsche*. If they could prove they served Hitler, then they got in. This proved they weren't Communists."

Describing the Jewish leadership at that time as "spineless," Friedman linked their self-imposed silence on the issue to meetings with Chancellor Konrad Adenauer to obtain reparations money for victims of Nazism.

"There were attempts by Jewish organizations to cover up," he told me. "Israel made a deal to get reparations—a tacit deal to cool down the war criminal complaints. I would find out about criminals here and Jewish organizations and JTA would refuse to make an issue about it. They felt it was more important to get reparations. When I wrote about the subject of Nazi war criminals for *The Nation*, I got calls from JTA telling me not to do so," he said.

Morris U. Schappes, the 75-year-old editor of *Jewish Currents*, a monthly magazine published in New York City, agrees with Friedman that reparations deals were at the root of the silence of JTA and the organized American Jewish community. "Our theory was that agreement between Adenauer and Israel on reparations involved a playing down of anti-Nazism," he told me at the *Jewish Currents* office on October 30, 1981. "This struggle rent the American Jewish community and the Jewish community in Israel as nothing else since World War II. There were mass demonstrations against the reparation plan. All of the organizations began to play down the war and the Holocaust, because if you're going to get billions of marks, you have to treat Adenauer like a repentant gentleman."

Not only were sensitive reparations negotiations ongoing, but from 1951 until 1963, JTA was funded by the Jewish Agency. Before the State of Israel was created in 1948, the Jewish Agency was, in effect, the government of pre-Israel. Although it later became "nongovernmental," even today its support of the World Zionist Organization and implementation of social services in Israel are tightly linked with the Israeli government.

On August 2, 1963, the *JTA Daily Bulletin* reported that, "The relationship between the Jewish Agency and the Jewish Telegraphic Agency was explored by Sen. J. W. Fulbright, chairman of the Senate Foreign Relations Committee, during his questioning of Jewish Agency representatives, as part of his Committee's study of non-diplomatic activities of representatives of foreign governments."

The JTA article further stated that Eleazar Lipsky, then president of JTA, sent a letter dated July 31 to Senator Fulbright on behalf of the JTA Board of Directors, reviewing the relationship between the Jewish Agency and JTA. Quoting this letter, the article states:

> "In 1951," Mr. Lipsky wrote, "the JTA was in acute financial difficulties which severely constricted its operations and, in fact, jeopardized its continued existence. To prevent the total collapse of this news service which was considered vital to the well-being of the Jewish community, the Jewish Agency was requested by the JTA to intervene and provide the funds to permit JTA to continue functioning on what was expected to be a provisional basis. It became nominally the owner of the Jewish Telegraphic Agency through ownership of the voting

shares by transfer from the late Jacob Landau, founder of the JTA. For a long time, the JTA regarded advances by the Jewish Agency as interest-free loans.

"The Jewish Telegraphic Agency is grateful to the Jewish Agency for having made it possible to continue its operations and render important services to the Jewish community. We believe that the American Jewish community is under a deep obligation to the Jewish Agency for having preserved this service for it."

Lipsky goes on to say that an agreement was reached in 1960 for future reorganization of JTA as an "independent entity." But at the time of his 1963 letter to Senator Fulbright, "some technical details remain to be effected," and the change-over from funding by the Jewish Agency "is now nearing completion." [4]

Lipsky's 1963 letter to Senator Fulbright (quoted in the August 2, 1963 JTA article) said of JTA: "Its sole purpose and its sole function has been to report as accurately and objectively as human frailties permit those developments any-where in the world of special concern or interest to the Jewish people, to bring to light information which their wellbeing required and to provide the information on which Jewish leadership could take informed action." The topic of Nazi war criminals in America undeniably falls into all of these categories, but the Jewish Agency's "human frailty" of placing the priority on need for reparation money may have served to prevent JTA from reporting this news "accurately and objectively."

Former JTA editor Boris Smolar denies any connection between the Jewish Agency's ownership of JTA and failure to report on the issue of Nazi war criminals in America. "I didn't know anything about the Nazi war criminal issue until David Horowitz (see Chapter 8) drew my attention to it regarding the Trifa case in 1971," he said in a phone con-versation with me from his New York City apartment on November 9, 1982. "It was brought to my attention for the first time by Horowitz. He started the campaign journalisti-cally."

Reminded that JTA's own Milton Friedman wrote about the issue in *The Nation* as early as 1952, and also in several Anglo-Jewish newspapers, and that Charles R. Allen, Jr. and *Jewish Currents* launched a major exposé in 1963, Smolar said, "I don't remember Milton Friedman writing about it. Maybe he mentioned it. I don't remember. If Friedman had written about it, why should I not want to print it? Milton had to be checked very often on libel in his articles. Maybe this was why. I don't remember Allen's 1963 booklet. Nobody must have paid any attention to it, none of the Jewish organizations. Horowitz went at it very strongly. He was the one who came to me. I don't remember that Friedman had columns in Jewish papers that didn't go through JTA."

Allen told me he remembers speaking with Smolar on the telephone during August, 1962. He was doing research for his Nazi war criminal series and thought JTA would have information in back issues of the *Daily Bulletin*. "Smolar didn't want to talk to me," Allen says. "I thought he didn't want to talk to a person writing for a Communist magazine. I didn't realize that Milton Friedman's articles on the subject weren't carried by JTA. When my *Jewish Currents* articles and booklet came out in 1963, I personally brought press releases on them to the JTA office."

With regard to the Jewish Agency's financial control of JTA, Smolar told me, "JTA not printing articles on Nazi war criminals had nothing to do with reparation talks or ownership by the Jewish Agency. The Jewish Agency never interfered in JTA's editorial matters. They didn't influence our situation in any way."

Compounding the Jewish community's concern about damaging delicate reparations negotiations was their fear of being called Communists, if they exposed the "anti-Communists" otherwise known as Nazi war criminals. Because McCarthyism was then in its heyday and Schappes was a Communist, JTA and the organized Jewish community were not interested in either him or *Jewish Currents* (*Jewish Life* until 1958). Hard facts on Nazi war criminals living here, investigated by left-winger Allen and published by Schappes, were termed "Communist propaganda."

"We tried to interest major Jewish organizations in the issue of Nazi war criminals in America, but we got rebuffs continually," Schappes says of the 1960s. "I was outside the Jewish community—in the doghouse." Well into the 1970s, some American Jewish leaders tried to dismiss the entire question of Nazi criminals living here by labeling it "Soviet manipulation" or "Communist-inspired," he told me.

From 1928 to 1941, Schappes was a faculty member of the English Department of City College in New York. He was one of over thirty teachers and staff members removed from the campus after an anti-Communist investigation conducted in 1941 by the Rapp-Coudert Committee, officially called the New York State Legislature's Joint Legislative Committee to Investigate State Monies for Public School Purposes and Subversive Activities.

Because he refused to be an informer against his colleagues, Schappes spent thirteen and one-half months in The Tombs, Sing Sing, Dannemora and Walkill prisons. The sole basis for his incarceration was his political association and beliefs, compounded by his unwillingness to publicly recant and inform. It was not until forty years later, on March 9, 1981, that the Faculty Senate of City College apologized for his dismissal.

Schappes believes that the 1961 trial in Jerusalem of Gestapo Chief Expert on Jewish Affairs Adolf Eichmann was the event that focused his interest on the issue of Nazi war criminals in America. In his "Issues and Events" column in the July–August 1961 issue of *Jewish Currents,* Schappes discussed both that trial and the presence of other Nazi war criminals in Europe, South America and the United States. "In the United States, in West Germany, in Austria there are war criminals crying to be tried," he wrote. This was the first time that the subject was mentioned in this magazine, and only one Nazi living in America, Andrija Artukovic, was mentioned.

In his September, 1962 "Issues and Events" column, Schappes added other names, taken from Charles R. Allen, Jr.'s work in progress. His list follows:

> Andrija Artukovich, [sic] former Minister of the Interior for the Nazi state of Croatia, mass murderer of Jews,

wanted by the Yugoslav government as a war criminal, now living near Long Beach, Calif.

Viorel Trifa, now Bishop Valerian D. Trifa of Detroit, denounced May 3 in Tel Aviv by Romanian Chief Rabbi Dr. Moshe Rosen, wanted in Romania as a pogrom-instigator and Nazi.

Nicolae Malaxa, 1158 Fifth Ave., N.Y., wanted in Romania as a mass murderer of Jews.

Anastas Ludivicas Impulavicius, Lithuanian fascist and mass murderer of Jews, now in Philadelphia and wanted by the Soviet Union.

Other Lithuanian war criminals wanted: Bishop V. Brizgis, Prof. Baziska, J. Slepetys, J. Ambrozevicius, (now Brazaitis), all living in U.S.A.

Emmanuel Yasuk of Byelorussia, convicted of war crimes against Jews and others, now in U.S.A.

Karl Linnas, 21 Goldsmith Ave., Greenlawn, L.I., N.Y., an Estonian charged with helping kill 12,000 Soviet citizens including 2,000 Jews.

The Polish Capt. Franciszek Kuschel, now living as Gen. Kuschel at 853 Alabama Ave., Brooklyn, who as a Major in the Nazi Army committed war crimes in Byelorussia; wanted by the Soviet Union.

Sergei Hutyrczyk, another criminal in Byelorussia, now at 104 French St., New Brunswick, N.J., wanted by the Soviet Union.

He ended his column with the following question: "Why should these Nazis not be deported and extradited to stand trial and be brought to justice?" [5]

Four _____

Dr. Charles Kremer
The Persistent Dentist

Dr. Charles Kremer's obsession with one Nazi war criminal, Archbishop Valerian Trifa, began over three decades ago. At the age of 84, Kremer, a retired New York City dentist, along with Nazi hunter Simon Wiesenthal, was presented with an award on March 31, 1981 by the Committee to Bring Nazi War Criminals to Justice in the U.S.A.[1]

According to the blurb on the dinner invitation, Kremer is

> Founder and President, Romanian Federation of America Inc. and Committee to Bring Nazi War Criminals to Justice In U.S.A.; hunter of Nazis; responsible for exposing activities of pogromist Rt. Reverend Valerian Trifa, which led to his surrendering his American naturalization certificate and standing trial for deportation . . . .

While Dr. Kremer had been instrumental in the battle against Trifa and had devoted years of his life to seeking justice for this accused Nazi war criminal, his efforts have been almost exclusively directed against only one alleged Nazi war criminal. As president and founder of the Committee to Bring Nazi War Criminals to Justice In the U.S.A., he is, in effect, the organization.

Since 1951, Dr. Kremer has been obsessed with his pursuit of this single admitted Nazi war criminal, later archbishop of the Rumanian Orthodox Church of America. At a meeting

Dr. Charles Kremer (center) and Simon Wiesenthal (left) receive procla-
mations from New York City Mayor Edward Koch, March, 1981.

of the United Rumanian Jews of America that year, Dr.
Kremer learned from two Rumanian clerics that Trifa was in
America. Bishop Andrei Moldavan and Father Gucherie Mor-
aru had come to the Rumanian-Jewish meeting in New York
City to inform members that Trifa had entered the United
States as a displaced person in 1950.

The clerics were especially disturbed that an unfrocked priest
had recently called a congress which had elected Trifa a vicar
of the church. Although Trifa was condemned to life imprisonment in Rumania and could never return for the required anointment by the church patriarch, the same congress
was now attempting to elect him a bishop.

As president of the student movement of the fascist Iron
Guard, Trifa was accused of inciting the January 21, 1941
Bucharest pogrom. His speech a day earlier is said to have

touched off four days of rioting, during which at least 200 Jews were murdered by the Iron Guard. Because of Trifa's alleged involvement in the pogrom, Bishop Moldavan and Father Moraru assumed that at the 1951 meeting, members of the United Rumanian Jews of America would join in seeking his deportation to serve a life sentence in Rumania.

But the clerics were wrong. When a vote was taken at the end of the meeting, the organization voted nineteen to one to take no action. The one was Dr. Kremer; he says he vowed to himself that night he would bring Trifa to justice on his own.

Dr. Kremer had first heard Trifa's name in New York City in February, 1941 at an emergency meeting of the executive committee of the United Rumanian Jews of America, called because of news of the Bucharest pogrom. At that meeting, the organization's president read from two uncensored Jewish Telegraphic Agency pogrom reports, datelined Sofia (Bulgaria), January 29 and 30, 1941. The first dispatch from correspondent Leigh White read:

> This, I believe, is the first eyewitness account to reach the outside world of the Iron Guard horror in Rumania.
>
> It was necessary for this correspondent to come to Sofia to send out details of the revolt because the Bucharest censorship refused to pass anything but milk and water versions of the insurrection and banned any mention whatever of the well-organized anti-Jewish pogrom carried out simultaneously with the disorders last week . . . .
>
> Dozens of Jews—women and children as well as men—were literally burned alive. I am not speaking of those who were burned to death in hundreds of buildings to which the Guardists set fire, after shooting and beating the inhabitants and looting the contents of their homes. I am speaking only of Jews who were beaten senseless on the streets, robbed, then doused with gasoline and set afire . . . .
>
> Perhaps the most horrifying single episode of the pogrom was the "kosher butchering" last Wednesday night of more than 200 Jews in the municipal slaughterhouse.
>
> The Jews, who had been rounded up after several hours of Iron Guard raids, were put into several trucks and carried off to the slaughterhouse. There the Greenshirts forced them to

undress and led them to the chopping blocks, where they cut
their throats in a horrible parody of the traditional Jewish
methods of slaughtering fowls and livestock . . . .[2]

In the second article, the JTA correspondent accused Trifa
and others; he added details of the pogrom to the earlier
article:

> The "general staff" which ordered the massacre consisted
> of Vice-Premier Horia Sima, chief of the Greenshirt Legion,
> Dimitry Groza, boss of the "Legionary Workers Corps," com-
> posed of "Lumpenproletariat" and completely lacking in skilled
> or organized workers; and Viorel Trifa, leader of the frenetic
> Greenshirt "student movement." [3]

Dr. Kremer left his native Rumania in 1919 because of
more subtle forms of anti-Semitism. As a medical student at
the University of Jassi in 1918, he and thirty other Jewish
students had to crowd along one side of a dissection table;
eight Christian students shared the other side. He recalls being
beaten daily by anti-Semites on his way home from the university. Earlier, in secondary school in his hometown of Braila,
numerus clausus restrictions permitted only two Jews, Dr. Kremer and another, to enter a class of some four hundred
students.

When Rumania became involved in World War I, Dr. Kremer, his father and brothers were placed in a concentration
camp by the Rumanians. Father and sons were incarcerated
as "foreigners" from September, 1916 to January, 1917, because Dr. Kremer's father was a native of Austria. (His mother's family were Rumanian natives for many generations.) Dr.
Kremer remembers concentration camp life as daily marches
in bitter cold, routine beatings, and sleeping quarters unfit
for animals.

After his degrading experiences in the concentration camp
and then in medical school, Dr. Kremer decided to leave
Rumania in 1919 as a stowaway on a British ship. He didn't
know his destination until the ship landed in Port Said, Egypt.
From there he journeyed to Liverpool, England, and ultimately
to New York.

Even at the age of twenty-two, Dr. Kremer must have possessed the drive that has seen him through many years of bullheaded determination against formidable odds. Although he could not speak a word of English, with the aid of a Liverpool rabbi he obtained the position of translator on a ship sailing for America. Not only did he get free passage, but he also received a salary.

By the time Dr. Kremer returned to Rumania in 1947, he was a successful New York dentist who had graduated *Phi Beta Kappa* from the University of Pennsylvania in 1923. (He worked his way through school as a waiter at the Beaux Arts nightclub.) As treasurer of the Rumanian American Medical Relief Organization, he went back to Rumania in 1947, at his own expense, to bring crates of penicillin.

When Dr. Kremer is asked today why he has been so determined to bring Trifa to justice, he often cries on cue and says he "lost seventy-seven members of my family because of the Holocaust." But his family lived in Braila, not Bucharest, and he found in 1947 that his only close relative left in Rumania, a sister, had survived. His parents were then living in America. His father's family had lived in Poland and perished there during the Holocaust, but his mother's family came to America before World War I.

After a reunion with his sister in Braila in 1947, Dr. Kremer spent time in Bucharest. He heard gruesome eyewitness accounts of the January, 1941 pogrom. The names of the alleged leaders of that pogrom, Horia Sima and Viorel Trifa, were repeated by many of the survivors. People told him that Sima was then in Spain, but no one knew Trifa's whereabouts. Four years later, in 1951, Dr. Kremer learned from the clerics at the meeting of the United Rumanian Jews of America that Trifa was living in America. Before Trifa's July 17, 1950 arrival here, he had lived in Italy for five years, teaching history at a Catholic college in Pesaro.

When Dr. Kremer learned Trifa was in America, he became determined to bring him to justice—singlehandedly, if necessary. He spoke with the Anti-Defamation League of B'nai B'rith and the American Jewish Congress, both of which he assumed would be natural allies in his efforts to deport Trifa. Dr. Kremer says that officials of these organizations were polite

and seemed interested, but they claimed the lack of an extradition agreement between America and Rumania prevented
them from taking action.

Meanwhile, Dr. Kremer waged a political campaign within
his own organization, the United Rumanian Jews of America,
and was elected president by the several hundred members.
He was then able to use official stationery to write a barrage
of letters about Trifa to congressmen, senators, other government officials, and journalists. In reply, he received either
polite form letters or indication that his letters had been
forwarded to the Immigration and Naturalization Service (INS).

On April 23, 1952, Dr. Kremer received a telephone call
from a Rumanian priest who would not give his name but
who volunteered the information that in four days Trifa would
be consecrated as a bishop. Trifa was to be anointed by the
archbishop of the Ukrainian Orthodox Church in Pennsylvania. The priest explained that this anointment by the archbishop of another Orthodox church would supposedly legiti-
matize Trifa's consecration in the Rumanian Orthodox Church.

Immediately after this phone call, Dr. Kremer sent a tele-
gram to the INS informing them of the forthcoming ceremony
and urging them to advise the Ukrainian archbishop "not to
consecrate Viorel Trifa until your own investigation is completed."

A reply dated April 24, 1952, from Floyd E. Ault, officer
in charge of INS in Cleveland, said, "I regret that your request
that we intercede to prevent the consecration of Mr. Trifa as
a bishop cannot be granted. I am sure that you realize that
this Service, being a government agency, cannot interfere in
religious matters even though this Service may be interested
in the individual concerned."

With Trifa a bishop (and his name changed from Viorel to
Valerian), there were now two bishops of the Rumanian Orthodox Church in America, and the church split into opposing
factions. Bishop Moldovan still led the established Rumanian
Missionary Orthodox Church of America, while Trifa headed
the Rumanian Orthodox Episcopate of America. On July 6,
1952, Trifa's group forcibly took over Moldovan's Grass Lake,
Michigan headquarters, some fifty miles west of Detroit.

In 1954, at the age of fifty-seven, Dr. Kremer gave up his dental practice and went to Israel with his teenage son. In Israel, he spent two years speaking with Jews from Rumania and collecting documents and eyewitness testimony for what he calls his eighty-eight "exhibits."

When Dr. Kremer returned to America, he says he learned that Trifa, at the invitation of Vice President Richard M. Nixon, had delivered the opening prayer before the United States Senate on May 11, 1955. "That happened because I was in Israel," Dr. Kremer explained to me twenty-four years later, with characteristic bravado. "If I had been here, it never would have happened. Because I would have let people know who he was."

During Dr. Kremer's absence, not only had Trifa gained prestige, but the United Rumanian Jews of America had lost interest in his case. In the fall of 1957, Dr. Kremer resigned and founded his own organization, the Roumanian Jewish Federation of America, Inc. Trifa had become a naturalized citizen on May 13, 1957, and Dr. Kremer was more determined than ever to have him deported.

As president of his new organization, Dr. Kremer submitted his eighty-eight "exhibits" against Trifa to the INS. When the INS took no action, he sent copies to the president, senators, congressmen, other government officials, Jewish organizations, journalists, Rumanian-Christian societies, and the parishes in Trifa's episcopate.

In reply to his letter to President Nixon, Dr. Kremer received an answer dated December 22, 1971, from James F. Greene, associate commissioner of operations for INS:

> President Nixon has asked me to respond to your recent letter to him concerning the immigration status of Bishop Valerian D. Trifa, since this is a matter within the jurisdiction of the United States Immigration and Naturalization Service.
>
> Bishop Trifa was admitted to the United States for permanent residence on July 17, 1950, as a Displaced Person. Subsequent to his admission numerous allegations and charges were levelled against him including those to which you aver in your letter. These charges were exhaustively examined and extensively investigated by this Service over a period of years. A study

was made of all the available evidence and the conclusion was reached that grounds for the institution of deportation proceedings or that he was excludable at the time of his entry had not been established.

Bishop Trifa subsequently applied for naturalization and all avenues of inquiry into the charges brought against him were thoroughly explored. All such charges, accusations, and adverse information were presented for consideration of the Circuit Court at Jackson, Michigan, at an open and public hearing on his petition but the court found him qualified for naturalization and admitted him to citizenship on May 13, 1957.

Between 1965 and 1972, Dr. Kremer made five more trips to Rumania and Israel to obtain additional documents and eyewitness accounts about Trifa's 1941 activities. He continued to write letters to INS and major Jewish organizations. He specifically requested from INS their file on the "extensive investigation" and "exhaustive inquiries" preceding Trifa's entry and naturalization. In reply, he was sent form letters and told the files could be released only with Trifa's written consent.

On March 23, 1972, Dr. Kremer finally received a different answer from an INS official. In response to repeated requests for a copy of Trifa's testimony at his "open and public hearing" of petition for naturalization, Lowell R. Palmes, assistant director for citizenship (Detroit), wrote:

> At the time of the naturalization hearings oral testimony was taken, and there was no record made of the testimony given. The only record in the Court was the order granting citizenship which was signed by the presiding judge.

Armed with this new information and furious about the INS failure to record the hearing, Dr. Kremer launched a new letter-writing campaign. He sent over 800 letters to government officials, Rumanian-Christian groups, the forty-four branches of Trifa's church, the branches of the Rumanian Missionary Orthodox Church, and Detroit newspapers. He enclosed articles about Trifa published by David Horowitz in the *United Israel Bulletin*, and pointed out that Trifa was slated to be honored June 30–July 2, 1972, at a celebration honoring his fifty-eighth birthday and his twentieth anniversary as bishop.

On August 27, 1972, Dr. Kremer heard on the radio that Trifa had "confirmed he had been the top leader of a fascist youth movement sympathetic to Hitler's Germany." According to the radio announcement, the information came from a front-page interview with Trifa by religion writer Hiley H. Ward in *The Detroit Free Press.* The article said that Trifa admitted to membership in the fascist Iron Guard and to leadership of the 16,000-member National Union of Rumanian Students in 1941. But he denied killing anyone. "I have never in my life killed anyone, neither Jew nor Christian, nor a member of any faith," he told the *Free Press.*[4]

Dr. Kremer sent the INS this article, and subsequent articles published in the *Detroit Jewish News* by Philip Slomovitz. When there was still no action on Trifa, he wrote to INS Associate Commissioner Greene on February 21, 1973:

> . . . Don't you think that the presentation on my part on behalf of the Roumanian Jewish Federation of America containing a personal letter dated November 24th, 1972 and the memorandum dated the same date, containing 88 exhibits, running into many hundreds of pages, *deserves a written answer* and at least a show of interest on your part? Why don't you delegate a person in either your Washington or New York City office to examine and discuss my file and thus give me an opportunity to compare my file with yours. THIS HAS NEVER BEEN DONE—WHY?
>
> I cannot help but be frustrated that since April 28th, 1952, as per a letter signed by James E. Reilly, Enforcement Division of the Department of Justice I have received the same lack of cooperation . . .

In the fall of 1973, Dr. Kremer thought his frustration might be coming to an end. He received the following letter, dated September 28 and signed by Charles Gordon, general counsel of the Department of Justice:

> Your letter of August 28, 1973 to Dr. Henry Kissinger, and your letter of August 19, 1973, as well as a copy of your letter

of July 14, 1973 to the Attorney General, regarding Valerian
D. Trifa have been referred to me for reply . . . .
This office will conduct a new investigation into the matter,
giving full consideration to all material recently submitted by
you. You will be advised of the results of the investigation and
the conclusions of this Service.

But Kremer's frustration did not end in September; it became more intense. Although he had received the INS investigation notice, the government did not begin action until
the following spring. On May 30, 1974, INS Investigator Sam
Zutty called Dr. Kremer to his New York office and told him
the government had begun interviewing witnesses. However,
not until a year later, on May 14, 1975, did the INS file
denaturalization proceedings. On that date, a U. S. attorney
filed a complaint in U. S. District Court, Eastern District of
Michigan, in Detroit. The government charged that Trifa had
withheld information about his past when he entered the
country in 1950. He would be subject to denaturalization and
deportation if the government proved that he concealed from
immigration officials his membership in the Iron Guard.

Although the case was filed in 1975, no trial date was set
for over four years. Dr. Kremer spent that time badgering
the Justice Department and officials of major Jewish organizations, most of whom dismissed him as a "crank" and a
"pest." He kept up his letter-writing campaign, and talked to
whomever would listen—media, synagogue groups, government and community leaders.

In 1977, he founded the Committee to Bring Nazi War
Criminals to Justice in the U.S.A., largely a letterhead organization devoted to justice for only one accused Nazi: Trifa. As
president of both this organization and his Roumanian Jewish
Federation of America, Inc., Dr. Kremer continued to seek
allies for his cause. Often his domineering single-mindedness
and desperate antics made him more enemies than friends.

When there was no court action by January, 1979, Dr.
Kremer decided it was time to dramatize the situation. To
mark the thirty-eighth anniversary of the Bucharest pogrom
on January 21, and to focus attention on the Trifa case, he
organized a demonstration of some twenty people in front of

the White House and handcuffed himself to the fence. Dr. Kremer, then eighty-two, was one of seven demonstrators arrested by park police, booked for disorderly conduct, fingerprinted, photographed and fined $10 each.

Because of poor timing, Dr. Kremer's demonstration did not create the stir he anticipated. Sports-minded confidants had counseled him to choose another date, if he wanted media coverage; January 21 was Superbowl Sunday, and the eyes and ears of the nation were not on Dr. Charles Kremer but on Pittsburgh vs. Dallas. Other than giving him lively subject matter for subsequent appearances and a thicker FBI file to brag about, the demonstration accomplished nothing.

On June 25, 1979, Dr. Kremer was again in Washington, this time with another purpose in mind. As a member of a group of individuals concerned about the issue of Nazi war criminals, he met with Walter J. Rockler, the newly-appointed head of the Justice Department's Office of Special Investigations. Although the meeting was intended as a briefing by Rockler, Dr. Kremer insisted on making opening remarks and launched into a tirade about Trifa. Other members of the delegation, equally committed to the cause, said later they were embarrassed by his emotional outburst and pushy manner.

Not convinced that Rumania had authenticated all of the necessary documents on Trifa, Dr. Kremer pressed Rockler for specific information on these papers. When Rockler said he was unable to give out that information, Dr. Kremer decided to pursue the issue on another level. He left for the Rumanian Embassy.

In fluent Rumanian, he told the deputy ambassador that he wanted to know what documents the Rumanian government had authenticated for the Trifa case. The official replied that he did not even know what documents his government had given the United States, as this was not within his jurisdiction. Never willing to give up, Dr. Kremer then asked if Rumania would authenticate certain documents in his possession, if he gave them to the Embassy. "Then I'll know that Rockler has the ones he should have," he explained. Polite and seemingly cooperative, the official said he would give no promises, but would make the request of his government. To reinforce his "request," Dr. Kremer pointed out that Rumania's Most Favored Nation status was then pending and that he had "helped them" before in trade issues through his Roumanian Jewish Federation of America.

When Dr. Kremer realized at the end of the meeting that he was stranded at the Embassy with no cab to take him back to Capitol Hill, he was, as usual, undaunted. "Tell your boy to drive me back—I'm an old man with a cane," said the robust octogenarian. Honoring his request, the deputy ambassador had the Embassy chauffeur drive Dr. Kremer back to the Capitol.

During the spring of 1979, Dr. Kremer was also dealing with another facet of the Trifa case. On May 1, Trifa had been interviewed for forty-five minutes on Radio Free Europe, a broadcast organization (funded by Congress and connected with the Central Intelligence Agency) which beams programs into Communist countries in Eastern Europe. The occasion was the fiftieth anniversary of the Rumanian Orthodox Church in America.

"How can we allow Radio Free Europe, a government-funded broadcasting organization, to use American money to give a platform to an accused Nazi war criminal? " Dr. Kremer asked. "The government does not want to try this case and this is their way of saying it. . . . It really doesn't matter what Trifa said. What matters is that our government gave forty-five minutes of its broadcast time to this butcher of Jews," he told me.[5]

And Dr. Kremer was off on another letter-writing streak to government officials, major Jewish organizations, and the media. He even became involved in internal accusations of anti-Semitism within the Rumanian desk of Radio Free Europe, waging a secondary battle in defense of two Munich-based Jewish employees of Radio Free Europe, Jacob Popper and Edgar Rafael. (The two had been dismissed from their positions and later alleged they were targets of anti-Semitic superiors.)

Meanwhile, the Trifa hearing date was finally set for July 30, 1979 in U. S. District Court, Detroit. In June, Trifa's attorneys asked Federal Judge Cornelia Kennedy to dismiss the government's suit, contending that the federal law barring entry to persons who "advocated or assisted in . . . persecution

. . ." was too broad and vague, and thus unconstitutional.[6] They further claimed that the government was aware of the charges against Trifa when he entered the country, and that he had been denied due process because of the thirty-year delay in bringing charges.[7] On October 30, 1979, the judge denied Trifa's request for a summary judgment in his favor.

In December, Dr. Kremer tried still another approach. He organized a demonstration outside a New York City church affiliated with Trifa's Rumanian Episcopate of America. As people came to worship at St. Dumitru Orthodox Church on West 89th Street on Sunday, December 9, they were handed literature summarizing Iron Guard activities and headlined: "Archbishop Valerian Trifa—If this man is *your* archbishop and head of *your* church, then you should know that he is a MASS MURDERER!"

To encourage people to join his demonstration, he distributed a flier that read:

> We must be there to state to this church that their support of such a leader is the height of immorality. It is the purpose of this demonstration to embarrass the church by informing its members of the infamous past of their archbishop, and not to interfere in any way with the exercise of anyone's religious rights. This should not be a confrontation, but be prepared for anything, keeping in mind this is a religious service.

Dr. Kremer did have a "confrontation" that day, with a priest named Florin Galdau. In a summons dated December 19, 1979, he was charged by the priest with harassment and menacing, and ordered to appear in criminal court on February 29, 1980. A second summons, issued on April 14, 1980, charged Dr. Kremer with aggravated harassment and ordered him to appear on May 29. He was then ordered by a July 16, 1980 summons to appear on July 31 at the Institution for Mediation and Control Conflict Resolution Center. The case was eventually dismissed "without prejudice."

Suddenly Trifa surrendered his naturalization papers on August 25, 1980 to federal authorities in Detroit, in effect relinquishing his citizenship. His denaturalization case had been set for October 14, 1980 before Federal District Judge Horace

W. Gilmore, who had replaced Judge Kennedy. In a statement released on August 25, Trifa said: "The relinquishment of my citizenship is in no way to be considered an admission of the Government allegations in any manner, form or substance." [8]

Dr. Kremer's reaction was that he was pleased Trifa had surrendered his papers, but he was determined to continue his fight against the archbishop.

On September 3, Judge Gilmore officially revoked Trifa's U.S. citizenship, ending the denaturalization phase of the government's case. U. S. attorneys said deportation proceedings would begin as soon as the proper papers were drawn up. Dr. Kremer told reporters outside the Detroit courtroom that day that he was unhappy the government didn't file papers immediately, and that he would not feel vindicated until Trifa was deported.

After voluntarily consenting to denaturalization on September 3, Trifa filed an appeal on the consent judgment. In May, 1981, with the government's motion to dismiss or advance the hearing pending before the Sixth Circuit Court of Appeals and a denial of Trifa's appeal anticipated, Dr. Kremer felt the case was all but completed.

"There's nothing left to do on the Trifa case," he said to me on May 18. "This summer I'm going to Israel to get evidence on another alleged Nazi war criminal, Tscherim Soobzokov." Dr. Kremer added that he had "made a deal" with OSI head Allan A. Ryan, Jr., claiming that Ryan had told him he would reopen the case if new evidence was forthcoming from the Israel trip.

This was denied by Ryan, who wrote Dr. Kremer a letter dated June 1, 1981 which said:

> I would very much appreciate your making clear to the people with whom you speak that you are acting purely as a private citizen and that by providing you the information [on Soobzokov] above (which is public) I am not authorizing you to act in any way on behalf of this Office or the United States government.

At the age of 84, Dr. Kremer left for Israel to begin a new battle. He brought with him for the archives at Yad Vashem Holocaust Memorial his exhibits, documents and correspondence about Trifa. They had previously been housed in his rented room in a Manhattan apartment, literally piled to the ceiling and falling in disarray as he discussed the Trifa case with journalists.

On October 7, 1982, Dr. Kremer heard Trifa's attorney agree in a Detroit courtroom that Trifa would leave the United States. A civil deportation proceeding against him had begun three days earlier, before Judge Bellino D'Ambrosio. Under an agreement with the federal government, Trifa admitted to lying to immigration authorities about his fascist activities when he entered the United States in 1950. Trifa's attorney said Trifa wanted to avoid dragging on a "no-win situation," and that Trifa requested deportation to Switzerland. Switzerland denied his request. The OSI then approached Italy and West Germany, both of which refused to accept Trifa.

In April, 1983, the Justice Department asked Israel to take Trifa. Negotiations broke down when Mark Richards, deputy assistant attorney general, refused to attend an official meeting in the East Jerusalem office of Israel's Attorney General, Yitzhak Zamir.[9] (The United States does not recognize East Jerusalem as part of the State of Israel.) Three months later Dr. Kremer went to Israel, planning to convince authorities there to accept Trifa and to try him as a war criminal.

By the time he returned to America in August, however, Dr. Kremer had changed his mind. "It is to Rumania or to the Vatican City where Trifa should be deported and not to Israel," he wrote. "Why does U.S. justice attempt to impose on Israel to accept him? What jurisdiction does Israel have over a former Rumanian and American citizen? . . . True, Israel should have such privilege but not such responsibility."[10] At age 86, Dr. Kremer was still stirring things up, sometimes muddying the water in the process.

Kremer has publicly stated, "In 1975 I succeeded to finally bring [Trifa] to trial."[11] But he did not accomplish this alone. As early as the 1950s, others were also actively seeking justice for Trifa, as well as for other Nazi war criminals living freely in America.

Five _____

"Nazi War Criminals Among Us"

Charles R. Allen, Jr.'s 1963 *Jewish Currents* articles and booklet, *Nazi War Criminals Among Us,* were the first thorough documentation published here on the issue of Nazi war criminals in America. Because the topic was then either unknown or hushed up by most Jewish organizations and government officials, Allen was a pioneer. The early advocates of justice that he mentions, and Allen himself, were heroic in speaking out on such an unpopular and obscure issue. For their accusations against so-called "anti-Communist" Nazi war criminals, they also risked being labeled Communist sympathizers during the McCarthy era.

Three congressmen are singled out by Allen for their exposure of the issue before 1963: Rep. Seymour Halpern (R-N.Y.), Rep. Frank Kowalski (D-Conn.) and Rep. John F. Shelley (D-Calif.). In the March 1, 1962 *Congressional Record,* page 2844, Halpern, as quoted by Allen, describes Trifa as one among "some of the leading culprits" who participated in the 1941 Bucharest pogrom, and who "remain unpunished, enjoying life in Spain, in Latin America, and one of them in the United States itself. This man walks the streets of one of our great cities freely."

Halpern explained to the House of Representatives that Trifa played a leading role in the fascist National Union of Rumanian Christian Students and was president of the group during the 1941 pogrom. "Trifa and his organization contributed significantly through speeches, manifestos and demonstrations to inciting the pogrom and there is no doubt of their active participation in it," Halpern said. "I have learned that despite this heinous background, this person was admitted to the United States as a displaced person in July of 1950." Allen writes in his 1963 booklet:

> U.S. Congressman Seymour Halpern shed additional light on this significant part of the Valerian [Trifa] case in his March 1 speech.
>
> Cong. Halpern learned that in 1951, after he was admitted to the United States as a Displaced Person . . . Trifa "was 'ordained' as a member of the clergy of the Romanian Orthodox Church, and, as Bishop Valerian, he is now serving in Detroit.
>
> "I put 'ordained' in quotes," the Congressman continued, "because the circumstances of his so-called ordination are highly questionable. According to a statement of the Romanian Orthodox Missionary Episcopate in America, [Trifa] was ordained by an unfrocked priest, and charges of simony [that is, criminal fraud in 'buying' ecclesiastical preferment] have been registered by the Episcopate against both Trifa and the 'priest' who 'ordained' him.
>
> "Apparently," Cong. Halpern declared, "the ceremonies of this suspect consecration were carried out despite a Federal court injunction sought and obtained by the Episcopate."
>
> Calling the presence of Trifa in the United States "appalling," Cong. Halpern demanded: "Has not the time come for public opinion to be clearly aware of Trifa's background and of his presence in our midst?
>
> "Should not the circumstances of his admission and continued free residence in our country be re-examined by the appropriate authorities? " [1]

On April 16, 1962, Rep. Kowalski exposed another Rumanian Nazi war criminal, Nicolae Malaxa. Allen's booklet reported on Kowalski's remarks in the *Congressional Record* (p. A2935) of that date, concerning the presence here of the former financier of the Rumanian Iron Guard and corporation partner of Nazi war criminal Hermann Goering. According to Allen:

Congressman Frank Kowalski (D-Conn.) exposed Malaxa April 16, 1962 with unassailable proof.

Malaxa, he said, "is living in this country solely because of the activities of several top-level personages of our Government."

Malaxa, Cong. Kowalski charged, was the "financial mainstay" of the Iron Guard at the time of the 1941 pogrom.[2]

In the October 5, 1962 *Congressional Record* (p. 21486), Kowalski again attacked Malaxa. "It is my understanding that Malaxa is only one of many fascist genocides who have bought their way into the United States," he said.[3]

In the same *Congressional Record* (pp. 21483–4), Rep. Shelley discussed Malaxa's connections with Albert Goering (Hermann's brother) and the Rumanian Iron Guard during World War II, as well as Malaxa's later connections with Richard M. Nixon when Nixon was the junior senator from California. Allen said:

> Cong. Shelley then reprinted the complete text of a letter sent Sept. 14, 1951 by Nixon and the then senior California U.S. Senator, William F. Knowland, to the Defense Production Administration (DPA). Nixon marked the letter on Malaxa's behalf "urgent" and told the DPA that "it is important strategically and economically, both for California and the entire United States," that the Malaxa application [to build a plant essential to Korean War materials] be approved.

As part of the deal, Malaxa was to be admitted to the United States with "first preference quota," because he was indispensable in building this plant. Shelley described Malaxa as "bloodstained and dangerous," and said he was "dismayed by the thought that such a person has been extended the hospitality and protection of the United States . . ."[4]

Kowalski and Shelley died in the fall of 1974. Halpern, now a New York City attorney, recalled to me in a May 27, 1981 interview his 1962 attempts to expose the presence of Trifa. "I remember that I got a letter that year, asking if I knew there was a Rumanian war criminal in this country," he said. "The letter said Trifa got in under false pretenses, had been ordained, and had become a bishop. I couldn't believe it, and

I wrote back for proof. I can't remember the person's name, but he sent me clips and other material. I got in touch with INS, who in turn went to their head man—I was a congressman. Their response was that they didn't have real evidence, no proof. This angered me. You'd think they would at least investigate!

"I asked for an investigation. Nothing happened," Halpern continued. "So I made a speech from the floor [recorded in the March 1, 1962 *Congressional Record*]. This speech appeared in Trifa's hometown newspaper, and played havoc with his parishioners. They sent me letters, and some of them were vicious. There was a newspaper article or editorial, criticizing me for making an issue of it and for defaming a 'great and holy man.' The article said Trifa had disproved the charges against him, and that I was trying to politically exploit him. I also remember there were letters from Cleveland criticizing me."

Halpern told me that at the time of his speech on the floor of the House, he was the only Jewish Republican member of Congress. He believes this may have been the reason that letters about Trifa were sent to him. Despite his exposure of Trifa in Congress, there was no action from INS for some time. "The effort of the INS got nowhere," he recalled. "Then there was word from INS five or six years later. They had never notified me they had investigated. But they said that as far as they could ascertain, there was not enough evidence to deport Trifa."

Besides documenting the early efforts of Halpern and his two colleagues in Congress to expose specific Nazi war criminals, Allen in his 1963 articles and booklet covered the work of several journalists on the subject.

The writings of then JTA Washington correspondent Milton Friedman in the March 1, 1952 issue of *The Nation* and in the June 21, 1960 *Jewish Floridian* were discussed in a previous chapter. Although JTA refused to carry Friedman's articles on Nazi war criminals in America, Allen singles out several individual Anglo-Jewish weeklies and editors that covered the subject. In discussing Artukovic, Allen says:

On September 20, 1962 the Chicago *Sentinel*, a Jewish weekly, reported that the U.S. Immigration and Naturalization Service "has continued its efforts to obtain a travel document for deportation to some other country but to date has been unsuccessful."

In the same magazine Jan. 18, 1962, J. I. Fishbein, its editor, pondered the meaning of the Artukovic case to Americans. "Here is a mystery that is indeed difficult to understand. What are the powerful forces behind Artukovic able to give him this kind of protection? Great musicians, scientists, professors of all kinds have been denied admittance to the United States on the basis that at one time or another, they were identified with Red causes. Yet, this notorious Nazi continues to find haven in Surfside, California.

"Isn't it about time that the American people insisted that he be turned over for judgment? " [5]

In what he describes as "a significant piece on the Bishop," Allen quotes extensively from an article on Trifa in the *National Jewish Post and Opinion* dated June 22, 1962:

Trifa admitted . . . that "he fled Bucharest on Jan. 21, 1941 and sought political asylum in Transylvania where he was captured by the Germans for extradition to Romania," where he was wanted by the Antonescu dictatorship. "For some reason," Trifa told the *Post and Opinion*, "I was not extradited but imprisoned by the Germans."

In interviewing Trifa (before writing his 1963 articles), Allen used this piece as a basis for his questions in *Nazi War Criminals Among Us:*

I then began to quote from a passage in the aforementioned article of *The Post and Opinion:* "Bishop Valerian . . . asserted that history was cluttered with flagrant misrepresentations of the Romanian 'Iron Guard Terror' of Jan., 1941. Among those misrepresentations, he declared, was the baseless charge that the terror took the form of pogroms against the Jews. He said that there was no violence of any kind in Bucharest on Jan. 20, 1941 . . . ."

Had he said this to *The Post and Opinion?* "Yes! " he screamed over the long-distance wires: "The Jews were never touched! "

Wasn't he aware of the fact that absolute proof of the 1941
pogrom came from German Nazi and Romanian archives? He
yelled:

"God-damn you! You Communist!!"

And with that, Viorel D. Trifa, now known as Bishop Valerian, hung up.[6]

Another newspaper (now defunct) is also mentioned by
Allen:

Feb. 9, 1953 the Yiddish daily, *The Day* reported: "One of
the worst Romanian Nazis and Jew-baiters who helped murder
6,000 Jews in Romania is at this time a Bishop in America."

Asserting that Trifa had been one of the "youth" leaders
of the 1941 pogrom, *The Day* quoted from a leaflet which the
Iron Guard issued on the eve of the mass murders in which
Trifa stated: "It is the duty of every Romanian to destroy and
extinguish Jewish lives!"[7]

In addition to these publications that specialized in news
for Jewish readers, Allen discussed in 1963 the writings of
syndicated columnist Drew Pearson, one of the first to expose
the presence of Nazis here. Allen quotes a nationally-syndicated
Pearson column dated June 7, 1962, which equates Artukovic's
decrees with those of Himmler and Hitler.[8] Allen also said
that Pearson "reported that Artukovic has now become 'the
center of a national high-pressure lobbying campaign' [by]
. . . a Who's Who of the Ultra Right in the United States
(*The National Jewish Post and Opinion*, June 29, 1962)."[9]

Because of fears about lack of reparation money from Germany, and McCarthyism in America, the major Jewish American organizations did not speak out militantly on the issue
of Nazi war criminals living here (see Chapter 3). Allen had
almost nothing to report about their pre-1963 activity. He
said, "There has been very little broad concern over the
Artukovic case yet in the United States. At its 1959 convention,
the Jewish War Veterans passed a resolution insisting that
Artukovic 'be deported at the earliest opportunity' and the
American Jewish Congress is also on record to this effect. Yet
no national indignation over this case can be reported."[10]

An editorial, which followed the third of Allen's *Jewish Currents* articles and was entitled "The Cry for Justice," further discussed the Jewish War Veterans' stand on the issue. The editorial said:

> Shortly after the first article by Mr. Allen appeared in our Jan. issue, the Jewish War Veterans of the United States of America acted. Its National Commander Morton London inquired of the Attorney-General what Gustav Hilger was doing in the United States. Weeks have passed without an answer. The J.W.V. at the same time urged Senator Philip A. Hart, Chairman of a Special Senate Subcommittee on Refugees and Escapees, to secure legislation that would plug the loopholes through which such Nazis and Fascists as Artukovic have slipped into our country.

The editorial added:

> And then there are the Jewish organizations, national and local. Will they follow the initiative of the Jewish War Veterans? Can Jews read this documented account by Mr. Allen without a special constriction of the heart, a special gritting of the teeth, a special determination not to rest until justice is done? . . . Will voices be raised to insist that Washington act to help bring the accused to trial? [11]

Six

Charles R. Allen, Jr. Steps In

Charles R. Allen, Jr. is not a Jew. He is, in fact, a WASP (White Anglo-Saxon Protestant) whose ancestors came to America in 1644. But since 1962 he has possessed, in the words of *Jewish Currents,* the "special determination" that the Jewish organizations seem to lack, "not to rest until justice is done." [1] Allen was the first to document sixteen known cases of Nazi war criminals living here, in most instances complete with interviews of the accused. At a time when even most of their surviving victims were ignoring the presence of Nazis here, how did Allen come to write his landmark documentation?

The immediate catalysts were Morris U. Schappes, editor of *Jewish Currents,* and Chaim Suller, editor of the *Morning Freiheit* [Freedom], a Yiddish daily published in New York City. Both publications were, until 1967, affiliated with the Communist Party of the United States of America (CPUSA). Like Schappes, Suller, a Communist, was an educator until he lost his job to McCarthyism. (The ethnic communist papers were the first to give the subject attention. The Lithuanian newspaper *Laisve,* edited by Anthony Bimba in New York, is a notable example.)

Suller began working at the *Freiheit* in 1953. "I had been director of a secular progressive Jewish school in New York from 1945 to 1952," he recalled to me thirty years later. "[Senator Joseph] McCarthy put it on his list and it had to close." Suller was born in White Russia in 1902 and came to

the United States at the age of twenty. Before directing the
New York City school, he was a teacher in progressive Jewish
schools in Chicago, Philadelphia and New York City.

Suller said in a June 29, 1981 interview at *Morning Freiheit*
headquarters that at the end of 1962 he started to write a
Yiddish series on Nazi war criminals for that newspaper. "I
had the idea that when I finished, the *Freiheit* would publish
the series as a booklet," he says. "But I met with Morris
Schappes and said to him, 'This is such an important issue,
you should do something about it in *Jewish Currents.*' He agreed
with me and commissioned Charles R. Allen, Jr., who had
written earlier investigative articles for him. Allen came to
see me, but he already had whatever information I could give
him."

Schappes concurs about the genesis of Allen's 1963 articles
and booklet. "Allen had done a McCarthyism series for us in
Jewish Life [in the 1950s], and we asked him to look into this,"
Schappes told me. "The *Freiheit* had material about some of
them [Nazi war criminals] getting into the United States. War
criminals were being tried in East Germany in great numbers
and in the Soviet Union, and this had been reported in the
Freiheit. We got our materials mainly from the *Freiheit,* but
Allen was a real investigator and got down to things they
didn't know about."

Asked where he got his material, Suller says: "Allen did
better than I did. He went out and spoke to the Nazi war
criminals. I hadn't done anything of the sort. What I did was
get in touch with people in the Soviet Union and countries
that had been occupied by the Nazis—either people who were
victims or had documents. What started me off was out of
the blue. I saw a little item in *The New York Times,* about
someone accused of being a Nazi war criminal. I got to thinking
that if there was one, there might be others. I started asking
around. I got Drew Pearson's articles on Artukovic. I went
to Washington, to the embassies of the Soviet Union, Hungary,
Poland. I asked for help and got very little."

Suller did, however, have a unique channel for information
on war criminals. "I started to get letters from Soviet Yiddish
writers and others in the Soviet Union who wanted subscriptions to the *Morning Freiheit,*" he says. "They were not allowed

to pay for these subscriptions, according to Soviet law. So I asked in exchange for the subscriptions to have them send me information on Jews in their areas, and on atrocities committed in their areas during the Nazi occupation. One man from Riga sent me a whole lot of material. He sent me Soviet newspaper reports about trials that took place, and among them were names of people who live here, for example, Maikovskis and Linnas. He sent me an original photo of Maikovskis, and his signature in a book."

Because *Jewish Currents* published Allen's booklet on war criminals, Suller switched his theme to anti-Semitism, but included the topic of Nazi war criminals. A total of 8,000 copies of Suller's booklet, entitled *What Price Silence?*, was published in 1963 in both English and Yiddish. After he published the booklet, Suller followed up with articles on Nazi war criminals in the *Freiheit*.

When asked whether his own work or the *Jewish Currents* articles and booklets made any impact on the Jewish community, Suller says, "For a few years I heard nothing. I didn't get an echo. I don't think the leadership of the major Jewish organizations did anything. There's a tendency to hush it up, whether because the government is really protecting Nazi war criminals, or whatever the case may be. The Jewish community does a lot about Soviet anti-Semitism and I'm not against this. I stress that I myself was disturbed about anti-Semitism in the Soviet Union. But the Jewish community here is not doing anything about war criminals in America. I'll give them the benefit of the doubt—maybe they're pulling strings.

"Why aren't they doing anything?" Suller asks rhetorically. "I'm just supposing they don't want to rock the boat. Many are close to the government. Some individual leaders of Jewish organizations are in with the government. The government finds it necessary to cover up, because it uses these Nazi war criminals for the Cold War. Many Jewish organizations are Cold War people. They hate the Soviet Union more than they love the Jewish people."

Suller is aware that his own connection to communism has made him *persona non grata* in the "organized Jewish community." "The *Freiheit* is still known as the 'Red paper'—the Communist Party paper," he says. "On the whole, I'm ignored because of my connection with the *Freiheit*. The paper considers itself a socialist paper, in support of communism as expressed in some European countries such as Italy and Spain. It's a left-wing radical Yiddish newspaper. I personally consider myself a Communist, but I don't think there is communism in the Soviet Union today."

Regarding the issue of Nazi war criminals here, Suller says, "The main thing is that no one wanted to touch this subject matter itself. No one but left-wing organizations would touch it. Frankly, I had a personal interest. I lost a lot of my family—uncles, aunts, cousins whom I had known personally before I came here. As a Jew, I am very much interested."

Allen, as a non-Jew and a left-winger, was also "very much interested" in 1962 and since. He is quick to point out that he is not a Nazi hunter, and that his investigative writing on Nazi war criminals is "consistent with and incidental to" his anti-fascist, anti-racist work. He recalls in detail the events leading to his writing on Nazi war criminals for *Jewish Currents*, and described them to me in a January 15, 1983 interview.

"In 1962 I was deeply into the first draft of my book, *Heusinger of the Fourth Reich: The Step-by-Step Resurgence of the German General Staff*," he says. "My friend, Morris Schappes, called and said someone (whom he didn't identify and who is still anonymous to me) had dropped off some documents about alleged Nazi war criminals now living in the United States. Morris said the packet was given to him by someone who had just returned from one of the Baltic countries. I told Morris I was too busy, and that I didn't believe there were Nazi war criminals living in the United States."

Allen's writing for *Jewish Life/Jewish Currents* had begun ten years earlier, while he was on the editorial staff of *The Nation*. "In 1952–1953 I did for *Jewish Life* a series of articles on McCarthyism," he says. "The first was 'McCarthy and Anti-Semitism', and the second was 'McCarthy: Enemy of the Negro People'. I had always assumed that *Jewish Life* was a publication of the CPUSA. I didn't know it for a fact, and I didn't care. My principle has always been that I'll work with you—no matter who you are, including a raving Communist—so long as you are anti-fascist, anti-Nazi, anti-racist, and anti-anti-Semite.

"Those articles were instant 'best sellers' in the broadest sense of the word," Allen recalls. "They were reprinted on the front pages of either Anglo-Jewish or black American newspapers. Most of the Jewish leaders denied what I said about McCarthy being anti-Semitic, and denounced it as communist propaganda.

"Soon afterward, I found out that *Jewish Life* was an organ of the CPUSA's Commission on the Jewish Question. Morris called me and said he wanted me to meet an 'important person,' and in the late fall of 1953 I went to the offices of the magazine. I was introduced to the chairman of CPUSA's Commission on the Jewish Question, but he was not identified as such. Since I was not a member of the party, it was not revealed to me that he was Schappes' and the magazine board members' party superior.

The chairman was introduced as 'a concerned friend of the magazine,' and said he wanted to critically reassess certain aspects of my articles. He said that as a Marine Corps veteran, McCarthy was therefore a militarist. I knew he didn't know what he was talking about. At this time, I was in my early twenties, had a short temper, checked in at 210 pounds off my professional football years, and was considered by many to be a 'certified homicidal maniac'. My attitude was, 'What will I learn from this nobody?' I cursed him out, asked him how he dared to presume to tell me about my work, and walked out of the meeting."

Allen tells this story to explain his skepticism about Schappes' call almost ten years later, regarding the Nazi war criminal documents. "In 1962 we were still in the throes of McCarthyism, and it was difficult to live in the United States on the Left. But I loved it," Allen says. "I got up every morning looking forward to a day of doing combat against these wahoos. So after Morris called a few times and reminded me, I finally dropped by at the magazine office to look at the documents."

Allen recalls that Schappes showed him Latvian and Lithuanian newspapers and magazines, and what looked like crudely translated excerpts from them. "The one that caught my eye reported on a war crimes trial in Lithuania. It cited a fragment of a Nazi administrative decree. Roman Catholic Bishop Vincentas Bryzgys was quoted as forbidding all clergy (including nuns) in his Lithuanian diocese from aiding and abetting Jews in any manner. The excerpt asserted that Bryzgys was living in Chicago. I told Morris that most of the translation was popularized communist propaganda, but that this alleged order intrigued me.

"I took the stuff home to study, and soon called a friend at Columbia University, whom I'd known there in graduate school," he says. "I asked if he knew anyone who could handle Russian, Latvian and Lithuanian, and he referred me to someone at Columbia's Russian Institute. I gave this person the materials and forgot about them. At the time I was caught up in the production stages of my *Heusinger* book, and I had other things on my mind.

"But then the translator from Columbia got in touch with me and said, 'I want to see you—you've got authentic stuff here'. Certain propagandistic slants by which the Latvians and Lithuanians were trying to reach out to *émigrés* abroad had to be disregarded. I instantly saw their propaganda intent; it was a powerful weapon to say Nazi war criminals were living among friends of the homeland in the United States, Western Europe and Canada—some running their *émigré* organizations. But I also saw a great degree of truth from their point of view, and I respected it. And I thought we might be dealing with factual documentation on the war criminals. My friend at Columbia agreed, even though he was pro-State Department during those horrible and essentially irrational Cold War years."

Allen's next step was to check the Nuremberg War Crimes Tribunal archives at Columbia University. "Searching the archives was blissful joy for me—I love that kind of research," he says. "I found there a basic document in which Bryzgys' activities in collaborating with the Nazis were thoroughly described by the U.S. prosecution. The Russian and Lithuanian materials Schappes had given me were translated from original German documents, as were the American translations at Columbia. When I saw that they matched, I knew they were authentic."

To determine whether Bryzgys was living in Chicago, Allen called the diocese there. Upon confirmation of his presence, Allen tried more than a half dozen times to interview Bryzgys, but the bishop refused. This case propelled him into his dedication to the issue. He investigated sixteen alleged Nazi war criminals over the summer of 1962, interviewing fourteen of them, and then in September wrote his seminal three-part series for *Jewish Currents*. His *Nazi War Criminals Among Us*, which in April, 1963 reprinted the three articles and additional material, sold out three printings before the summer of that year.

"When the 1963 articles and booklet appeared, they created a sensation," Allen says. "In the 1960s there was a much more definable left-wing press than now. I was also on national radio and television, including seven minutes a day for a week on NBC's 'Monitor'—prime time for a declared 'lefty' in a communist publication!"

Allen's writings triggered three mass rallies in 1963–64 in Brooklyn, Chicago and Los Angeles. At the Brooklyn meeting on May 8, 1963, Allen spoke before an audience of 2,000. The meeting was held at the De Luxe Palace in Brownsville, and other speakers were Gedalia Sandler, billed as a "Jewish leader and lecturer;" Mrs. Thelma Hamilton, a black Brownsville leader who was executive secretary of the Parents Workshop in Brooklyn; and Rabbi Chaim Rabinowitz.

Sponsors, hardly "major" Jewish American organizations, were: Ralph Aronoff Society, Brooklyn Cultural Society, Brownsville and East New York Benevolent Society, Crown Heights Cultural Club, East Flatbush Fraternal Society, Flatbush Cultural Club, David Lapidus Fraternal Society, Premier Aid Society, and Williamsburg-Biller Society.

After Allen spoke, he made his way through the hall, surrounded by several friends. "People called one friend, filmmaker Larry Mischel, 'Baby Bull', and they called me 'Big Bull'," Allen recalls. Another friend accompanying him was the film director and producer Larry Moyer, with whom Allen had co-authored *The Moving Finger*, winner of the 1963–64 San Francisco International Film Festival and other awards.

"As we started to walk out, four or five guys walked right up to us in the main aisle," Allen says. "One of them, with an intent crazy look in his eye, put his chest right up to mine and said, 'Danzig' [the Nazi "free" city, a Nazi rallying cry]." Allen replied with an unprintable curse, and the man said, "Danzig, Danzig, Danzig, you Communist!"

PROTEST   PROTEST
AGAINST NAZI WAR CRIMINALS
IN OUR MIDST
HELP GET THEM OUT OF THE U.S.A.

COME AND HEAR ABOUT THESE NAZI MURDERERS WHO
SLAUGHTERED MILLIONS OF JEWS AND OTHER PEOPLES,
INNOCENT MEN, WOMEN AND CHILDREN

ONE OF THEM LIVES RIGHT HERE IN BROWNSVILLE!

COME HEAR THE FACTS.....AT A MASS RALLY

**WEDNESDAY, MAY 8, 1963 at 8:15 pm
at the
DE LUXE PALACE   Howard and Pitkin Aves.
Admission: FREE**

Speakers

● CHARLES R. ALLEN, JR.
Author: "Nazi War Criminals Among Us"

● GEDALIA SANDLER
Jewish Leader and Lecturer

● MRS. THELMA HAMILTON
Exec. Sec., Parents Workshop in Brooklyn
Negro Leader in Brownsville

● RABBI CHAIM RABINOWITZ

You will hear authentic facts, names and descriptions of at least 25 NAZI WAR
CRIMINALS who have found a haven in our country.

We ask: WHY ARE THESE MURDERERS PROTECTED IN OUR LAND?

THEY MUST BE BROUGHT TO JUSTICE!

WE MUST NEVER FORGET AND NEVER FORGIVE THOSE WHO
BELIEVE IN WAR, DESTRUCTION AND MURDER.

A 1963 poster announcing one of the first demonstrations against Nazi war criminals in America.

Allen and his friends drove away, but were tailed by the group who had accosted them. Allen says he pulled the car over, and the other car stopped behind them. He and Mischel got out and beat up their pursuers. Searching the car, Allen and his friends found two pistols. "We took them and threw them in the river as we drove over the Brooklyn Bridge," he recalls.

Because of this incident, Mischel became Allen's self-appointed bodyguard for a May, 1963 rally in Chicago. At that meeting, Mrs. Dagmara Vallens, a 34-year-old Latvian national, created a panic when she released ten white mice into the audience. A group of American Nazi party members then took off their "civilian" shirts to reveal swastika-adorned uniforms, and tried to storm the podium. Allen says that he, Mischel and two union participants "worked them over" thoroughly. "I know I broke the jaw of one of them," he recalls. "My punch went cleanly through it."

The Chicago rally was sponsored by the National Committee Against Nazism and Nazi Criminals, of which Allen was a charter member. The Committee was founded and led by Rabbi S. Burr Yampol of Chicago, whom Allen describes as "an Orthodox rabbi who ran a nursing home for old, poor Jews. I met him on one of his trips to New York and instantly liked him," Allen says. "He had read my series and told me he was 'totally bowled over.' We formed the committee in the early 1960s with him as national president. Sam Pevsner ran the New York City branch. Some members were Communists, but not everyone—for example, Yampol and myself. The rabbi tried mightily to get Congress to do something. He devoted the balance of his life to seeking justice for Nazi war criminals in the United States."

Rabbi Yampol died in October, 1969. In 1983 his granddaughter, Lani Yampol Gershon, traced his involvement from his collected papers. "His motivation came from the issue of [high-ranking Nazi General Adolf Ernst] Heusinger's appointment [as chairman of the NATO Military Committee]," she says. "He was very proud of being a United States citizen and responded strongly."

The rabbi arrived here by an unusual route. With his mother and father, he fled his native Russia for China. In 1915 at the age of eighteen and already an ordained rabbi, he brought his parents from China to California. From his youth, Rabbi Yampol had been responsible for his parents; his father had been shot and blinded in the aftermath of anti-Tsarist activities.

Rabbi Yampol moved from California to New Brunswick, Canada, where he met and married his wife. He later served as rabbi for Orthodox congregations in Harrisburg, Pa. and Nashville, Tenn. He moved to Chicago to become an administrator for the Hebrew Theological College. In 1952, he founded the Sovereign Kosher Nursing Home there, and was rabbi for an on-premises synagogue.

Rabbi S. Burr Yampol, right, founder of the National Committee Against Nazism, on a trip to Eastern Europe.

Like Allen, Rabbi Yampol was willing to work with anyone (including Communists) who believed in combatting nazism. He organized the National Committee Against Nazism and Nazi Criminals, a coalition of groups that had not formerly worked together. His other accomplishments include publication of *Combat* (an anti-Nazi periodical with a mailing list that included government leaders here and abroad); work on the Trifa case; protesting the 1965 expiration of the West German statute of limitations for Nazi war criminals; meetings with U.S. government officials; and organizing rallies and conferences on Nazi war criminals and related issues.

In his capacity as head of the committee, Rabbi Yampol traveled to the German Democratic Republic, Lithuania, Israel, Russia, West Germany, Belgium, Poland and France. In the fall of 1969, he went on a mission to East and West Germany, bringing copies of Nuremburg Tribunal evidence from the American archives. According to his granddaughter, both governments had requested his help. This important journey was to be Rabbi Yampol's last. Suffering from internal bleeding, he flew home for treatment. Two weeks later, he died.

While in Chicago with Rabbi Yampol for the 1963 rally, Allen appeared on "The Kup Show," a syndicated four-hour television talk show hosted by Irving Kupcinet, syndicated *Chicago Sun-Times* columnist. Other guests were Hugh Hefner, Dick Gregory, cartoonist Jules Feiffer and Larry Moyer. "Remember that while in the midst of all of this Nazi war criminal controversy, Larry's film *The Moving Finger* had just been released, my *Heusinger* book was just out, and Moyer and I were also writing for such publications as *Playboy*," Allen says.

"Kupcinet revealed on that program that he had talked with then Attorney General Robert F. Kennedy, who told him I was 'motivated and probably a Communist agent'. All of my efforts on the Nazi war criminal issue, and those of our Committee Against Nazism, were from the first investigated and systematically thwarted by the FBI and Kennedy."

Allen's FBI files, obtained by him through a Freedom of Information Act (FOIA) request, contain the following statements:

> "Informants who have furnished reliable information to the Bureau in the past and who are familiar with some phases of Communist Party activity in the New Jersey, Pennsylvania, New York and Northeastern states area were contacted, and they advised us the subject is not known to them. Subject's photograph was shown to informants. The subject is not known to them." (1955–1969 reports)
> "Subject is not being recommended by the Bureau for interview by agents, inasmuch as a review of the file does not anywhere indicate Communist Party membership for the subject, or that he is an officer in a front group of the party . . ." (March 6, 1956)

The Department of State's Office of Security in one instance even protected an actual German Nazi war criminal by placing Allen under surveillance. Through FOIA requests, Allen learned in the summer of 1979 that he was the subject of a memorandum between the Department of State and the FBI during the August, 1969 visit to the United States of then

West German Chancellor Kurt Georg Kiesinger. As deputy director of Hitler's broadcasting department, Kiesinger had been responsible for the dissemination abroad of anti-Jewish propaganda broadcasts.

Remarks in the memorandum regarding Allen say that he was a "member of a delegation from demonstrating group organized by Committee to Combat Nazism and Anti-Semitism and picketed the West German Republic Consulate in NY. 2/3/65 delegation submitted message of protest to German Chancellor."

The purpose of the demonstration and message referred to in the memorandum was to protest the expiration of the statute of limitations for Nazi war criminals in West Germany, a fact that the State Department neglected to mention. (The statute was extended at that time, and extended again indefinitely in 1979.) In addition to Allen, members of the New York Department of Jewish War Veterans were leaders of the protest at the Consulate.

In another document dated October 16, 1967, the Criminal Division of the Department of Justice directed the FBI to continue an investigation they had begun on Allen. According to Allen, one prominent New York attorney, who successfully reversed FBI procedures against civil rights leaders at the Supreme Court level, told him in 1979 that this document meant that a "veritable frameup" was in the making against him.

In 1982, Allen successfully sued the Central Intelligence Agency under the Federal Tort Claims Act for admitted violations of his constitutional rights under the First and Fourth Amendments while he was investigating Nazi war criminals here and abroad as early as the 1960s. In a formal settlement, the CIA conceded having broken the law "as a result of the activities of the defendant [CIA] in opening certain letters of the plaintiff [Allen]."

The outcome of the illegal letter openings by the CIA was a settlement of $1,000 plus court costs. The letter openings were discovered by Allen as he perused documents released to him under the Freedom of Information and Privacy Acts, on requests about alleged Nazi war criminals living here. Analyses of the materials secured by Allen clearly show that the CIA had intercepted his cables, telegrams and "other electronic communications," including "satellite research," for nearly ten years. The agency had also carried out personal surveillance of him both overseas and at home while he worked as a journalist.

The documentation showed the CIA had intercepted, opened, copied and processed into the intelligence community nineteen pieces of specific correspondence to and from such cities as Moscow, Berlin, Paris, Amsterdam, Copenhagen, London, New York, Washington, and Chicago. Heavily marked copies of articles, booklets, speeches, radio and television broadcasts by Allen, as well as book reviews, commentary and news reports about him and his writings were used by CIA analysts, along with the illegally-procured materials. The CIA opened (and presumably processed) not only Allen's communications, but those of Rabbi Yampol's National Committee Against Nazism and Nazi Criminals.[2]

Seven _____

Charles R. Allen, Jr.
"A WASP Kid Who Went Haywire"

On May 24, 1980, at a *Jewish Currents* dinner held in his honor, Charles R. Allen, Jr. described to guests his "Basic Commandments of the true social revolutions of our times." He said:

> Those injunctions state: Thou shalt not commit anti-Semitism. Thou shalt not commit anti-black or anti-Hispanic or anti-Chicano or anti-Asian or anti-native American racism. Thou shalt not commit any bigotries nor ghettoize spiritually any man, woman or child because of race, creed, color, national, ethnic or religious origin or preference. Thou can not truly achieve a just revolution for humankind—namely, the liberation of the world's working classes—unless these Commandments are obeyed.

"I learned these Commandments from many sources, but primarily from my own Episcopalian and Quaker heritage and experience," he added. In some ways Allen's "heritage and experience" made him a natural for the Nazi war criminal issue; in other ways, they seem contradictory.

Allen grew up in suburban Philadelphia, and can trace his family's arrival in America to the seventeenth century. The son of a successful physician, he attended the prestigious

69

Episcopal Academy in Philadelphia. "When our Founding Fathers marched to Carpenter Hall to ring the Liberty Bell, students from the Episcopal Academy were in the leading contingent. That's my tradition—that and Quaker," he described his background to me.

From 1938, at the age of nine, Allen kept a history scrapbook on events leading to World War II. He also kept a diary of his athletic activities, and says, "I was a professional jock from the time I was nine." Recalling Allen's early scholastic and academic accomplishments, a former classmate told him recently, "Sometimes you were a little too much."

As one of two Philadelphia area students in an experimental program, during his last semester at Upper Darby High School Allen instead attended Swarthmore College (a Quaker school). Although he stayed only for that term, he met someone there who sparked his interest in anti-Semitism and the Holocaust.

"When I was at Swarthmore, a member of St. Giles Episcopal Church, which I attended, told me I should meet a Jewish refugee girl who went to the college," he recalls. "I met her one day on campus—her name was Lilo Teutsch. She was highly intellectual, slender, with reddish-brown hair. We immediately began a friendship, and I asked her questions about her memories of life in Germany. Five years earlier, she and her family had fled to America from Nuremberg, where her father had been a lawyer.

"Lilo described in detail her memories of *Kristallnacht* [November 9, 1938, The Night of Broken Glass]," Allen says. "When I asked her why her parents didn't leave earlier, she said, 'Nuremberg was our city. My family had lived there since the 1500s.' I loved her dearly and thought her wonderfully attractive, but I identified most intensely with what she had been through and escaped from," he says. "We read together, went to lectures and concerts. It was an idyllic love affair. We just held hands."

On one occasion, Allen defended Lilo from an anti-Semitic remark, but she never knew it. "I was still technically in high school, but worked out with the Swarthmore team," he says. "During practice, a member of the team made a crack about Lilo—that she should have stayed in Germany where she belonged, and Hitler would have taken care of her. I punched him out. I almost got thrown out of Swarthmore. Lilo knew about the fight, but not that it had anything to do with her.

"At around the same time, I told my parents that I had no intention of staying at Swarthmore. Instead I entered Kenyon College. Lilo and I said goodbye on campus in 1944, and I didn't see her again until the spring of 1981. She was living in Atlanta, and I contacted her while taping a Ted Turner Channel News Network television show there with Allan Ryan and Elizabeth Holtzman."

Two other women had deep and early influences on Allen's dedication to fighting anti-Semitism, racism and fascism. Dr. Elizabeth Allen Bower, his great-aunt, died at the age of 104 in 1974. She was a physician and the senior partner in his father's practice. An advocate of women's liberation before its time, she was one of the first women to be licensed as a physician in Pennsylvania. Her staunch Quaker morality taught Allen to stand up to all forms of social injustice.

Sophie Weissblatt, the eighty-year-old grandmother of a neighbor, arrived in the area when Allen was ten. She had barely escaped the Nazis, and told him about her family's experiences on *Kristallnacht*. He says her descriptions left an "indelible mark" on him.

At Kenyon, Allen was a Rhodes Scholar-elect and his scholastic and athletic proficiency continued. He even became the subject of a research paper entitled "The Natural Superiority Complex." A fraternity brother who majored in psychology was studying inferiority complexes. When the class was assigned a paper on that topic, he asked his professor if he could instead write about someone who had a "natural superiority complex" and was completely unabashed about it. That someone: Charles R. Allen, Jr.

Perhaps such a complex was "natural" for Allen. He came from a Main Line Philadelphia family, was exceptionally intelligent and attractive, and excelled in sports and scholastics. With his capability, background and family connections, he could have been successful and wealthy in virtually any prestigious profession. Instead, he chose critical and unpopular journalism as a career, writing progressive and radical articles and books. "You can't make a lot of money out of this, and if you do, you've failed," he says today. "I'm not a Nazi hunter. As even the FBI has characterized me, I'm just a WASP kid that went haywire! "

In college, the superior but haywire WASP kid set all kinds of athletic records. He was the only underclassman there to be elected to the sports Hall of Fame, and the only major four-letter man in the history of Kenyon at that time (earning varsity letters in one year for football, basketball, track and baseball). He was named to All-Ohio Conference teams in these sports for three straight years. He was a nationally-ranked sprinter in track. He was also on the Associated Press Little All-American football team. In basketball, he established the highest points-per-game average and single game ever scored up until that time. Now in his 50s, Allen is still a "jock," proud of his athletic prowess and physique. He jogs every morning and works out in a gym every evening. He prefers that friends call him "Chuck," the nickname his Kenyon football coach gave him.

After college, from 1946 to 1948, Allen was in Army Intelligence as a political analyst and contacts officer for the Political Advisory Group to the American delegation of the U.S.-U.S.S.R. Joint Commission for the Unification of Korea. Based in Korea, he had top-security clearance and traveled throughout the Far East on various missions. After his discharge, in opposition to U.S. policy in Korea and the Far East, he testified in 1949 before the United Nations Commission on the Unification of Korea.

During his two and one-half years in the service, Allen played football in Seoul with the 20th Army All-Stars. He had signed to play with professional baseball and football teams after graduation. While at Columbia University graduate school, he played football with the Bethlehem Bulldogs, a minor-league affiliate of the National Football League.

Scoring points on ball fields did not keep Allen from pursuing his writing career. "I love to write, and I'm fascinated by the discovery of truth through rigorous journalistic processes," he says. "The idea of being privileged to serve by writing social criticism is one of the most exciting things in the world." Allen studied law for a year at University of Pennsylvania Law School, as background for his investigative writing.

Even while in college, he wrote for *The New Republic* and *The New Yorker*. His first pieces were on music (classical and jazz), and he was a student intern on the famed *Kenyon Review*. After graduate studies, he was an investigative reporter for the prize-winning newspaper *The Gazette and Daily* of York, Pa. He won national honors uncovering anti-Semitism, racism and fascism, with pieces on the Ku Klux Klan and the American Nazi Party. During the same period, cooperating closely with the Anti-Defamation League of B'nai B'rith, he did extensive and dangerous undercover work to expose numerous anti-Semitic and neo-Fascist organizations and individuals. His investigations and writing were incorporated into the book *A Measure of Freedom* by Ben Epstein and Arnold Forster, published by Doubleday in 1951.

As the youngest senior editor of *The Nation*, he contributed articles on McCarthyism, anti-Semitism, racism and other bigotries. Throughout the 1950s, he also wrote major exposés for more than 200 other magazines and newspapers, including *The New Republic, The Atlantic Monthly, The New Statesman* (London), *Colliers, The Saturday Evening Post* and *Look*.

His 1952 *New Statesman* articles, entitled "America's Concentration Camps", detailed for the first time the detention camps set aside for American dissenters under the 1950 McCarran Act (Internal Security Act). His 1968 work on that subject, *Concentration Camps, U.S.A.*, sold over a million copies. The book was widely cited during congressional debate as contributing to opposition to the McCarran Act, when it was declared in part unconstitutional and its detention camp provisions repealed outright in 1971.

His investigative writings also resulted in the parole by the State of New Jersey of Clarence Hill, a black man who had been imprisoned for life for three double murders allegedly committed in the 1930s. After Allen proved the entire case was a frameup, New Jersey set Hill free in 1961.

Allen's *Heusinger of the Fourth Reich: The Step-by-Step Resurgence of the German General Staff* was published at the end of 1963, the same year as his *Nazi War Criminals Among Us*. The *Heusinger* book detailed the wartime record of this high-ranking German general who served in Hitler's Third Reich, and who after World War II was appointed to a high rank in NATO.

Heusinger was published in twelve languages and sold some seven million copies worldwide. Allen felt his work uncovered more than enough documentary material to justify the Soviet Union's demand that Heusinger be tried as a Nazi war criminal.

Throughout the years, Allen's left-wing orientation and affiliations have led to accusations that he is a member of the Communist Party of the U.S.A. (CPUSA). He denies such charges, and says, "I've been involved with lots of causes, leftist and otherwise, most of which were not connected with the Communist Party." FBI reports on Allen corroborate his denials. For example, an FBI report covering the period October 12, 1953–January 29, 1954 says: "Informant advised [FBI] that he regards the subject [Allen] pleasing personality, well-groomed, assumes responsibility. . . . He stated he had no reason to suspect subject's loyalty as an American at any time" (see also Chapter 6).

Allen sticks by his principles, regardless of consequences. "I don't care what people think, as long as I know in my heart that what I'm doing is right," he says. While working full-time on the staff of *The Nation* in 1953, he was assigned to edit and rewrite an anti-Tito three-part series by a Columbia University professor who had just returned from Yugoslavia. "I refused to do so, and that ended my full-time job there," he says. "I wouldn't truck with this McCarthyite garbage, especially in a liberal magazine."

He served the magazine part-time until 1957. "By then, I was tired of the charade," he says. "And at around the same time, my good friend I. F. Stone said, 'What the hell are you doing staying on at *The Nation?* It's Bloomer Girl journalism— get out and strike out on your own.' Many other friends also influenced my thinking then, for example Otto Nathan, executor of Albert Einstein's estate; writer Albert Kahn; artist Rockwell Kent; Carey McWilliams, Editor of *The Nation;* journalist Edward R. Murrow; Angus Cameron, editor-in-chief of Little, Brown & Co.; Julio Alvarez del Vayo, foreign minister of Loyalist Spain."

After Allen left *The Nation,* loyalty oaths plagued him. "I was interviewed for jobs by Murrow of CBS-TV, *Time* Magazine, Lester Markel of *The New York Times Magazine,* NBC-TV News and *The New York Herald Tribune,*" he recalls. "They all wanted to hire me, but in each and every instance there was a loyalty oath. 'Are you now, or have you ever been . . . etc.'. I remember the one at the *Times* was four pages long. I said, 'I'm not going to sign one of those things—not ever.' So no one would hire me."

With no journalistic staff job in sight, he successfully free-lanced in major magazines. He also contracted to write a book on McCarthy and McCarthyism. In 1957, Allen became public relations director of the United Electrical Radio and Machine Workers Union (UE). "The reason I was asked to take that post was to handle the union's public relations campaign against the Subversive Activities Control Board, a McCarthyite creation of the 1950s," Allen says. "That board had ruled the UE was 'Communist dominated.' It was called 'The Red UE.' In 1959–1960, the courts threw out this so-called finding of that McCarthyite board.

"The UE, on the contrary, was in direct opposition to the policy of the CPUSA regarding a merger with the AFL-CIO, while I worked there until 1961," Allen adds. "During that period, it was CPUSA's policy to go into the AFL-CIO. The UE was a national independent union of some 200,000 workers that successfully opposed and fought this policy."

Allen's UE position involved him in major free speech and right-to-organize struggles, as well as some barroom brawls and fisticuffs. He remembers as most exciting the 1960 vote at the Lynn, Massachusetts General Electric plant. "Our public relations job was so effective that the competing union sent in goons," he says. "We lost, but there were 14,000 workers and we came within less than 200 votes of throwing them out. It was democratic militancy at its best. We lost by a hair."

While still employed by the UE, Allen on July 27, 1961 delivered a speech at a New York City rally sponsored by the left-wing Citizens Committee for Constitutional Liberties. (A reprint says, "Mr. Allen spoke for himself, not for the UE.") Entitled "Will You Fight for American Democracy? ", the speech was against the Supreme Court's decisions that the membership section of the 1940 Smith Act was constitutional. Allen stated "as unequivocally, as urgently and as aggressively as I can that we had better make certain that the American

Communist Party is assured full and equal rights—or else every single one of us will eventually be denied these rights! "

Recalling that speech today, he says, "I don't care if they were Communists or not. The law was unconstitutional." Ironically, his 1961 speech triggered a demand by the UE that reminded him of his 1957 job-seeking experiences. The UE national board ruled that it had the right to approve in advance any speeches or written matter by Allen. "They asked me to sign a statement to that effect, and I refused and walked out," he says. "It was another loyalty oath."

With unemployment insurance his only income, Allen began his *Heusinger* book and wrote magazine articles. In 1964–65, he spent six months traveling in the Soviet Union and wrote a small book on trade unions there. With two foundation grants, he was preparing in 1966 to write a large book entitled *Since the Revolution.* When he "got the long shuffle from Soviet bureaucracy" about his need to do research in model Communist cities, he scrapped the book—at a cost of $20,000 in monies he had to return for advances received for the study.

Allen's 1949 marriage came to an end in 1967, when he was "thrown out of the house." In 1966–67 he had been in East and West Germany, on a trip sponsored by the Peace Council of the German Democratic Republic (GDR). While trying to get his *Heusinger* book published in West Berlin, he was arrested.

In East Berlin, Allen, Paul Wohl and British trade unionist George Pavett met with Walter Ulbricht, the Chairman of the Council of State of the GDR. The meeting was reported by Wohl on October 24, 1966, on the front page of *The Christian Science Monitor.* As a result of the trip, Wohl, Allen and ten others founded the American Society for the Study of the German Democratic Republic. "The GDR didn't even exist in the State Department's view," Allen says.

The trip may have put the finishing touch to Allen's marriage. "I always have dug women, and they've dug me, but I really fell in love that year in the GDR," he says. "The woman I met there symbolizes a lot of the reasons I do what I do. She was a teacher and a member of the Socialist Unity Party (GDR Communist Party). As a teenager after the war, she had worked cleaning the rubble in West Germany. She then worked in various factories and was blacklisted for her trade union activism. She had put her husband through medical school, but he left her when he became a successful doctor. She couldn't get a job, so during the years when everyone else was seemingly fleeing west, she fled east.

"In the GDR, she became a teacher and member of the party. She married again, this time an Angolan revolutionary who was convalescing in a GDR hospital. They had a son, and her husband returned to Angola to continue the struggle against Portuguese rule. He was murdered there for his revolutionary activities.

"This woman represented for me the struggle against fascism on German soil. When I returned home from that trip, I knew I didn't want to live with my wife," Allen says. "After she threw me out, I went to Europe and filed lots of copy in 1968. But my heart and mind were in the political struggle back home. I returned to America in the spring of 1968 with no money and no job."

One reason Allen returned was his deep love for his son, Derek, then a teenager. Describing him as "the apple of my eye," Allen says he "consciously tried to shape him to become a great scholar/athlete—which in fact he became." Allen also speaks proudly of Jacob and Benedict Carton, the two college-age sons of Elizabeth Hall, with whom he later had a long-term relationship. Today he considers them an integral part of his extended family.

To finance his son Derek's education, in 1968 Allen put his political writing on a back burner for several years and entered the high-paying world of international corporate public relations. By 1974 he had returned to his writings on fascism, including the Nazi war criminal issue, and quickly reestablished himself as an internationally recognized political journalist.

Eight

David Horowitz
Always a Man with a Cause

United Nations correspondent David Horowitz says, "Just to exist isn't enough; one must live for a cause." And he has always done so. A passionate crusader for justice, he was motivated by a 1971 trip to Israel and Rumania to join the effort against Nazi war criminals in America. He recalls that he first learned of their presence here in 1966 from the Swedish Ambassador to the United Nations.

Beginning with the March, 1971 issue of his *United Israel Bulletin* (published three times a year), Horowitz printed charges against Iron Guardist Valerian Trifa. Horowitz reviewed in that issue of his independent newspaper the charges against Trifa originally reported by Walter Winchell and Drew Pearson. In addition, he quoted Congressman Seymour Halpern's statement on Trifa from the March 1, 1962 *Congressional Record* (see Chapter 5).

In the July, 1971 issue, Horowitz published a letter from Trifa disclaiming the charges in the March issue and asking for substantiation of the allegations against him. Along with Trifa's letter, which called the March article "libelous," Horowitz ran photos of Trifa as he appeared then and in 1941. Under the 1941 photograph of Trifa in Iron Guard uniform, Horowitz quoted from Trifa's January 21, 1941 speech (which Horowitz said was at that time printed in the Iron Guard daily, *Bune Vestire*): "Even if Adolf Hitler had done nothing

David Horowitz, United Nations correspondent who exposed Trifa in his
World Union Press.

else than initiate his life struggle of National Socialism, which
leads to the unmasking of the fight against Judaism, he still
would have risen to the great peaks of history, as he blazed
a new path." [1]

Horowitz also printed a facsimile of the Rumanian court
decision sentencing Trifa to life imprisonment.

On a trip to Israel in January, 1972, Horowitz met Rabbi
Zvi Guttman, a survivor of the January 21, 1941 Bucharest
pogrom (which Trifa is accused of inciting). After interviewing
the rabbi, Horowitz returned more determined than ever to
expose Trifa's activities as an Iron Guardist student leader.
He reported in the February, 1972 *United Israel Bulletin:*

> Rabbi Guttman, trembling and in near tears, recounted in
> minute detail the unspeakable horrors he, his family and tens
> of thousands of other Jews in Romania had experienced during
> those tragic and horrifying three days of the bitter freezing
> month of January, 1941 when Viorel Trifa, now a Bishop in
> Detroit, commandeered the rebellious pro-Nazi Iron Guard
> butchers in a pogrom that saw husbands, wives, and children
> slaughtered like cattle, and in some cases, hung up on sharp
> hooks in slaughter-houses.[2]

The rabbi told Horowitz that his two sons were shot and
murdered by Iron Guardists while holding onto their father's
arms. "Trifa had led this pogrom," Rabbi Guttman avowed
to Horowitz.

Along with the interview of Rabbi Guttman, Horowitz ran
an article condemning Trifa, written in Rumanian by a Ru-
manian-American priest. Throughout 1972–1974, he published other articles about Trifa in both English and Rumanian.
In January, 1974, he also wrote two articles on Trifa for the
Jewish Telegraphic Agency.

Horowitz's relentless journalistic pursuit of Trifa was a substantial factor in the government's activation of the case in
1974. While Dr. Charles Kremer often takes full credit for
bringing the case to trial, the government was reacting to
pressure from many sources, including both Kremer and Horowitz. Horowitz says that the dentist has often taken credit
for information on Trifa originally published in the *United
Israel Bulletin.*

An article by Wolf Pasmanik in the summer, 1974 issue of
the *United Israel Bulletin* announced Horowitz's role in INS's
reactivization of the case:

> The initiative and persistent efforts taken by the editor of
> this publication in exposing the Iron Guard activities of the

Rumanian pogromist Bishop Valerian D. Trifa—through a series of articles appearing in the *United Israel Bulletin* during the past five years—are bearing fruit. . . . The *Bulletin* editor's exposés, based upon data gathered from witnesses whom he had interviewed in Israel and in Rumania—data which produced documentary evidence pointing to Trifa's direct role in the pogrom-rebellion—kept the issue alive and provided Dr. Charles Kremer, president of the American Federation of Rumanian Jews, with the ammunition he needed to further his own anti-Trifa campaign.

Up until the *Bulletin* began its exposés, national Jewish organizations, among them the ADL [Anti-Defamation League] of B'nai B'rith and the American Jewish Congress—which had in their files dossiers on the Bishop and on the basis of which they had tried years ago to expose him—had let the whole matter rest in the belief that not much could be done in the face of the Immigration Service's negative attitude.

But the *United Israel Bulletin* and its editor persisted with publishing exposés which were also syndicated by the World Union Press for wider circulation in the English-Jewish press.

Mentioning articles in *The New York Times,* the *New York Daily News* and the *Detroit Free Press,* Pasmanik said, "All these dailies, in the main, republished material which had already appeared in the *United Israel Bulletin* during the past five years." [3]

Horowitz's campaign against another alleged Nazi war criminal, Ferenc Koreh, resulted in a libel suit in 1978. An attorney who resides in Englewood, N.J., Koreh was a member of the Hungarian fascist Arrow/Cross Party and wrote anti-Semitic articles during World War II. In Budapest, he was found guilty of Nazi collaboration and sentenced as a war criminal to one and one-half years of imprisonment and five years loss of civil rights. Like Trifa, he has been employed by Radio Free Europe.

Based on a spring, 1977 article in the *United Israel Bulletin,* Koreh in 1978 sued for three million dollars: $1,000,000 each from the World Union Press (Horowitz's syndication), the *United Israel Bulletin,* and the editor. According to Koreh's attorney, Horowitz's article contained these libelous statements:

First, responsible for the murder of thousands of Jews and Rumanians in Transylvania during the Horthy occupation of Hungary. Second, sentenced to death by high courts for war crime. Third, a Hungarian from Transylvania who had helped the fascist organization known as the Cross and the Arrow. Fourth, that the Supreme Court of Hungary passed the death sentence upon him for his war crimes against Jews in Transylvania.[4]

At an appearance before Judge Thomas P. Griesa in Southern District Court, New York, on September 21, 1979, Paul O'Dwyer, Horowitz's attorney, conceded that the second, third and fourth statements were incorrect. The first statement was not retracted. In the course of a discussion about "having this document turn into a polemic for either side," [5] the case was settled and did not go to trial.

By the time Horowitz took up the issue of Nazi war criminals in 1972, he was sixty-eight years old and a veteran of a lifetime of other causes. His autobiographical *Thirty-Three Candles,* published in 1949, relates the story of his life from 1914 through 1944. Filled with Horowitz's dreams, visions and prophecies, the book is a testimony to his determination and tenacity.

Born in Sweden in 1903, Horowitz came to America in 1914 with his mother and five brothers and sisters. His father (a Russian-born cantor) and his two older siblings had come to this country earlier. An ardent Zionist during his teenage years in Wilkes-Barre, Pa., Horowitz organized and led the Galileans, a Zionist youth group.

By 1921, Horowitz decided he wanted to go to Palestine. After working on a New Jersey farm until 1924 to gain experience and save money for his passage, he sailed for Palestine. Once there, he worked at the Mikveh Israel Agricultural School.

In December, 1927, Horowitz met the "prophet" Moshe Guibbory in the Jerusalem Sanhedrin cave. The "prophet" became a cause that changed the course of his life and occupied him body and soul until 1943.

In the cave with "his" Moshe, Horowitz says he saw thirty-three candles that changed in formation from the Hebrew letters for "Jehovah" to those for "the hand of God." He believed this was an omen. His encounter with Moshe answered his "irresistible lifelong quest of God." [6] For the next sixteen years, he devoted himself to editing and publishing Moshe's version of the Bible, *The Bible in the Hands of Its Creators.*

The book (published in 1943) sees the original Hebrew Bible as written in code, never properly understood. Despite a lack of funds, almost superhuman demands from Moshe (who stayed in Jerusalem and sent Horowitz back to New York) and personal difficulties with some of his supporters and sometime friends, Horowitz managed not only to publish the book but also to found a society supporting its beliefs. He promoted both the society and book throughout the country.

During those years, Horowitz kept a diary in which he recorded his dreams. Two of his dreams, described in his autobiography, explain in part his later dedication to the fight for justice for Nazi war criminals:

> Of the hundreds of visions and dreams experienced in the early part of 1942, I had two that were very vivid. One dealt with Hitler, the other with a human slaughter-house. In the former, I found myself the prisoner of Hitler deep in an enormous underground pit. . . . In the other dream, I was somewhere near a big house and saw several human beings hung up on hooks like slaughtered animals. Their skin was flayed but they were alive. I dreamed this the night of February 21, 1942. . . . I didn't realize that scenes such as I saw in my dream were being enacted in real life by the Nazis on their prisoners in a number of European "butcher shops." [7]

Horowitz became disillusioned with "his" Moshe and other associates in the Society of the Bible in the Hands of its Creators. He founded another organization, the United Israel World Union, through which he still publishes his *United Israel Bulletin.* The purpose of the Union is to propagate the ideals of the Hebraic heritage on a universal scale, according to Horowitz. He explains that he founded the organization to "expose the big lie." He told me in an April 9, 1981 interview at his U.N. office: "The suffering we [Jews] have gone through for 2,000 years in exile because of the deicide charge greatly disturbed me. I decided I must expose this lie."

Horowitz maintains his firm religious faith in Mosaic Law. He considers the edicts of the bibilical Moses as a "blueprint for life," not only for Jews but for all humanity. Through his Union and *Bulletin,* he says he endeavors to bring to people in Africa, Eastern and Western Europe, and Latin America an understanding of Israel, universal peace and the world order outlined in the Bible.

Accredited as a United Nations correspondent in 1946, Horowitz remains one today. In addition to his *United Israel Bulletin,* he syndicates a column, "Behind the Scenes at the U.N.," for twenty Anglo-Jewish newspapers in the United States, Canada, South America and Italy. He is a past president of two international press organizations, the Foreign Press Association (1966), and the 250-member United Nations Correspondents Association (1981).

Horowitz is still the staunch Zionist of his youth. Books, awards and memorabilia with Jewish and Zionist themes line the shelves of his United Nations office space. He proudly tells visitors that his area in Room 373 of the United Nations Secretariat building is the only corner there that is pro-Zionist. But Horowitz has adopted new causes in addition to Zionism and the Nazi war criminal issue. Among them are the plights of the three million Kurds in Iraq and the South Moluccans within the Indonesian archipelago.

When pressed for a personal reason for his outspoken and courageous fight against the many forms of fascism and racism, including anti-Semitism, Horowitz refers to three experiences detailed in his autobiography. During his childhood in Sweden, he recalls:

> As the only dark-haired child in the class and having to arrive at school one half-hour late in order to bypass the religious services, I entered shyly and fearfully under the wondering, antagonistic gaze of my blond classmates. In their heart was a common objection: "Here comes the Jude." [8]

On a visit to Poland in 1928, Horowitz was awakened one March night by shouts of "Kill the Jews! " The ensuing pogrom was his first taste of violent anti-Semitism. [9]

Fifteen years later, he traveled to Washington, D.C. with a black associate and was shocked by the racism he found there. He says in his autobiography:

> I had heard a great deal about the division made in the South between Negroes and the whites, but that there should be such a schism between human beings in the Capital of the United States greatly shocked me and I realized more than ever that there was still a lot of work to be done for a better way of life in this nation.[10]

But Horowitz has a deeper, more personal reason for his fight against Nazi war criminals, a reason he does not often discuss. While he was in Palestine in 1927, he fell in love with and married a Polish Jew named Pola Kleinowa. The reason for his trip to Poland in 1928 was to visit her parents, before continuing on from Palestine to America.

Horowitz spent six months with Pola's family in Poland, and his son, Emmanuel, was born there on April 28, 1928. When he left for America that May, he decided to go alone and later send for his wife and infant son. His wife continued to postpone her departure for America for ten years, and died of a tumor in Poland in October, 1938.

When Horowitz learned of his wife's death, he wrote to his father-in-law and requested that Emmanuel, then ten, be sent to him in America. The boy's grandfather refused to part with him, and wrote Horowitz that he would have to wait until Emmanual grew up. But he never had a chance to grow up. After World War II, Horowitz learned that Emmanuel had been murdered by the Nazis at Auschwitz.

Nine _____

DeVito and Schiano
The End of a Beautiful Friendship

Anthony DeVito and Vincent Schiano, once best friends, no longer speak to each other. Both of the former Immigration and Naturalization Service (INS) employees are tough-talking and street-wise. After growing up in New York City in Italian-American working class families, they served in the Army during World War II.

As colleagues working on Nazi war criminal cases in the INS, DeVito and Schiano were the first to discover and expose the agency's inadequacies. Schiano resigned on December 7, 1972, and DeVito retired on June 28, 1973, both charging the INS with interference.

The only point the former friends seem to agree on now is that their silent feud began February 2, 1977, when they were waiting to tape a "McNeil-Lehrer Report" television program about Nazi war criminals in America. Interviewing DeVito in his Westbury, Long Island home on July 17, 1981, and Schiano in his Wall Street law office on August 24, 1981, I heard both sides of the story.

Each accuses the other of initiating the silent treatment. DeVito says: "I met Schiano in the Channel 13 waiting room. He came with his two kids. They said hello to me, but Schiano turned his back. I said to myself that something's up. I didn't know what."

Former Immigration and Naturalization Service investigator Anthony DeVito, in front of awards he has received for his efforts, 1981. (photo by author)

Schiano says, "He never said a word to me in the waiting room. He never looked at me before we went in."

Either man may have been reacting to the aftermath of the publication of Howard Blum's *Wanted! The Search for Nazis in America*, a pseudo-journalistic account of the issue based largely on DeVito's information to Blum, then a reporter for *The Village Voice*. Federal and state libel suits resulted against Quadrangle Books, *The New York Times*, CBS, Inc., Fawcett Books and Blum by Tscherim Soobzokov of Paterson, N.J., a Circassian accused of concealing his collaboration with the *Waffen SS* and his participation in Nazi atrocities in and around Krasnodar, in the Transcaucasus. (In 1979 the Office of Special Investigations filed a complaint seeking Soobzokov's denaturalization, alleging he concealed membership in proscribed Nazi

Former Immigration and Naturalization Service attorney Vincent Schiano.

military units during World War II. OSI withdrew its action "with prejudice" in 1980.)

Soobzokov and his attorney, Michael Dennis, were appearing on the 1977 "McNeil-Lehrer Report" program with DeVito and Schiano in New York. Blum and Rep. Joshua Eilberg, (D-Pa.), then chairman of the House Judiciary Subcommittee on Immigration, participated in the program via a Washington, D.C. studio hookup.

DeVito, the central character in Blum's book, now says of *Wanted!*, "The book had an impact like no other book in America. Blum has been denied his due credit by his critics. When the Blum book came out, Schiano was not happy. If Schiano was starred, it might have been different."

Schiano says, "Blum tampered with a delicate and important subject. There's no question the publicity surrounding the book generated interest in the issue, but it was not a good interest. Tony [DeVito] is hungry for glory. Blum needed a central figure to hold his book together and used him. If there was any cover-up in INS, Tony is responsible for bringing it about. He lost sight of everything, because of the book and his desire for publicity."

Schiano describes the book as "almost anti-Semitic." He told me that Blum "took the lead from DeVito and chastised the Jewish community. But it's a question of American law. DeVito thought the Jewish INS supervisors should come to our aid. His attitude was, 'Look, Mr. Jew, what we do for your people!' That's bullshit. We do it for our morals and standards. The issue of Nazi war criminals is not one of Jewish vengeance but of immigration law."

Among examples of the book's "almost anti-Semitic" approach is the incident of DeVito's report to Sol Marks, INS district director, of theft of some Nazi war criminal records. Blum writes that DeVito later said to Schiano, "I told Marks but he didn't seem shocked or anything. He didn't flinch a muscle. I finally had to scream, 'You're a Jew, don't you care?' " [1]

Another instance: when Marks and Ben Lambert, assistant district director of investigations, insisted that DeVito give them a list of alleged Nazi war criminals and his sources, DeVito described the two men as part of a *Judenrat*. (During World War II, the Nazis appointed *Judenrate*, or Jewish Councils, who expedited Nazi orders in the ghettos, and were sometimes considered collaborators.)

Blum continued:

> [DeVito] stared at Lambert and Marks, men he had known for nearly all his professional career, and tried to decide why two Jews were doing this. For DeVito, this was an important

question. Then for some unavoidable but unknown reason his mind flashed on that scene in Dachau: the inmates in the awning outfits attacking a fellow Jewish prisoner. DeVito stood *[sic]* in front of his two superiors, furious, pacing the room in anger. In his mind it was clear: One Judenrat had been replaced with another; one generation of Jewish collaborators had been replaced with another.[2]

Blum also has DeVito speaking of "the Judenrat which runs the Immigration Service," [3] whom he calls "the new collaborators, the new enemy," and the "moral descendants of the *kapo* [prisoner who oversaw other prisoners] he had seen thirty years ago being stoned in Dachau." [4] Any Jew not interested in pursuing Nazi war criminals is a "collaborator," according to DeVito.[5]

Asked about his statements in Blum's book, DeVito does not deny them; he told me, "All the stuff I gave him, he rattled off in pretty good fashion."

DeVito's and Schiano's differences about *Wanted!* were festering when they met at the "McNeil-Lehrer Report" taping. Schiano recalls that he "blasted" DeVito on the program, reminding him, "You didn't quit; you retired. I resigned."

Their friendship began in 1952, soon after both became investigators in the INS New York district office. They had passed a civil service exam for U.S. Treasury enforcement agents, and INS had offered investigatory jobs to 80 qualifiers. Before 1951 Schiano, a graduate of St. John's University and Brooklyn Law School, was an attorney with the New York Children's Society. His INS assignments included undercover work in Harlem and Canada; cases dealt with Cuban and Chinese immigrants and the Mafia, and later with Beatle John Lennon.

Schiano not only investigated but also presented cases, and says that he "created" the position of trial attorney for himself as he left INS in 1960. "I was an investigator and also a supervisor, and presented subversive, criminal cases. I wore many hats," he recalls. He left in 1960 after a promised promotion to Washington headquarters was changed into a position in Anchorage, Alaska. "They didn't like my answers," he says of the change in assignment.

"In 1953–1954 there were a lot of Communist cases, but no Nazi cases," Schiano told me. "The 1952 Immigration Law put emphasis on the Leftist movement. Before 1952 the internal security laws barred Nazis, but the 1952 law was oriented toward the Communist menace. It ignored Nazis— the government didn't seem to think there was a problem. I did have a *kapo* case at the time, and this got me interested in the issue of Nazi war criminals and collaborators."

In addition to the *kapo,* the one Nazi war criminal case Schiano dealt with in the 1950s was that of Nicolae Malaxa, financier of the Rumanian Iron Guard and one-time business partner of Albert Goering (see Chapter 5). Malaxa entered the United States on September 29, 1946 as a member of the Rumanian Government Trade Mission; he may have made a deal with an agent of the American Office of Strategic Services (OSS) to get in.

"In 1955 I was called to Washington to handle the Malaxa case, and this was the beginning of my troubles," Schiano says. "There is no question there was an attempt to fix this case. The Board of Immigration Appeals (BIA) decision was contrived. They changed the facts to fit the decision, and wouldn't let me appeal the case. Malaxa refused to answer my questions. I should have become bitter and disaffected, and said 'This is the way of life.' But it didn't go down right. It gave me a good education into the Nazi war criminal issue. The nature of the government's thinking was that there was some value to attacking Malaxa's ties to Communist Rumania, but not in his Iron Guard and Nazi attachments."

Malaxa formally applied for permanent residence in 1948, under the Displaced Persons Act. Using former government officials and their law partners to fight his legal battles, he was able to reclaim millions of dollars that had been frozen as enemy assets, and at Immigration hearings he defended himself against allegations of his Iron Guard connections. In 1951, the then junior senator from California, Richard M. Nixon, introduced a private bill to allow Malaxa to remain in the United States. The bill was defeated.

With industry under wartime control during the Korean War, Malaxa organized in May, 1951 the Western Tube Corporation, using the same address in Whittier, California as that of Nixon's law firm of Bewley, Kroop and Nixon. Officers of Western Tube included two of Nixon's friends, law partner Thomas Bewley and political supporter Herman L. Perry.

With Nixon's request for "first-preference quota" admission granted because of Malaxa's purported usefulness in the defense industry, Malaxa went to Canada to get his visa. In September, 1953, he was admitted from there (under this special first-preference petition) as a permanent resident. After the application for Western Tube was approved, the corporation ceased to function. Meanwhile, Malaxa had his official and legal "in" to the United States.[6]

Schiano was given the case when Malaxa tried to reenter the United States in 1955, after spending ten months in Argentina. At hearings before the House Judiciary Subcommittee on Immigration, Citizenship, and International Law on July 21, 1978, Schiano discussed his role in the case. When asked by then Chairman of the Subcommittee Eilberg what he had prosecuted Malaxa for, Schiano said:

> That was an exclusion process upon his return from Argentina in 1955. I demanded he take the witness stand since he was an applicant for a readmission to the United States. He refused to answer any of my questions and throughout those proceedings which took 60 days of trial, never answered a single question of mine. I asked it be made a rule of law he answer those questions. In fact, I said if we are wrong in our position, then we should have a hearing *de novo;* the entire tribunal was at fault.

Schiano also told the subcommittee about a bribe offer in connection with the Malaxa case:

> A Romanian came to see me, . . . and the way he put it very artfully, he said he had $100,000 or $200,000 [with] which he was going to dispose of this problem and asked me for suggestions as to what I should do with the money, how to dispose of it. I told him, being poor, I had no use for it, but he had adequate counsel and he should not trouble me about these questions. There was never a direct offer saying, "Here is a hundred thousand dollars; what can be done?" [7]

Malaxa was ordered deported in 1958, but the decision was overruled by the BIA. He lived in the United States until his death in 1965. Recalling the case today, Schiano says with characteristic swagger and humor, "I would not take bribes. Not because of honesty, but because of arrogance."

When Schiano left INS temporarily in 1960, he practiced law in Paul O'Dwyer's New York City firm. In 1963 he returned to INS as a trial attorney. In that capacity he was assigned in October, 1971 to the deportation phase of the case against Nazi war criminal Hermine Braunsteiner Ryan. DeVito was appointed his investigator late in the case.

Ryan, a Queens, N.Y. housewife, was a supervisor of Nazi concentration camp guards. The Austrian native married an American soldier in 1958 and then entered the United States from Canada. She was the first American resident turned over to West Germany for prosecution for war crimes.

As the Justice Department was about to begin her denaturalization trial in 1971, she relinquished her citizenship. According to DeVito: "The fix was in on the Ryan case." He testified before the House Judiciary Subcommittee on July 20, 1978:

> The Nazi female's [Ryan] lawyer was being fed material right along in that case, and if we were to direct our inquiries through him, then the central office personnel would know what is going on in the case, and advise the counsel accordingly. You see, Mr. Chairman, in my view, there was no question that there was a fix in the Nazi female's case. There was a fix just as sure as I am sitting here now. Namely, go ahead and yield, consent to the agreement to relinquish her citizenship, and we will give you a superficial deportation hearing, well, a super, super. The deportation hearing they got wasn't expected, especially when the foreign witnesses appeared on the scene.[8]

Before entering the United States, Ryan had been convicted in Austria for crimes committed at Ravensbruck, a slave labor camp for women and children. According to Schiano, records of her conviction were acquired through subterfuge by a Central Intelligence Agency agent in Austria. He told me, "Washington had her files and didn't let anyone in on the secret of how her conviction files from Austria were obtained. They were not supposed to be available, according to the privacy laws of Austria. In addition to the legal question of how they were obtained, there was the security question of exposing a CIA agent in Austria, and the problem of authenticating the records' correctness."

Testifying to the House Judiciary Subcommittee about the CIA's role in the Ryan case, DeVito said on July 20, 1978:

> When the story broke in the United States on that female Nazi case, immigration was caught off guard. The public became aroused. The press had a heyday. How could this "wardress", SS wardress wind up in America? So that at the beginning the public clamoured for action. Then somebody at immigration apparently called on the CIA saying, look, we are stuck, we need this conviction record in Austria in order to get going. We have not got it, the Austrian Government refuses to relinquish it, and the female refuses to grant us a waiver. In short, the CIA was called upon to obtain Mrs. Ryan's Nazi criminal record, a conviction record in Austria and so they did it.[9]

Asked by the subcommittee on July 21 to give a "thumbnail statement" of Ryan's crimes, Schiano told them:

> She was at Ravensbruck, she was convicted, I think, after a course of conduct in Ravensbruck for beating inmates, but she was never tried or convicted, [for] a course of conduct at Maidanek Concentration Camp in Poland. Remember this, the charge against her for deportation was not necessarily a course of conduct during that period of time, but a conviction in Austria for a crime involving moral turpitude. Now, that was important in light of this memorandum, because if the only charge was that she lied when she got a visa concerning herself, it would have been obviated as she said, as 241(f) which in substance says if you are married to a citizen we automatically excuse you from your fraud.[10]

Schiano testified he did not know whether or not INS had ever made a deal, or whether formally or informally that agency had agreed not to deport Ryan in exchange for her consent to denaturalization. Discussing with the subcommittee the memorandum he referred to in his testimony, he termed it "obstructive." [11] It's an open question whether there was an agreement not to deport Ryan if she relinquished her citizenship.

On May 1, 1973 Judge Jacob Mischler ordered Ryan extradited to West Germany to stand trial. Mischler's decision to extradite her came after months of investigation by DeVito and Schiano. Often on their own time and skirting official channels, they contacted the West German and Polish governments to find witnesses and additional evidence, and to encourage both countries to request extradition. To avoid State Department red tape, they went directly to the Polish Embassy in Washington. They also communicated with the German office (in Dusseldorf) responsible for prosecution of war crimes committed at Maidanek, a Nazi extermination camp near Lublin, Poland. Schiano recalls that a Judge Auerbach of Dusseldorf even came to America and discussed the Ryan case with him.

"When I read the documents about Ryan, they dealt with Ravensbruck and were about brutalities and medical experiments, but not about her participation in murders," DeVito told me. "But I caught the name Maidanek, and focused on that. It was primarily an extermination center, and I thought there was the possibility she might be implicated in this death factory. Before long, the case was rolling. We got witnesses here in the United States who knew Mrs. Ryan, and also a key witness from Paris and a dentist from Warsaw, who broke the case wide open with his testimony here."

Ryan's trial in West Germany began in November, 1975 and continued for five and a half years, the longest war crimes trial in West Germany. She was found guilty of crimes that included child murder and the selection of Maidanek inmates for the gas chamber. At the age of 61, Ryan was sentenced on June 30, 1981 to two consecutive life sentences.

Schiano and DeVito succeeded in the Ryan case despite the INS. Besides obstructions that Schiano discussed with the judiciary subcommittee, he described to them the setup of his quarters during the time he worked on Nazi war criminal cases:

While I was involved in the prosecution of one of these cases, I felt oppressed. We were denied a telephone, an office, any funding or even courtesies. The oppression reached the point where we were placed in a cubicle which "shrunk" from week to week. For two of us to occupy that office, one of us would have to climb over the desk. This is not an exaggeration. The press was witness to this. This is where we interviewed the witnesses, and also representatives of foreign governments.

From here we ran across the hall and waited for the use of a telephone or went into the public hallway and the coin box became our office telephone. An apt observation made of these doings was expressed by one who is now an Immigration judge. Shaking his head and with a wry smile he remarked, "If I had money I would put it on Broadway." I failed to ask whether he considered it a comedy or a tragedy. . . . My cubicle got smaller. I can only imagine that someone at the central office was in the midst of reading Edgar Allan Poe's "The Cask of Amontillado." [12]

DeVito attributes obstructions and the lack of cooperation to an ODESSA-like organization created to assist Nazi war criminals. (ODESSA is an acronym for *Organisation der ehemaligen SS-Angehorigen,* a now-defunct Nazi escape group that functioned after World War II.) He insists that his files were rifled and stolen, and that his wife received a threatening phone call. As portrayed by Blum, DeVito considered the situation "actions in a coordinated plot." [13] "Odessa has struck again," he says of his missing files in *Wanted!.*[14]

Schiano disagrees with DeVito's conspiracy theory. He told the subcommittee, "I think his [DeVito's] allusions to Odessa go beyond the horizons of mere sobriety. I do not think they can be expanded upon. I say it is an exaggeration. I do not believe in any 'theater of widespread cooperation *[sic]* in the Immigration service.' " [15]

Schiano also denies that files were missing in the Ryan case. "No files were missing or stolen," he told me. "My notes were taken, but they probably thought the notes had to do with an investigation of me. Tony exaggerates and out-and-out lies. He said his wife was threatened. This is a lie, and I have him on tape saying so."

According to Blum, who states in "A Note to the Reader" that *Wanted!* is a "documented" and "true" story, the name "Soobzokov, Tscherim" was on a list of 59 Nazis living in America given to DeVito by Dr. Oscar Karbach of the World Jewish Congress (WJC). Blum describes Dr. Karbach as "president" of the WJC. He was a staff researcher.[16]

During the Ryan case in 1973, DeVito was contacted by Ruby Fier, a Social Security investigator in Baltimore. A retired Jewish New York City policeman, Fier, while checking on possible social security violations by Soobzokov, discovered Nazi allegations in Soobzokov's file. Because DeVito's name was in the press in connection with the Ryan case, Fier came to see him about Soobzokov. DeVito supposedly matched Soobzokov's name with the list that the WJC official had given him.

"When DeVito said Soobzokov's name was on a list, he told a lie," Schiano says. "This man was never on any list Tony had. Tony got the name from Ruby Fier and gave it to me. I may be a witness against DeVito in the libel action. If the Soobzokov case goes to trial, Tony won't look good. It gives me no great pleasure, but I may testify against him. The government has that list, and Soobzokov is not on it." [17]

DeVito explains away the question of the list by saying there were two lists—one written and one typed. He says Soobzokov's name was on the handwritten list, whereabouts unknown. In Soobzokov's state libel case against Blum *et al.*, DeVito was one of the defendants. After he was sued for libel, he made three trips to the Soviet Union to gather evidence against Soobzokov. DeVito says his unofficial trips to the Soviet Union to learn more about Soobzokov's wartime activities were for the purpose of defending himself in the state libel case.

These trips caused him difficulties when he was called as a defense witness in the March, 1980 federal libel suit against Blum and others, in which he was not a co-defendant. Acting as his own attorney, he refused to answer a question by Michael Dennis, Soobzokov's attorney, about the source of funds for his trips to the Soviet Union, on the grounds that he had promised not to reveal the source. Although he says he offered to give the information in a sealed envelope to the judge, he was held in contempt by U.S. District Judge Gerard Goettel.

DeVito was sent to the Metropolitan Correction Center in Manhattan on March 25, but received an Easter furlough in April. After his discharge, he was fined $250 a day, later reduced to $50 a day, for 46 days. The fine was dismissed on appeal.

DeVito is bitter about his experience. "This is idiotic," he told me in July, 1981. "The hunter goes to jail and the Nazis are running around." But he seems to enjoy playing the role of hero and reciting his troubles, as he chain smokes and drinks black coffee at home.

Although his experience was limited, DeVito professes expertise on the Nazi war criminal issue. He seems to believe it revolves around him. At the July, 1978 judiciary subcommittee hearing, he said that the GAO and other government investigations of the subject which did not consult him could not be effective.

"In all of these investigations, nobody came to Tony DeVito," he said. "I was their main catalyst, wasn't I? Nobody came to me to ask me questions, hey, where did the difficulties lie, what happened, nothing, nobody. So what kind of investigations have we got here?" [18]

When asked how he became interested in the Nazi war criminal issue, DeVito talks about his days as a soldier in World War II: "Here I am, a nice healthy Italian boy in New York's Hell's Kitchen, and I get a 'Greetings' letter," he recalls. "I go to Egypt, where I'm in the middle of the Egyptian and Libyan deserts fighting against Rommel. Then to Italy and ultimately to Nazi Germany. I saw a lot of dead bodies on the way to Germany—a lot of American blood. I said to myself, how silly it is that man has got to fight man. Good young American bodies dead. For what?

"I walked into Dachau concentration camp and saw the sight soon after its liberation. Then the meaning of World War II began to play a more vital role in my life."

DeVito met his future wife, Frieda, while he was passing through the town of Erlangen, Germany soon after the war. He took his discharge in Germany, married Frieda, and lived for a while in Erlangen, near the site of the Nuremberg war crimes trials. He remembers that once he even went into the courtroom in Nuremberg, but had no credentials and was asked to leave.

"From that point on, I was interested in Nazi war criminals," he told me. "I went out of my way to read about the subject. In 1947 I came back to America, and the subject drew me to it. Occasionally I would read in the paper about Artukovic, and thanks to Dr. Kremer, about Trifa."

DeVito appears to be a typical suburban retiree, enjoying his home and grandchildren. (He was sixty-three on July 17, 1983.) But his involvement with the Nazi war criminal issue and public exposure through Blum's *Wanted!*, television appearances, newspaper interviews and lectures have changed his life. DeVito is proud of his display of awards and citations from Jewish organizations, and seems concerned that his critics term him paranoid or fanatical.

"I'm not a nut. I'm a determined officer," he says. "I took an oath and I did a job. I consider myself a good law enforcement officer. You'll see as time goes on that the statements I made are confirmed by events."

Schiano's lifestyle is much less tranquil than DeVito's. A partner in a Wall Street immigration law firm, Schiano is a youthful sixty-one and still has the mien of his professional boxing days on Coney Island. Along with his collection of awards from Jewish organizations (for his work on the war criminal issue) and the usual college and law school degrees, his office boasts a prominent display of inscribed photographs of beautiful women.

Schiano and his wife, from whom he was never legally divorced, have two grown sons. He also lived with another woman, with whom he had two daughters. Schiano says she left him at the time of the Ryan case because of the pressures of an INS investigation of him. He believes the investigation was an attempt to end his criminal work. "I said I was going ahead with the case unless they stopped me in writing. They didn't like me," he recalls. "They figured they couldn't fix the case while I was the prosecuting attorney."

Whatever the reason, INS did conduct a grand jury investigation of Schiano in 1973. "They investigated my private life—women and money," he told me. "Their accusations were not true and put pressures on my family and harassed me. My sister died of cancer at the time, and my brother six months later. I left the government on December 7, 1973 with seventy-five cents in my pocket, owing $5,000, and with two families to support. It also affected my health; I have high blood pressure."

Schiano was in the infantry during World War II, but he says his war experience has nothing to do with his attitude toward Nazis. He was captured during the Battle of the Bulge and struck by an SS officer. While running away, he was shot and left for dead. The graves registration detail tagged him for burial and sent his dog tags home to his mother. "My mother knew I wasn't dead, though," Schiano says.

He traces his interest in the Nazi war criminal issue to two people who influenced him in his youth: his grandfather and a nun who taught him at St. Augustine's Academy in Brooklyn.

"When I was ten years old, there was a bully on my block who picked on me—he was bigger," Schiano says. "I told my grandfather, and he said to me, 'Unless he's going to kill you, don't give in to him. If he's going to kill you, it will be his problem.' So next time he grabbed me, I said I'd get a knife and kill him. Otherwise he should kill me, and that would be his problem. He never bothered me again.

"Since then, I have never accepted any kind of persecution and I cannot take the idea of living in fear. When I was in high school, I belonged to the Catholic Evidence Guild. We made speeches on street corners against Communists and against Hitler—we considered them both our enemies."

The nun strengthened him in another way. "She had been a countess in Czechoslovakia, and her husband was killed on her wedding day," Schiano told me. "She instilled in me the idea that I should do what I believe in, that if I have to fight, I must conquer or die. I was a romantic, starting at that age."

Schiano's sense of right and romance took him in a new direction in 1980, when he agreed to represent an alleged Nazi war criminal, Mikhail Dercacz. The Office of Special Investigations brought denaturalization proceedings against Dercacz, accusing him of beatings and executions of unarmed Jewish civilians in Lvov, Ukraine.

Asked why he would represent an alleged Nazi war criminal, Schiano says, "It is an insult to the Jews to prosecute this man. I don't think this man was capable or in a position to do what he is accused of. There were Jewish leaders who probably did more harm than he did.

"I chose to represent him, because it is my obligation to protect the system. I don't have to like my clients. But no one can make him guilty before trying him. No lawyer has that right. The belief that he is guilty is a social problem, not a legal problem." Schiano has since dropped the case, because "this kind of case takes too much time and I lose money on it."

Quick with a joke, Schiano says he always stood up for what he thought was right at school, and often got in trouble for it. He recalls with a smile, "I always seemed to sit alphabetically next to a kid named Schwartz—the Jew and Italian teamed up to protest the injustices."

Ten

Elizabeth Holtzman Forces the Issue in Congress

As a member of Congress, Elizabeth Holtzman was sometimes criticized for her inability to compromise—a quality that served her positively in her relentless push to force the government to act on the issue of Nazi war criminals in America. Her detractors and some of her friends have termed this quality "inflexibility," but admirers describe it as "tenacity."

Holtzman refused to give in on this issue, which she says she brought to the attention of Congress in the spring of 1974. Her vigilance continued until she left Congress at the end of 1980. By then, the OSI was firmly established as an investigative and prosecutorial force.

Born in Brooklyn on August 11, 1941, Holtzman and her twin brother Robert (a Brooklyn neurosurgeon) are the only children of Sidney Holtzman, a criminal lawyer, and Filia Holtzman, former chair of the Hunter College Russian Department. Elizabeth was raised in Brooklyn, graduating from Radcliffe College *magna cum laude* and Harvard Law School.

Like many other women who have reached the top politically, Holtzman is single. A fighter for feminist causes, she was a founder and co-chairwoman of the Congresswomen's Caucus, a bipartisan group created to improve the social and legal status of women. A nameplate in her Congressional office, probably the gift of an admirer with a sense of humor, read: "Elizabeth Holtzwoman, Congressperson."

Former Congresswoman Elizabeth Holtzman, leader of efforts in Congress.

Entering Congress at the age of thirty-one in January, 1973, she was the youngest woman ever elected to the House. (She won against twenty-five-term Congressman Emanuel Celler in the 1972 Brooklyn Democratic primary.) The freshman congresswoman soon gained a seat on the Immigration Subcommittee of the House Judiciary Committee (which Celler had chaired). Her aggressive questioning during the televised Watergate hearings made her well-known.

Although she likes to be addressed as Liz, the nickname doesn't match her contained and formal manner. She projects cool professional competence that sometimes gives an interviewer the impression she is wearing armor to ward off a strike at a vulnerable spot. With her image of independence, propriety and intensity, Holtzman is hardly the stereotype of a baby-kissing, back-slapping politician.

She says she first became aware of the presence of Nazi war criminals here in early 1974, when people (non-Jews) told her the INS had a list of such criminals but was doing nothing about it. "My first reaction was one of disbelief," she told me in 1978. "But when I asked the Immigration Service about it, they said there was such a list. Then I asked what they were doing about it, and there was silence."

When Holtzman received the status reports on the cases, the lack of information there revealed the government's inaction. "I looked through the file of one case—call him 'Mr. X'—and the file listed no eyewitnesses that had been questioned," she said. "And there was no documented evidence. What did the file say? It said, 'Mr. X is in good health.' In all of the case files, I found the same thing. It seemed clear that the Immigration Service was not interested in the violation of immigration laws, but had become a 'public health agency,' concerned about the health of these individuals."

She added that no witnesses had been questioned here or abroad, and no one was in charge of any kind of investigation, despite allegations dating as far back as the 1940s. "Our government had no professionals assigned to investigate these cases on a full-time basis, and they had no lawyers. In many cases they refused to collect evidence, or there was the most half-hearted unprofessional kind of investigation imaginable, and certainly not worthy of this country or worthy of the problem.

"When I originally exposed this in the spring of 1974, I thought the best way of dealing with Nazi war criminals in this country was to create a special task force in the Immigration Service, so that people could develop expertise and deal only with this problem. In the summer of 1977, Immigration Service agreed to set up a task force." [1]

Holtzman's office for over three years sent out a barrage of press releases and letters to INS and others, before INS agreed. On April 3, 1974, along with other subcommittee members, she questioned the INS at Immigration Subcommittee hearings, after which she stated to the press:

> It is outrageous that the Immigration Service has been dragging its heels on the investigation of alleged Nazi war criminals living in the United States.
>
> Since last August, the New York office of the Immigration Service has been the "control office" for Nazi war crimes investigations. It has had information concerning these 38 alleged criminals. Yet officials admitted to me today that in a period of over nine months, they have virtually done nothing. They conceded that they have not interviewed one single witness in any of the 38 cases. They have not initiated any deportation proceedings . . . .
>
> In view of the charges that political pressure has stifled INS investigations in the past, this failure of the Immigration Service to act against these alleged war criminals is a particularly serious problem. The American people expect expeditious action from the Immigration Service . . . .[2]

This press release was followed by a May 20, 1974 Washington news conference, at which Holtzman made public a letter and memorandum addressed to Leonard F. Chapman, Jr., commissioner of INS, asserting the investigation of alleged Nazi war criminals by INS "reveal[s] inaction, disorganization and lack of direction."

Holtzman said at the press conference that people on the INS list of alleged Nazi war criminals living in the United States were charged with "horrendous crimes against humanity." As one example, she mentioned Andrija Artukovic, originally brought to the attention of Congress in 1962 by then Representative Seymour Halpern (see Chapter 5).

Holtzman's letter and memo to Chapman asked that the following steps be taken: immediate deportation or extradition of Artukovic; review of evidence in cases of Bishop Valerian Trifa and Boleslavs Maikovskis to determine if deportation proceedings could be instituted; cooperation with West Germany on extradition of all individuals wanted there for war crimes; and reinstatement of investigations that had been unjustifiably cancelled.

The memo also asked Chapman why the INS had failed to commence any investigation of at least these three reported war criminals. Holtzman further charged the INS with "failure to conduct a vigorous, result-oriented investigation." Eyewitnesses whose names were available to the INS were not interviewed in at least fourteen cases, she said. Status reports indicated that no substantive information had been obtained for eleven cases, and that none had been obtained for several months in eight additional cases. In six of these nineteen cases, witnesses' names had been provided but none had been interviewed.

Holtzman called for a "substantial overhaul" of the administration of the investigation, recommending the following steps: creation of a special War Crimes Strike Force within the INS with full responsibility for conducting the investigation and deportation of alleged Nazi war criminals; assignment of a full-time expert lawyer to direct and guide investigations; establishment of investigation priorities and timetables; and development of a systematic method for contacting all foreign and domestic governmental and other sources.[3]

On June 11, 1974, Holtzman's office released to the press her letter written the previous day to Chapman, in response to his June 5 answer to her May 20 communication. In a statement to the press which accompanied the letter, Holtzman said:

> Commissioner Leonard F. Chapman's June 5th letter and memorandum confirm my analysis that the Immigration and Naturalization Service (INS) has failed to conduct a thorough, result-oriented investigation of alleged Nazi war criminals living in the United States.
>
> I am profoundly disappointed that despite my detailed analysis of the status of the investigation sent to the Commissioner, the INS has yet to take steps that will result in the immediate deportation or extradition of Andrija Artukovic, interview all available witnesses, check systematically all foreign official and

private sources, and assign personnel on a full-time basis to direct this investigation.

In fact, it appears that whatever additional action INS has taken was not the result of a more vigorous and systematic investigation but was solely in reaction to my initial inquiries or in response to them.[4]

To back up her charges that INS was ineffective in administering the investigation of war criminals, Holtzman said in her June 10 letter to Chapman:

I presume that the INS status reports are prepared for the purpose of enabling some kind of administrative review of the investigation. Since you admit they are deliberately condensed and lacking in detail and therefore cannot form an adequate basis for *my* analysis of the investigation, I fail to understand how they can form an adequate basis for *your* analysis (or that of any other INS officials).

Holtzman ended her letter to Chapman:

You can be assured of my continued interest in this matter. I welcome your invitation to examine the files in the New York office. I also look forward to meeting with you to discuss these issues more thoroughly, in the sincere hope that the progress of this investigation can be substantially furthered.[5]

Rep. Joshua Eilberg (D-Pa.), who served as chairman of the House Judiciary Subcommittee on Immigration from 1973 through 1978, says that he and the subcommittee were well aware of the presence here of Nazi war criminals before Holtzman's 1974 "exposure." "I took a personal interest in the subject even before I became chairman," he told me in a January 9, 1983 telephone interview. "Almost as soon as I became chairman in 1973, I called a meeting and had INS Commissioner Chapman come before the subcommittee. It became increasingly apparent that INS was doing nothing."

Describing Holtzman as a "solo player" who made her own contacts with INS rather than working within the subcommittee, Eilberg says that as chairman he also had many contacts, and that the issue was a continuing project for him. Eilberg's

first term began in January, 1967. He became a member of
the subcommittee in 1969, succeeding Peter W. Rodino, Jr.
(D-N.J.) as chairman in 1973, when Rodino became chairman
of the full Judiciary Committee. Eilberg lost his bid for re-
election in November, 1978, amidst allegations that he received more than $100,000 in a conflict of interests involving
work his law firm did for Philadelphia's Hahnemann Hospital.
When Congress reconvened in January, 1979, Holtzman became subcommittee chairwoman.

The next month Eilberg pleaded guilty to charges that he
had illegally accepted money for helping the hospital obtain
a federal grant. He was fined, placed on probation for five
years, and barred for life from seeking federal office.

Eilberg, who today is the director of Brith Sholom, a Philadelphia communal organization that provides community,
civic welfare and minority rights services, repeats the charges
against INS and much of the information in Holtzman's releases. "The issue was never hers, but the subcommittee's,"
he says. "I would have loved to have her input, instead of
her keeping it to herself. She never fully recognized the
committee system." He believes the issue became known as
"hers" because her Brooklyn Jewish constituency expected her
to take the lead.

A chronology of Nazi war criminal activities prepared by
the Immigration Subcommittee summarizes Eilberg's involvement in 1974 and early 1975 as follows:

> Mr. Eilberg addressed a letter to the Secretary of State June
> 1974 expressing concern that the Department of State failed
> to cooperate with [the Department of] Justice in the investi-
> gation of the alleged war criminals and requested a detailed
> report on State Department efforts and assistance in consulting
> foreign governments regarding extradition requests. The State
> Department response was inadequate, and Mr. Eilberg ad-
> dressed another letter in July concerning Soviet consultation
> and obtaining statements from potential eyewitnesses in West
> Germany . . . . A letter to the President August 1974 was
> sent from Mr. Eilberg concerning the lack of coordination
> between INS and State [Department]. . . . During hearings
> before the Subcommittee March 1975 Mr. Eilberg questioned
> the priority given by INS to these investigations. . . . In April/

May 1975 Mr. Eilberg continued to press the Department of
State and INS for information on the alleged Nazi war criminals
and the need for more priority for this issue.[6]

Meanwhile, the tenacious, independent and sometimes ab-
rasive Holtzman was taking on Secretary of State Henry Kissinger. On May 20, 1975, she wrote him to complain about
his department's failure to cooperate with INS.[7]

On May 24, 1975, Eilberg and Holtzman were part of a
Special Study Subcommittee of the Judiciary Committee which
traveled to the Soviet Union. They discussed with officials
there Soviet emigration policies and cooperation with our
government in investigating alleged Nazi war criminals living
in the United States. Other members of the special study
subcommittee were Reps. Hamilton Fish, Jr. (R-N.Y.), Edward
Mezvinsky (D-Iowa) and Christopher J. Dodd (D-Conn.).

"There was a thaw in Soviet-U.S. relations then, and it was
a good time to go," Eilberg told me. "The Soviet Union was
granting visas to Jews entering the United States and they
wanted to help—it was to their political advantage. We met
in Moscow with the first Deputy Procurator General, Mikhail
P. Malyarov. In our long discussions about exit visas for Soviet
Jews, he was not especially friendly. But when I brought up
the issue of Nazi war criminals, he transformed into a grand-
fatherly type and was full of pathos. He said, 'Now you're
talking about something important,' and spoke of the millions
of Soviet citizens killed by the Nazis. We asked him about
cooperating by providing witnesses, and he said no approach
had ever been made by the United States. He agreed we
could come over and interrogate witnesses." [8]

On August 25, 1975 Holtzman wrote again to Kissinger,
saying that she was "frankly dismayed at the attitude of the
State Department." She called the "initiatives" taken by the
State Department "pointless duplication of INS efforts and
further delay," and she described as "plainly dilatory" the
State Department's decision to wait for "formal reply" from
the West German government before "formally" approaching
other foreign governments. She further accused the State
Department of "making every effort to avoid contacting any
Eastern European countries, including the Soviet Union, which

may have relevant information about Nazi war criminals," and reminded Kissinger that his Department had been asked to make these contacts for more than one and a half years by INS and by Eilberg.

Complaining that her May 20 letter to Kissinger had been answered by Assistant Secretary of State Robert J. McCloskey, and only after a delay of more than two months, Holtzman requested Kissinger to answer her "personally." "The Department's inaction and indifference is *[sic]* an affront to the Congress and the American people—especially now, as we mark the thirtieth anniversary of the end of the Second World War," Holtzman concluded.[9]

In July, 1975 Eilberg had written to Kissinger, requesting a detailed report on initiatives the State Department had taken to obtain the cooperation of foreign governments. McCloskey's response to him was a status report of the department's efforts in requesting assistance from the Berlin Document Center through the American Embassy in Bonn. In October, Eilberg received a letter stating that German-language documents had been received and were being translated. After assessing those documents, the State Department would decide if they should approach other foreign governments. Eilberg replied, requesting the report be expedited.

In November, 1975, Eilberg sent subcommittee staff to Israel to discuss with Israeli officials the possibility of locating eyewitnesses there. During oversight hearings the next month he asked Lawrence S. Eagleburger, deputy undersecretary for management, Department of State, if the department had yet contacted the Soviet government and why there was such a delay. He pointed out the assurances of cooperation which his delegation had received during their May visit to the Soviet Union.[10]

The following winter, when the State Department finally asked the Soviet Union for information on three alleged Nazi war criminals living in the United States, Holtzman said on January 30, 1976, "I am pleased to see that the State Department is finally seeking information on these cases from the Soviet Union. Because many of the cases under investigation involve crimes that allegedly took place in countries now a part of the U.S.S.R., the Soviets may have useful evidence. . . ."

Noting that the State Department used "justifiable caution" in forwarding only three cases to Soviet authorities, she urged further action, saying, "For the first time since the Nuremberg Trials, the United States Government is seeking evidence on alleged Nazi war criminals from the Soviet Union. I hope that the Soviets will cooperate, and that these cases can be resolved quickly and satisfactorily. I hope, too, that the State Department will proceed to contact the Soviets and other Eastern European countries with regard to the 47 other cases forwarded by the Immigration Service." [11]

INS announced on September 27, 1976 that as a result of interviews conducted in Israel by its attorneys, it would begin deportation proceedings within thirty days against three permanent resident aliens accused of Nazi war crimes. The Service also announced that it would, within sixty days, recommend to the Department of Justice that denaturalization be sought for four naturalized citizens. As was her usual dogged style on this issue, Holtzman released a statement that combined criticism of past inaction by INS with praise for their announcement of progress. She also took credit for this progress, saying:

> This is a very important development. I am very pleased that as a result of my criticism of the Immigration Service's foot dragging and indifference on the cases of alleged Nazi war criminals living in the United States, action is now being taken in at least seven cases. It is particularly gratifying that today's development is apparently the direct consequence of my insistence that the Service seek witnesses and documentation in these cases from sources in the State of Israel.
>
> Although the actions announced today do not make up for nearly 30 years of Immigration Service delay and neglect, they do offer the hope that the United States will no longer be a haven for persons accused of some of the most atrocious crimes in human history.[12]

Utilization of alleged Nazi war criminals by intelligence agencies was the subject of correspondence the next month. Holtzman and Eilberg questioned Chapman as to "whether intervention by the CIA and other executive agencies played any role in this outrageous laxity [of the INS] toward alleged Nazi war criminals." They wrote this in a letter to Chapman dated October 15, 1976, after reading in that day's *New York Times* that the CIA had contacted INS about a former employee and alleged Nazi war criminal, Edgars Laipenieks. The *Times* article cited by them said that Laipenieks had received a letter from the CIA, dated July 20, 1976, stating that the agency had corresponded with INS about his case and had been informed it had been dropped.

Bob Dorn, a reporter on the *San Diego Evening Tribune,* did the original investigation of this case, and his stories on Laipenieks (of San Diego) appeared in that newspaper in the fall and winter of 1976. Dorn described to Charles R. Allen, Jr. how Laipenieks had shown him and colleague Martin Gerchen the correspondence, while boasting that INS was not going to get him. Dorn said Laipenieks even carried with him photocopies of his letter from the CIA, which said, in part:

. . . we have been corresponding with the Immigration and Naturalization Service about your status. We have now been told that you are "not amenable to deportation under existing laws." It is our understanding that INS has advised their San Diego office to cease any action against you . . . . If such does not prove the case, please let us know immediately. Thank you once again . . . for your past assistance to the agency.[13]

After learning the details of the Laipenieks correspondence from the CIA, Holtzman and Eilberg wrote to Chapman:

. . . we find the willingness of the CIA to employ and contact the Immigration Service on behalf of a person alleged to have committed war crimes under the Nazis an intolerable affront to the decency of the American people, and we are deeply concerned that its action in this case may have been duplicated in others where deportation may be possible.

We, therefore, request that you report to us in detail, as promptly as possible, about any and all communications, written or oral, between the Immigration Service and the Central Intelligence Agency regarding persons about whom allegations of participation in atrocities under the Nazis have been made to INS. Your report should indicate what effect, if any, such communication had upon the progress of the investigation of any case, and whether it contributed to a delay in such an investigation. We further request that you advise us of any communication about alleged war criminals between INS and other executive agencies including the Office of Strategic Services, Federal Bureau of Investigation, Defense Intelligence Agency, National Security Agency, and National Aeronautics and Space Administration, and any action taken by INS in response thereto . . . .[14]

Holtzman was not satisfied with Chapman's answer to her and Eilberg's October 15 letter about Laipenieks. On February 7, 1977, she made public his reply, calling it "incomplete and evasive." [15] Holtzman that day also released her letter to Chapman, dated February 7. In a statement to the press accompanying her letter, Holtzman said:

Commissioner Chapman's failure to respond fully to my questions about executive agency interference in war criminal investigations points out again the need for a full Congressional inquiry into the Immigration Service's handling of Nazi cases. I hope that the House Immigration Subcommittee will act immediately to find out why INS failed for more than 25 years to act on the cases of alleged Nazi war criminals living in the United States.[16]

Holtzman had called for such investigations eleven days earlier, when on January 27, 1977 she and Rep. William S. Cohen (R-Me.), also a member of the subcommittee, wrote to Eilberg urging that the House Immigration Subcommittee investigate INS's "long failure to act in the cases of alleged Nazi war criminals living in the United States." Eilberg officially requested of the comptroller general such an investigation.

The Holtzman-Cohen letter said the investigation should uncover reasons for the "half-hearted, dilatory" efforts of INS on Nazi cases, and specifically should seek to learn who within INS and the Justice Department made decisions on Nazi cases; whether political pressures were put on INS to drop investigations of alleged Nazi war criminals; and whether the CIA, FBI or other executive agencies intervened in investigations.

Six months later, on July 26, Holtzman announced the formation by INS of a "high level task force to direct the investigation and prosecution of [Nazi war criminal] cases," something she had suggested three years earlier. Her announcement said she had been advised by INS General Counsel David Crosland that the task force then being formed would consist of five attorneys and supporting personnel based in Washington. The new team would be responsible for the supervision of five deportation and five denaturalization cases then under way, for bringing new cases, and for coordinating investigative efforts throughout the country. Holtzman said that the new task force "represented substantial improvement," and that she was "greatly encouraged" by this decision by INS.[17]

The announcement of the new INS task force may have prodded the State Department into showing some movement on the issue. On September 21, 1977, John W. DeWitt, deputy assistant secretary for consular affairs, wrote to Holtzman about the State Department's handling of requests to foreign governments for information about alleged Nazi war criminals living here:

> Currently, we have 68 names which have not yet been submitted to the U.S.S.R. We will forward these names to the Soviet Foreign Ministry within thirty days, indicating that we have received allegations about the individuals and asking for any pertinent information which the Soviets may have on hand. We will continue to request investigations by the Soviet authorities in cases of particular interest to the Immigration and Naturalization Service.
>
> Any cases which we receive in the future from the INS will be referred simultaneously to the Berlin Document Center, the Federal Republic of Germany and the U.S.S.R. as soon as they are received.

Taking at least partially-deserved credit for the State Department's action, Holtzman on September 30 issued a press release headlined "State Department Accedes to Holtzman

Demand for Stepped Up Action on Nazi War Criminals." She said in the release:

> I am pleased that the State Department has finally abandoned its dilatory procedures and has agreed to expedite the investigation of Nazi war criminals in the U.S. The assurance that all cases will be promptly forwarded to the Soviet Union is important. Since both the defendants and the eyewitnesses in many cases are very old, it is critical that there be no delay in completing these investigations.

In her May 20, 1975 letter to Kissinger, Holtzman had called "utterly incomprehensible" the State Department's failure to respond to the INS request. If she did not know then of State Department and other American intelligence-Nazi war criminal connections, she was certainly aware of them three years later. In January, 1977, Eilberg requested the comptroller general "to conduct a thorough investigation of this situation," and specifically asked him "to determine whether there was any evidence of deliberate attempts on the part of U.S. government agencies to obstruct or quash investigations and prosecutions of these individuals." [18] In compliance with this request, on May 15, 1978, the General Accounting Office (GAO), the investigative arm of Congress, issued a report entitled "Widespread Conspiracy to Obstruct Probes of Alleged Nazi War Criminals Not Supported by Available Evidence—Controversy May Continue."

Although the report stated there was no evidence of a "widespread conspiracy" within the U.S. government to cover up the Nazi war criminal cases, the FBI and the CIA did admit to the GAO that they "utilized" Nazi war criminals and collaborators. According to the report, the CIA admitted to having used Nazi war criminals and the FBI admitted having "contacted" forty-four Nazi war criminals and further admitted having employed seven of them. (These figures were based on a total of 111 samplings from the official INS list of 252 alleged Nazi war criminals and collaborators living in America.) [19]

When the GAO report was released in May, Holtzman in a press release called it "incomplete," because "The G.A.O.

did not have access to the files of the CIA and the FBI, but made assumptions based on summaries of those files. It is ludicrous to assume a report is conclusive and that there is no evidence of obstruction of prosecution when the source material has been concealed." She said that subcommittee hearings should be held on the matter.[20]

She and Cohen wrote on June 8, 1978 to Eilberg to "renew our request that the Immigration Subcommittee conduct an appropriate preliminary investigation—including a review of all relevant files—and then hold public hearings on this matter."

A series of such public hearings by the subcommittee (which did *not* include a review of "all relevant files"), began on July 19, 1978. Among those testifying were: Vincent Schiano, Anthony DeVito (see Chapter 9); officials of the GAO and Department of State; former INS Deputy Commissioner James F. Greene; former displaced persons officials; Sam Zutty, former officer in charge of the INS Nazi war criminal operation in New York City; and Charles R. Allen, Jr. (see Chapters 5, 6, 7, 15). Asked in November, 1978 about intelligence connections to Nazi war criminals, Holtzman told me:

> It's very troubling for me as an American and as a Jew to have found that our government permitted many of these Nazi war criminals to stay in this country, even though it was well aware of the allegations against them, even though in some cases it had innumerable witnesses. . . . There is no question that a number of these alleged Nazi war criminals did have connections with the CIA. . . . The GAO did say that more than twenty-five alleged Nazi war criminals were in fact hired by U.S. government agencies such as the Defense Department, the State Department, the FBI, the CIA, since the late 1940s, with full awareness of the backgrounds of these people. Why they were hired, nobody knows. What they were doing, nobody knows. But it seems incredible to me that our government, which fought a war against nazism, would not only encourage these people to come here and permit them to stay, but would actually employ them. . . .
> We had a GAO investigation which did a preliminary job. Their conclusion that there was no conspiracy seems to me to be unwarranted, since they never saw actual files. We need to hold additional hearings, as the report raised serious questions

that have to be explored further. It's premature to say we know the answer as to whether these alleged Nazi war criminals were permitted to stay here because they could be experts on communism and the Cold War, or whether they were permitted to come here because they claimed to be anti-Communist and we were willing to close our eyes to their atrocities and their war crimes. We don't know the answer to that. I think we need to hold additional hearings, and I would hope that additional hearings will be held. It's premature to say we know the answer. Serious allegations have been raised.[21]

Meanwhile, on October 30, 1978, a bill first introduced by Holtzman on December 19, 1975 was signed into law. Public Law 95–549 amends the Immigration and Nationality Act "to exclude from admission into, and to deport from, the United States all aliens who persecuted any person on the basis of race, religion, national origin, or political opinion, under the direction of the Nazi government of Germany, and for other purposes." The law gives explicit authority to INS to deport Nazi war criminals who have come here since 1952, closing a loophole which had existed for twenty-six years and had allowed Nazi war criminals to enter and live freely in the United States.

Holtzman said of this victory that it was "accompanied by tenacity, by hard work, by skepticism, by refusing to say we have to take what we were given." Speaking in Schenectady, New York on November 29, 1978, she said that the presence here of Nazi war criminals is a "pool of poison" that helps to create and further anti-Semitism. She received letters in which the "horrible anti-Semitic flavor of the thinking is dreadful," she said.

In her November 2, 1978 press release announcing the signing of her bill into law, Holtzman said:

This law puts our government squarely on record against providing sanctuary in this country to Nazi war criminals. Its enactment is especially appropriate at this time: a time of increased awareness of the horrors of the holocaust [sic]; a time when the past role of our government in affording a haven to war criminals has become a matter of public record; and a time of resurgence of Nazism and anti-semitism [sic] worldwide—in the Soviet Union, in South America, and in Skokie. . . .

This law will finally give the Immigration Service direct legislative authority to act against Nazi war criminals. INS officials have told me that my legislation will aid them in their present investigation of alleged Nazis, and will allow them to proceed against those who would otherwise be protected. . . .

Although the immigration laws exclude from the United States everyone from polygamists to marijuana users, from prostitutes to anarchists, until today our country's doors have been wide open to Nazi war criminals. This law is long overdue.

The sorry record of our government over the past 30 years in allowing known Nazi war criminals to live undisturbed in this country has been amply documented. This action confirms my belief that it is not too late to make our stand against war crimes clear and unequivocal.[22]

After Holtzman took over as subcommittee chairperson in January, 1979, she had more clout to push the Justice Department. On March 15, 1979, she criticized as "inadequate, half-hearted, and falling short of the legal requirements imposed by Congress" the Department's new plans to upgrade its Nazi war criminal investigations. Her press release of that date said that she had met for two days with INS and Justice Department officials, who agreed to set aside an additional $300,000 for the remainder of fiscal year 1979, and to authorize hiring another attorney and seven more investigators. Holtzman had set hearings on the issue for that day, and said, "The Department's sudden willingness—the day before my scheduled hearings on the matter—to set aside some additional funds does not alter the fact that the law has not been complied with. The full amount [of $2.052 million authorized by Congress] must be made available."

Holtzman's release also said she advocated transferring the war criminal task force from INS to the Justice Department, with it reporting directly to the attorney general. She said:

Given the 30 year history of indifference and incompetence by INS in dealing with Nazi war criminals in this country, it is inappropriate that the Task Force remain in the Service. In addition to short-circuiting the bureaucratic obstacles which

have plagued the Task Force since it was established, placing
it under the direct control of the Attorney General would
demonstrate the Administration's commitment to denying Nazi
war criminals sanctuary in this country.

She warned that "my patience is at an end, as is that of
my many colleagues in the Congress who are concerned about
the issue." Although Holtzman said Associate Attorney General
Michael Egan advised her he would not transfer the Nazi
Unit from INS, eventually this administrative change was made
(see Chapter 11).[23]

In 1980, Holtzman won the Democratic nomination for
U.S. Senator but lost the election to Republican Alfonse M.
D'Amato. Senator Jacob K. Javits, who traditionally received
heavy Democratic support, ran on the Liberal Party line and
split the vote. When the 97th Congress convened in January,
1981, Holtzman was no longer there to fight for "her" issue.
But her 1980 campaign, like her previous ones, was based on
Holtzman's commitment, ability and integrity. Her independent
attitude and early inattention to building bridges to the
New York State party establishment alienated such political
heavyweights as New York City Mayor Edward Koch, Brooklyn
Democratic leader Meade H. Esposito, and Erie County Democratic
leader Joseph F. Crangle (who all nonetheless supported
her). Never a backslapper by nature, she expected to win on
her record, not by charisma or personality. Even as she joked
privately about her sober image, she publicly projected such
an image at campaign rallies and speeches. She rarely smiled
even as she told her favorite joke about herself. "On the
Abscam tapes they said, 'Don't even try to bribe that Holtzman.
She's too honest to trust.' "

An article in *The New York Times Magazine*, containing interviews
of candidates for the Democratic primary, said, "Miss
Holtzman is offering herself as a technician with the devotion
of a Carmelite. She is supported by feminist groups, and
unquestionably she is a woman of today. But a blouse with a
round collar under a cardigan sweater says she is June Allyson
and it is 1946. This is part of her appeal, too." [24]

Soon after losing the 1980 senatorial race, Holtzman said
she would continue her commitment to the Nazi war criminal

issue, and that as a private citizen she would form a "broadly-based committee of public concern" to assure continuance of the OSI, monitor OSI trials, and "keep the issue before the American people." Although at this writing the creation of such a committee has not been announced, Holtzman continues to speak out on the issue.[25]

In the fall of 1981, Holtzman was elected district attorney of Brooklyn, the first female district attorney in New York City.

Eleven

Mendelsohn, Rockler and Ryan
Attorneys at Law

In the summer of 1977, the Immigration and Naturalization Service (INS) finally agreed to set up the first coordinated effort to pursue and prosecute Nazi war criminals in America. The first three directors of the unit were: Martin Mendelsohn (October, 1977–May, 1979), Walter J. Rockler (May, 1979–March, 1980), and Allan A. Ryan, Jr. (April, 1980–August, 1983). Other than their law degrees, the three attorneys have little in common.

When Mendelsohn was appointed head of the newly-created Special Litigation Unit (SLU), INS moved its Nazi war criminal operation from New York City to Washington. Depending on the time and source of the comments, Mendelsohn's directorship has been severely criticized, highly praised, or excused with rationalizations. He assumed the position after a thirty-year lapse in the United States government's effort to seek eyewitnesses and its lack of willingness to acknowledge that Nazi war criminals had come here and were utilized by various agencies.

Was Mendelsohn the wrong man for the job, or did he tackle the impossible? His questionable qualifications for the position and his slow progress show he may not have been the best choice to head the SLU.

Brooklyn-bred and Jewish, Mendelsohn was thirty-five years old when INS Chief Counsel David Crosland appointed him.

Special Litigation Unit Director Martin Mendelsohn (right) in Albany, N.Y. for trial of Vilis Hazners; shown with Rabbi Paul Silton, 1978.

He says that he doesn't want to talk about his background or motivation for heading the SLU. "That's all behind me now. You're one of the few that even remember I was involved," he told me by telephone on February 3, 1983. When pressed, he said he was "working on the Hill" before coming to the SLU. Others recall that his background was in Legal Aid in Illinois, and that he was active in local Democratic politics. He is currently counsel for the Simon Wiesenthal Center in Los Angeles.

As early as the end of October, 1977, it was apparent that newly-appointed SLU Director Mendelsohn and his staff were in over their heads. At the October-November denaturalization hearing of accused Nazi war criminal Vilis Hazners in Albany (one of the unit's first efforts), Mendelsohn and his staff attorney William Strasser were sharply criticized by presiding INS Judge Anthony DeGaeto (see Chapter 2). DeGaeto stopped the proceedings on November 1, the sixth day of the trial, when the SLU attorneys could not produce a copy of a statement given in 1974 to Israeli police by Shabtai Dolgizer, an Israeli witness for the government. "I do think the government has been a little lax. They should have had the documents and had their case prepared," I heard DeGaeto say.

The next day, DeGaeto had to adjourn for several hours because the SLU attorneys had failed to provide a sufficiently broad time frame for the testimony of another Israeli witness, Chava Ljak. Original allegations pertained to Hazners' persecution of Jews in the Dwinsk Ghetto, Riga, Latvia in June, 1941; Ljak testified about an August, 1941 allegation. (Strasser submitted this new allegation during the afternoon session.)

On November 3, DeGaeto charged Strasser with destroying the value of government evidence. He warned that this blunder might cause him "not to give a great deal of weight" to key testimony. Without DeGaeto's permission, Strasser had rearranged an exhibit of photographs that had previously been shown to witnesses.

When the Strasser photograph switch took place, Mendelsohn was back in Washington. In a telephone interview with Fredric U. Dicker of the Albany *Times-Union,* Mendelsohn said, "I'm dismayed at what's been happening." According to Dicker's article, an undisclosed source said that the INS effort to deport Nazi war criminals had been "severely damaged by sloppy preparation of cases." [1]

When the Hazners hearing reconvened in March, 1978, Mendelsohn acted as chief trial attorney. Dicker described the judge's impatience with him:

. . . DeGaeto clashed on several occasions with INS attorney Martin Mendelsohn, who is heading the Immigration Service's nationwide effort to deport alleged war criminals, and at one point accused Mendelsohn of not knowing an essential point of law.

"That is something you should have known when you went to law school," DeGaeto snapped at Mendelsohn. . . .

A further indication of the government's problems came when Mendelsohn called his last witness, government attorney William Strasser, who handled the Immigration Service's case against Hazners last fall.

Immediately, Hazners' attorney, Ivars Berzins, objected that a trial attorney could not also be a witness, an argument that won DeGaeto's support.

DeGaeto advised Mendelsohn to read sections of a federal Canon of Ethics for attorneys, saying they would prevent such an appearance.

Mendelsohn called Stasser *[sic]* in an effort to undue *[sic]* the damage caused in the fall when Strasser rearranged a critical piece of the government's evidence, a set of photographs which were shown to the Israeli witnesses.

At the time, DeGaeto accused Strasser of "destroying" evidence, although he later said he was satisfied the photographs had been returned to their original condition.

DeGaeto finally relented in the face of Mendelsohn's protests and instructed both Mendelsohn and Berzins to submit legal briefs on the propriety of the testimony.[2]

In March, 1978, the SLU had a staff of five full-time attorneys. Mendelsohn told me on March 9 that he expected to have twenty hearings underway by the end of that year.

The INS had 169 investigations in progress, according to Mendelsohn, but not all of the alleged war criminals were still living. He told me that he had stepped into the Albany hearing at that point because the original government attorney assigned to the case, Ralph Smith, became ill and his replacement, William Strasser, was "uncomfortable in the spotlight." Mendelsohn wouldn't comment on complaints by the press and Albany residents that Strasser's handling of the case was less than competent.

Asked what American Jewish communities and organizations could do to assist in bringing alleged Nazi war criminals to justice, Mendelsohn stressed the importance of having attorneys monitor hearings. "This lets the witnesses know that they have support," he said, "and it also makes the judges aware that they are being observed by competent professionals who will bear witness to any errors. This is an important and significant role that American Jews can play at the hearings."

Mendelsohn said he did not believe that picketing and demonstrations are positive approaches. "We have chosen, in this society, to deal with disputes through the law," he said, "and I think that this approach should be allowed to go forward."

He mentioned that there were demonstrations by such groups as the Jewish Defense League at the hearing of another alleged Nazi war criminal, Karlis Detlavs, in Baltimore. Those demonstrations received a great deal of publicity on television, he explained, but were not beneficial to the case.

Mendelsohn seemed determined to prove that Hazners should be deported, but whatever the outcome of the case, he said he believed that the hearing already served a twofold purpose. "First of all," he said, "the media coverage has given residents of the Albany area, and Americans in general, an education about Nazi war criminals. In addition, Hazners is no longer the secure and happy man that he was five years ago. Now he's worried about being deported, and this in itself is an accomplishment," Mendelsohn said.

Like the ten other denaturalization/deportation cases the SLU dealt with, the Hazners and Detlavs proceedings were started before that unit was created. The SLU did not initiate any case. Charles R. Allen, Jr. described the situation:

> Whenever the SLU did manage to get before a judge, the ineptness of the government lawyers often degenerated into a tragi-comedy of errors deriving from a lack of trial experience. In a "confidential" Congressional report it was noted that of the SLU's five lawyers, one—brought over from the State Department, notoriously the single-most derelict Agency in the whole history of the Nazi war criminal matter—had no trial experience; another only Legal Aid background and among the other three less than five years' experience as trial lawyers! [3]

On March 28, 1979, the Justice Department agreed to transfer control of the Nazi unit from INS to the Criminal Division, a move pushed by Rep. Elizabeth Holtzman. There the SLU became the Office of Special Investigations (OSI), and annual funding of $2 million was authorized for a staff of thirty-eight attorneys, investigators, researchers and aides.

Discussing the transfer with a Jewish War Veterans group in Syracuse, New York in April, then National Commander Nathan M. Goldberg said, "After almost two years of practically no effective results, the unit has been switched . . . [and] assured that it would receive full funding. . . . Now let them produce some results. It's time to put the unit on notice. Unless some concrete action is taken to prosecute accused

Nazi war criminals in the next six months, it's time for a new director and a new cast of characters."

The next month, the "cast" did change and there was a new "leading man." Walter J. Rockler, a senior partner in the prestigious Washington law firm of Arnold and Porter, was appointed OSI director and special counsel on May 6, 1979. Mendelsohn became his deputy.

At a meeting on June 25, 1979 in his temporary OSI headquarters, Rockler discussed with ten concerned individuals his plans for the OSI. It was immediately apparent that the new director, then age fifty-eight, was sharp and confident. With his background and personality, no one was going to push him around as they had the less-aggressive Mendelsohn. When I asked whether it had occurred to him that he was hired and the Nazi unit reorganized just to waste more time and further obstruct the issue, he said, "Yes . . . but that doesn't suit my purposes. I'm not going to be a paperhanger at this stage of my life."

Rockler had arrived at "this stage" of his life after a successful military and legal career. As a Marine Corps officer during World War II, he took part in battles on Kwajalein, Saipan, Tinian and Iwo Jima, and was awarded the Bronze Star. At the age of twenty-six in 1947, he became a prosecuting attorney for the Office of Chief of Counsel for War Crimes, U.S. War Department, at the Nuremberg war crimes trials. In 1948 he was appointed deputy director of the Economic Ministry Division, responsible for prosecuting Hitler's financial backers. Since 1949, he had been in private practice, specializing in federal tax law.

Rockler made it clear that he expected to reorganize, hire experienced trial lawyers, and see that the unit operated at top efficiency. He had already "parceled out" the files of the strongest cases, but results were likely to be "quite spotty," he said. "We must put on the tightest cases we can, but this may not make a difference. The problem will be convincing American judges. . . . Who cares if people were killed thirty-five years ago?"

At a second meeting on October 22, 1979, Rockler seemed just as committed to his assignment, but had begun to realize the enormity of the obstacles he was facing. "It's thirty-five

Former Director of Office of Special Investigations Walter J. Rockler, in his Justice Department office in Washington, February, 1981. (photo by author)

years too late already," he told me. "No matter what we do, we can never recreate the year 1950. These people have been living here, and will probably be buried here. Anything else is unrealistic.

"The worst thing to cope with is the federal government in general," he continued. "It takes a week to get a box of paper clips. I didn't have a messenger for two months. The lack of a messenger was more detrimental than the FBI not cooperating!"

A dynamic and high-powered man, Rockler seemed frustrated by his inability to control the time frame of the prosecutions. "They're all so damn old, and they've been sitting in the United States forever," he said. "We either have cases or we don't. If we sit long enough, all we'll have is a bunch of dead defendants. I'd rather bring a case and lose than do nothing. I'd rather win, of course. But never bringing the case is as zero as you can get. We'll win some."

Rockler called time his biggest problem, especially since the U.S. judicial process makes it possible for an alleged Nazi war criminal to stretch out a case and "fiddle around in court for five or six years." When asked about the oldest case he was handling (begun in 1951), Rockler said, "If we have to start a new trial, I'm not sure *I'll* live to see the end of it, let alone [Andrija] Artukovic!"

Rockler, who is Jewish, was sometimes criticized by Jewish community leaders for remarks they described as "insensitive." On the other hand, he complained of having to report to hundreds of people, including those in the Jewish community, who thought they were overseeing his work. He was especially incensed when he was blamed for thirty years of neglect, pointing out that his job was to move forward and not to apologize for past errors of others.

When he became OSI director, Rockler made it clear that his assignment would be temporary. On March 31, 1980, he resumed his private practice with Arnold and Porter. Before that date, Mendelsohn was removed from the unit and a new deputy director was named to replace him—amid much controversy.

On January 6, 1980, Rockler had announced that the next day Allan A. Ryan, Jr. would become deputy director. A thirty-four-year-old lawyer in the Solicitor General's office, Ryan would take over as OSI director when Rockler left on March 31. According to Rockler, the period of overlap would assure continuity in the OSI.

"In my opinion Ryan is a very bright and able guy, and I certainly recommended his coming aboard," Rockler told me that day. Asked about Mendelsohn's future, Rockler said that the former deputy had been offered "certain options" by the Justice Department, but that he had not yet made his decision.

Amid reports that Assistant Attorney General Philip Heymann (in charge of the Criminal Division) replaced Mendelsohn because his personality clashed with Rockler's, some people who had urged the government to act on the Nazi issue were upset by the deputy director's removal. Elizabeth Holtzman said she had told Attorney General Benjamin Civiletti that she was strongly opposed to Mendelsohn's removal. "To remove him would seriously impair the effective functioning of the office and would send the wrong signals to the federal courts and to foreign governments, which would see this as a sign that the U.S. is not really serious about these cases," she said.[4]

The Harvard Jewish Law Students Association sent a mailgram to President Carter, Civiletti, and Heymann, expressing "outrage" at Mendelsohn's ouster. Allen Wieder, the student association's president, declared that the group had "monitored" the OSI and "what has been accomplished to date is largely a reflection of Mr. Mendelsohn's skill, stamina and professionalism."

Wieder charged that "the loss of the litigation and management skills which Martin Mendelsohn has brought to his government service would severely impede OSI's progress when combined with the resultant destruction of the international goodwill which he has so carefully cultivated. His departure would almost surely cause a significant diminution in the pace of investigations. Time has been the Nazis' ally for too long, and additional delays can be ill-afforded."[5]

The Jewish War Veterans, Department of New York, said they were "gravely concerned over the recent transfer of the OSI Deputy Director Martin Mendelsohn, and its subsequent effect on the status of future investigations. . . . We have waited much too long for our government to become serious about the pursuit of Nazi war criminals, to have the investigations threatened by counterproductive forces . . . [and we seek] an answer to the question why Mr. Mendelsohn should not be reinstated forthwith." [6]

A characteristic editorial in the Anglo-Jewish press appeared in the *Jewish Journal* (Brooklyn, N.Y.) on January 11:

> We hope that Rep. Elizabeth Holtzman (D-Bklyn.) will speed-ily convene hearings on whether the switch of a key Justice Department Nazi hunter to other duties was a government attempt to derail the search for war criminals. . . .
>
> The man at the center of the controversy is Martin Men-delsohn, hired by the Justice Department in 1977, who was doing a commendable and successful job of tracking down Nazi criminals. [7]

Even columnist Jack Anderson got into the act (January 9):

> Philip Heymann, head of Justice's Criminal Division, was persuaded to sack the unit's most diligent Nazi hunter, deputy director Martin Mendelsohn. . . .
>
> After more than two years with the special unit, Mendelsohn had developed legal expertise in the often tricky handling of ex-Nazi cases. He also had important contacts with prosecutors in other countries, whose help in finding witnesses and doc-uments is frequently crucial.
>
> As one knowledgeable source put it, "The one man who knows the most about the investigations and can do the best job is being removed. Why? " [8]

Shortly before Rockler left his post on March 31, he dis-cussed with me his frustrations and accomplishments during his nine months as director. Regarding his differences with Mendelsohn, he was admittedly "bitter," blaming him for "impediments" and "harassments" that affected "working ef-ficiency."

Rockler named as his greatest problems the physical setup of the unit and internal politics. He said that he "started from scratch" with virtually no staff, and ended his term with some fifty people under him including twenty lawyers, fifteen to twenty investigators, and ten administrators. Not until the fall of 1979 was OSI finally housed under one roof, with files and staff centralized.

The obvious difficulties of time and distance in finding witnesses, as well as the "reasonably fair but unpredictable" attitudes of the courts, were also cited by Rockler. He stressed that deporting a Nazi war criminal was a lengthy process, and that it was unrealistic to think there was "a mechanism whereby waving an appropriate wand would get people deported."

Rockler said he had introduced organization and systematization into the investigation of war criminals. He referred to the four new denaturalization cases filed by OSI in November-December, 1979. He also mentioned as a major achievement during his tenure increased cooperation with foreign governments: West Germany, Poland, the German Democratic Republic, the Soviet Union, and Israel.

Rockler and Ryan visited Israel in January, 1980, and officials there promised the OSI "utmost cooperation in making files available." They met with Minister of the Interior Yosef Burg, Minister of Justice Shmuel Tamir, and other officials, and also spent time at Yad Vashem (Holocaust memorial and archives), exploring with the staff how to best use the information available there.

Part of their mission in Israel was to overcome Israeli anger at the OSI because of a January article in *The Jerusalem Post*, Rockler explained. Based on an interview with Mendelsohn, the article quoted the then OSI deputy director as saying that the Israeli government was not responding fully to the OSI's needs.[9] "We made it clear to the Israelis that these accusations were unauthorized and incorrect," Rockler said.

In August, 1980, Mendelsohn was named a counsel to the House Immigration Subcommittee by chairperson Holtzman. A staff aide said of the appointment that Mendelsohn would be primarily responsible for investigating why criminals were allowed to enter the United States. Holtzman described him as "one of the few people in the United States with the knowledge and experience to conduct such a historical inquiry."[10]

Meanwhile, Ryan on April 1 had become director of OSI. He told me in a February 19, 1980 interview in his Washington office that his earlier involvement with the Feodor Fedorenko case piqued his interest in Nazi war criminals. As an assistant to the solicitor general in 1978, he wrote the brief and argued

Former Director of Office of Special Investigations Allan A. Ryan, Jr., in his Justice Department office, February, 1981. (photo by author)

the appeal in the government's case against Fedorenko, an admitted *SS* guard at Treblinka concentration camp. While meeting with Rockler to discuss the Fedorenko case, he had asked to be considered for the OSI directorship at the end of Rockler's tenure on March 31.

Ryan, a *magna cum laude* graduate of the University of Minnesota Law School, where he was president of the *Law Review*, was serious and confident about the OSI's future accomplishments. In addition to his 1977–1980 position in the solicitor general's office, his legal experience included a clerkship for Supreme Court Justice Byron White, service as an attorney in the Marine Corps, and an association with the Washington, D.C. law firm of Williams, Connally and Califano.

"I took the job [with OSI] because I was convinced it was a job that needed doing," Ryan told me. "There are relatively few areas in law in which you can be certain every morning when you wake up that you are doing something important to see that justice is done. After having been through Yad

Vashem, I have no doubt that what I'm doing must be done. There are people still alive who took part in the Nazi process of inhumanity and some of them are in this country. I feel obligated to do everything humanly possible under the law to bring them to account.

"Ideally, the goal of the OSI should be to locate every Nazi war criminal and collaborator in the United States, denaturalize them if they are citizens, and deport them all," he continued. "As a practical matter, it's very unlikely we'll find every single one. They don't advertise their pasts."

Ryan was born after World War II and is not Jewish. He was speaking of himself when on April 1, 1981 he told an Indianapolis Anti-Defamation League group:

> The forty-and-under generation came of age with its own passions and tragedies: the assassination of John F. Kennedy, the struggle for racial equality, with Vietnam, Watergate, energy, the environment. Mention Nazis and eyebrows are raised. Nazis belong to history, with the Depression and the Model T., Lindbergh, Pearl Harbor, and even Joe McCarthy. We grew up with the Beatles, after all, not with Glenn Miller.

But unlike many people of his generation and younger, Ryan seems to have a deep sensitivity about the lessons to be learned from the Holocaust. On the same occasion, he said:

> My personal view [is] that those who believe that Nazism is an historical relic are dangerously mistaken. There is today throughout the world, and especially in Europe, a profoundly disturbing re-emergence of right-wing extremism, including actual neo-Nazism, with all its trappings: anti-Semitism, racist ideology and violent terrorism. . . .
>
> It is the sad truth of the post-war world, a truth with which we all are familiar, that repression and discrimination have been too much with us throughout the world. . . .
>
> The Holocaust was mass murder as political policy, and civilized people must reject it in every form, lest it appear as if we are forgetting it, or worse, legitimizing it. . . .
>
> What we are doing today is perhaps the last action that we as a people can take that is not merely symbolic—an action to demonstrate our commitment that this shall not be allowed

to happen again. For what we are doing is enforcing the law against the very people who violated it, the very people who violated not only the United States' law of immigration and citizenship, but the law of humanity. We can change in court only the former, but the latter can never be far from our minds. . . .

And so to those who ask "Why now? " I say, "If not now, when? " Shall we do nothing now and await instead, God forbid, some new Holocaust that will give us a new generation of Nazis, a younger, larger list of defendants? However late this date, it is still within the power of our nation, still within the reach of the law, to call to account those criminals who still live among us. It *can* yet be done. That is why it *must* be done.[11]

With Ryan, a bright young Irish-Catholic Dartmouth graduate, at the helm, the issue became less a Jewish one and more the American one that it should be. On another occasion, Ryan said:

We are proceeding against [Nazi war criminals] because we know that they are here and we know that they broke the law to get here. And if we were to do nothing and to ignore all of that, I think it could be taken as condoning or legitimizing what they did in the past. And I don't think that's a position the United States government ought to be in, or the United States people who lost 200,000 Americans fighting Nazism.[12]

In the winter of 1983, Ryan began concentrating on a specific Nazi war criminal, former *Gestapo* officer Klaus Barbie. Known as the "Butcher of Lyons," Barbie was expelled from Bolivia to France in February to face charges of war crimes. At the request of the Criminal Division of the Justice Department, Ryan took leave from his OSI directorship and began on March 15, 1983 to work full-time on the Barbie case.

Barbie had been employed by the U.S. Army Counter-Intelligence Corps in Germany from 1947 to 1951, and was then helped by the U.S. government to escape to South America. French Nazi hunter Beate Klarsfeld came to Bolivia in 1972 and publicized Barbie's presence. That year Barbie was protected from extradition by Bolivia's military government, but ten years later a new democratic government was more cooperative. Barbie was arrested in Bolivia and expelled to France to stand trial.

Ryan's 216-page report on Barbie, with 600 pages of supporting documents, was made public on August 16, 1983. In submitting his report to the Justice Department a week earlier, Ryan urged that the U.S. government apologize to France for lying about Barbie's whereabouts and obstructing his extradition thirty-three years earlier.

"The report's historic value comes from the fact that it is the first official admission by the U.S. government that it had used and protected from prosecution by an ally—in this case, France—a wanted, notorious war criminal, Klaus Barbie, executioner of French Jews and resistance movement heroes during World War II," wrote Charles R. Allen, Jr. While giving Ryan's report qualified praise, Allen and others were critical of several aspects. For example, Allen questioned Ryan's conclusion that the Cold War made it "defensible" for the United States to recruit and utilize Barbie. He also pointed out that Ryan failed to satisfactorily pursue the matters of "Vatican complicity" and CIA connections.[13]

While in the process of writing his Barbie report, Ryan on June 12, 1983 seemed to be making excuses for the government's inaction on that case. He said in a speech to the Anti-Defamation League:

> In the late forties and fifties, our greatest concern was not Nazism but Communism, and our greatest fear was of internal subversion by Communist agents. We can look back now and see that our concern sometimes became an unhealthy obsession and that the threat of internal subversion was probably never half as grave as we painted it at the time. But that is beside the point. Finding Communists was easy, perhaps too easy, and finding Nazis was hard, because the crimes had taken place in darkness, in Europe, and evidence was hard to come by, and of course many of the Nazi suspects were outspoken anti-Communists themselves. Lacking any strong direction from the Executive, the Congress or the public, there was little incentive for INS to spend great amounts of time on cases that were difficult to understand. Promotions and advancement came to

those who produced, not to those who fought the good fight, and by our inaction we let INS believe that the good fight against Nazis had ended in 1945.[14]

In the same speech, Ryan announced he would leave OSI and the Justice Department at the end of his Barbie investigation. He recommended as his successor Neal Sher, his "extraordinarily capable deputy" for three years, and acting director of OSI since March, 1983. Ryan said he planned to do some writing, and then either return to the Justice Department in another capacity or enter private law practice.

Sher was appointed OSI Director on November 29, 1983. A thirty-six year old Jewish graduate of New York University Law School, he has been with the OSI since its creation in 1979. In April, 1980, Sher was appointed deputy director in charge of all litigation. He tried the OSI's first case, that of Wolodymir Osidach, and was responsible for the first OSI depositions taken in the Soviet Union.

Twelve

Major Jewish Organizations NJCRAC

Given the vast network of major and minor Jewish organizations operating in America, it is ironic that the crusade for justice for Nazi war criminals living in the U.S. has been left, for the most part, to independent individuals. Until Reps. Joshua Eilberg and Elizabeth Holtzman put the issue on the agenda of Congress in 1974, the major American Jewish organizations, with few exceptions, did not publicly (nor, in many cases, privately) take this cause as their own.

Jewish communal life in America is highly structured and bureaucratic, with policies and agendas for action set by the top lay and professional leaders of some thirty-eight national organizations. All but the American Jewish Committee fall under the "umbrella" of the Conference of Presidents of Major American Jewish Organizations, which has "the cooperation, support and participation of all constituent members." [1]

The national organizations that have programs addressing government domestic and foreign issues also fall under the "umbrella" of the National Jewish Community Relations Advisory Council (NJCRAC), as do local community relations councils. Additional "umbrellas" unify these and other Jewish groups, with some national organizations under several.

Breaking through this tightly-woven mesh and maze of bureaucracy to place any issue on the agenda of a Jewish national

139

organization or umbrella group is no simple task. Although all feign democracy, in reality policy is made not through grassroots action, but by a small cadre of well-paid bureaucrats and monied *"machers"* (influential persons). An issue such as Nazi war criminals in America seems on the surface a "natural" for American Jewish organizations, and especially for NJCRAC, the community relations umbrella. Why, then, did NJCRAC wait until 1979–1980 to first include a statement on unprosecuted Nazis in the United States among its programs?

Two answers to this question are discussed in Chapter 3: fear of McCarthyism and the campaign to obtain reparation money from Germany. Through 1978, "other priorities" and "no evidence" (of the guilt of the accused) were among reasons for their inaction, according to various NJCRAC officials. Because the government utilized many of the alleged Nazi war criminals in Cold War activities, fear of being labeled unpatriotic (a holdover from McCarthy days) was also an unspoken element. Apathy, a reactionary attitude, and inherent conservatism cannot be ruled out either as reasons for the silence of NJCRAC and other Jewish organizations.

When NJCRAC belatedly acknowledged the issue in their 1979 statement, they gave "Jewish community relations agencies" (and therefore themselves) credit as the "background" for "a long campaign" to establish the Special Litigation Unit (SLU) in INS. It was against this "background" that Rep. Holtzman "led a successful initiative for the establishment of a Special Litigation Unit," according to NJCRAC.[2]

But Abraham J. Bayer, director of the International Commission of NJCRAC, told me on May 15, 1980 that his group neither raised the issue until "five or six years ago," nor actively met with officials in Washington on the issue until that time. This would place first efforts in 1974 or 1975, after Reps. Eilberg and Holtzman exposed the situation in Congress and thus made it officially "safe" for them to act. On January 13, 1980, Jacqueline K. Levine, then chair of the NJCRAC Commission on International Community Relations Concerns, and of its Subcommittee on Unprosecuted Nazi War Criminals, said that her subcommittee was created just three years earlier, in 1977.

NJCRAC's "long campaign" was nowhere in evidence until the end of 1978. On January 12 of that year, I wrote a letter to Albert D. Chernin, executive vice chairman (top professional) of NJCRAC, suggesting that the issue be included in the group's forthcoming annual plenary meeting in Tucson. I received no reply.

While attending NJCRAC's Tucson meeting as a representative of the Greater Albany Jewish Federation's Community Relations Committee, I introduced myself to Chernin, mentioned my letter, and asked why the issue of Nazi war criminals was not among the program listings. His answer was that today's issues were important, not what happened thirty years ago. As late as 1977–1978, this was the general attitude of leaders of most Jewish organizations here.

By May, 1978, NJCRAC's stance had not changed. In response to a letter I wrote to Bayer, which included clippings on Nazi war criminals, I received the following brief note from him, dated May 4, 1978:

> Thank you for sending the clippings on Skokie et al from Albany.
> I have passed them on to my colleagues.
> Your interest is appreciated. Best wishes.

(The clippings were not about neo-Nazis in Skokie, but about World War II Nazi war criminals.)

In the December 8, 1978 issue of *Sh'ma*, Holocaust historian Nora Levin reported she was unable to "prod Jewish agency staff people to take this matter seriously. They have told me, 'It is not a first priority on our agenda'. . . . Nor has the National Jewish Community Relations [Advisory] Council seen fit to put the matter of prosecution of Nazi criminals in the U.S. on its program agenda for 1978–79. Why not? one is bound to ask. Is it not as important to Jews as the Bakke case, or the abortion issue, or aid to parochial schools, and other issues over which our 'defense' agencies have poured out so much ink? "[3]

Between the time Levin wrote her perceptive comments and the time *Sh'ma* put them in print, NJCRAC evidently changed its policy on Nazi war criminals. On December 3, 1978, I wrote to Chernin:

> As the umbrella organization for Jewish community relations in the United States, NJCRAC should be deeply concerned with the issue of Nazi war criminals in America.
>
> Especially now, when Rep. Elizabeth Holtzman's bill will make it easier for the INS to bring the deportation hearings of Nazi war criminals to successful conclusions, and when Simon Wiesenthal is spearheading a worldwide effort to extend or eliminate the statute of limitations in West Germany, it is crucial that NJCRAC and its affiliates stand up and demand justice. . . .
>
> Under the direction of attorney Martin Mendelsohn, a special INS task force has been designated to find witnesses, investigate alleged criminals and prosecute them. NJCRAC should be at the forefront of a nationwide campaign to assist INS in its efforts by educating Jewish leadership, media, political leaders, teachers, and the general public about the proven fact that some of the murderers . . . are living in our midst. . . .
>
> I wrote to you last year about Nazi war criminals and never even got the courtesy of a reply. In light of new developments during the past year, the issue is of even greater concern. What can be of greater importance for Jewish community relations than removing from our midst the murderers of six million of our brothers and sisters? . . .

This time, Chernin not only answered (on December 18), but stated, "We share [your] concern and for that reason it has been a matter that has *actively* involved NJCRAC and its member agencies *for some time*" (emphases mine). He enclosed a copy of a report which he said had been sent to member agencies, and which he stated "does describe the nature of the activities of an NJCRAC subcommittee charged with responding to this particular situation."

Entitled "Unprosecuted Nazi War Criminals in the U.S.: Status of Cases," the report is by Subcommittee Chairperson Jacqueline Levine. It is purportedly a written version of her oral presentation to the NJCRAC Executive Committee meeting in New York on October 9, 1978.

The introduction says:

Since its last report to the Executive Committee more than a year ago, the NJCRAC Subcommittee on Unprosecuted Nazis has been monitoring the prosecution of Nazis living in this country. We have traveled to Washington, have met with Martin Mendelsohn, the head of the Special Litigation Unit created by the Justice Department and the immigration *[sic]* and Naturalization Service to expedite denaturalization and deportation proceedings against unprosecuted Nazis living in the United States. We met with Mr. Mendelsohn when he was first appointed in December, 1977, and again last September 8. Following the latter meeting, we were also in Washington again on September 28 to congratulate Congresswoman Elizabeth Holtzman (D-N.Y.) on the unanimous passage of her Nazi war criminal legislation in the House of Representatives and to meet with the Solicitor General, Wade McCress. Mrs. *[sic]* Holtzman's legislation "amends the Immigration and Nationality Act to exclude from admission into, and to deport from the United States all aliens who persecuted any person on the basis of race, religion, national origin, or political opinion, under the direction of the Nazi government of Germany, and for other purposes." The following gives background on the issue and substance of our meetings.

The four-page mimeographed report then presents this "background" and "substance" in a manner that is quite less than accurate. (Even in the above introduction, the date of Mendelsohn's appointment is wrong. See Chapter 1).

Jacqueline Levine is an intelligent and dedicated volunteer. She explained that the report was prepared under her name and sent out by the NJCRAC staff while she was out of town on vacation. It is generally accepted in Jewish organizational circles that one function of the professionals is to make lay leaders look good. In this case, NJCRAC did the opposite. In a telephone conversation with me from her New Jersey home on January 1, 1979, Levine said she had not seen the report.

A section of the report labeled "Background" states: "Efforts to get the Soviet Union and other Iron Curtain nations to produce documentation and testimony during the Cold War years were unfruitful." When asked about the accuracy of this statement, in light of the fact that Yugoslavia tried to extradite Andrija Artukovic since 1951 and the Soviet Union attempted to extradite at least half a dozen alleged Nazi war criminals in the late 1950s and 1960s, Levine replied, "That's not what that point goes to. It goes to the fact that the Americans were not particularly interested in working closely with the Russians. And as a matter of fact, until almost three or four years ago, I think that is due to the effect of the Cold War. The Americans didn't want to accept as valid any kind of information that would be secured from the Soviet Union." When it was pointed out to her that this was not the thrust of the statement in the report, Levine said that the statement was nevertheless true, "even given the instance of Yugoslavia."

Other minor and major errors abound throughout the report, which discusses alleged (some admitted) Nazi war criminals Feodor Fedorenko, Hermine Braunsteiner Ryan, Andrei [sic] Artukovic, Valerian Trifa and Ivan Nikolayevich Demjanuk [sic]. Ryan, the report says, was "a former Auchwitz [sic] guard" and was "successfully deported to West Germany." The facts are, however, that Ryan was not just a guard, was not only at Auschwitz, and was not deported. She was a supervisor of guards known for her ruthlessness at Auschwitz, Maidanek, and Ravensbruck. She was extradited upon agreement between West Germany and the U.S. When asked whether she knew that Ryan had been extradited, not deported, Levine admitted it was a "glaring error. I know that; I should have edited it," she said.

The history of the lengthy proceedings against Artukovic is even more garbled in the NJCRAC report. The report says, "He was found deportable from the U.S. on the basis of fraudulent entry in 1951, but was not deported on the grounds that he could not get a fair trial in Yugoslavia." In actuality, Artukovic's extradition was requested by Yugoslavia in 1951, based on a 1901 extradition treaty. He contested the validity of this treaty until 1959, when the Supreme Court ruled that it was valid. He was originally ordered deported in 1952, on the grounds that he had come to the U.S. as a visitor in 1948 and had overstayed the time for which he had been admitted, according to INS report #202–376–8353, issued on April 28, 1977. Thus there have been both extradition and deportation proceedings pending in regard to Artukovic (see Chapters 3, 5).

Regarding Trifa, the NJCRAC report says that he lived in Detroit when, in fact, he lived in Grass Lake, Michigan, which is fifty miles west of Detroit. "Our meeting with the National Council of Churches (NCC) in 1977 was to discuss Trifa's status as a delegate member of the NCC's Board. He was subsequently asked to leave the Board," the report states. Levine admitted that the statement "is not completely accurate." In actuality, Trifa, known as archbishop of the Rumanian Orthodox Episcopate of America, was asked to temporarily suspend his activities in terms of his participation on the board, pending the outcome of the case. He was not even asked to leave the board.

Although Levine clearly indicated that she knew how to spell Demjanjuk, the NJCRAC report consistently omitted the second "j" from his name. In addition, it identified him as "an SS guard at the infamous Sobibor and other concentration camps." A much more accurate description would state that he was a Ukrainian collaborator employed by the SS as a uniformed guard at Sobibor and Treblinka extermination centers, and operated the diesel engines of the gas chamber at the latter.

Levine confirmed during the phone conversation that NJCRAC was not planning to present a workshop on Nazi war criminals in America at their annual plenary meeting to be held that year in Cincinnati on January 21–24. "If you can tell me what you think people can do and how this could be a workshop subject, I'd be interested," she said. "I don't see it. I don't see it as a matter of public pressure. This is not to me, anyway, in the same category as Syrian Jews and Falasha Jews and all the other things I work on."

The NJCRAC report concluded, "We represent the very strong feelings of the Jewish community that it cannot rest until every murderer during the Nazi years is brought to full justice." But their activism and attitudes toward the issue have not been consistent with this lofty ideal.

In a March 23, 1979 press release, NJCRAC charged the Justice Department and INS with "defying the will and intent of Congress by withholding funds allocated for speeding up the investigations and trials" of Nazi war criminals living in the United States. This statement was soon followed by another press release that said:

> The National Jewish Community Relations Advisory Council today [March 29, 1979] hailed the Justice Department's decision to expend the full $2.052 million authorized by Congress for the investigation and trials of Nazi war criminals living in the United States as "a welcome and concrete step to bolster the assurance given us that Nazi war criminal cases would be expedited as soon as possible. . . ."
>
> Its Subcommittee on Unprosecuted Nazis, after numerous meetings in Washington with Deputy Attorney General Michael Egan; Martin Mendelsohn, chief of the Special Litigation Unit of the Immigration and Naturalization Service, and David Crossland [sic], General Counsel of the INS, had last week charged the Justice Department and the INS with "defying the will and intent of Congress by withholding funds allocated for speeding up the investigations and trials."

In case the intent to take largely undeserved credit was not obvious to some recipients of this second press release, an accompanying cover note from Bayer (dated March 29), sent to the NJCRAC Executive Committee and local community relations councils, said:

> On March 23 we sent you a news release reporting the NJCRAC's protest of the slow pace of the prosecution of Nazi war criminals living in the United States.
>
> The attached follow-up story, reporting the Justice Department agreement yesterday to allocate the full $2.052 million authorized by the United States Congress for the Special Litigation Unit, is self-explanatory.
>
> This is an encouraging development and we hope you will try to place the story in your local papers as broadly as possible.

By the time NJCRAC was planning its next annual plenary meeting (to be held in Philadelphia in January, 1980), Rabbi Paul Silton was ready to try to force them into action. Remembering the rabbi's infamous stunt of dressing as an *SS* officer at the United Synagogue Convention in November, 1979 (Chapter 2), Bayer was worried that Silton would disrupt

Rabbi Paul Silton (right) in concentration camp garb at Philadelphia demonstration, January, 1980. (photo by author)

the NJCRAC meeting. Bayer told me on December 12 of that year that he tried to get a workshop on Nazis added to the agenda, because he knew Silton would "do something." He said he told the leadership he expected such an interruption, but his request for a workshop was turned down.

True to form, Rabbi Silton "did something" in Philadelphia. First, he attempted to organize a mass rally at the site of the Liberty Bell to protest the presence here of Nazi war criminals. Because there had been demonstrations in defense of alleged Nazi war criminals living in Philadelphia, the rabbi even wore a bullet proof vest for the occasion. But there were few supporters, fewer media people and no adversaries at this gathering on Sunday afternoon, January 13, at which the rabbi said:

> We are here in the city of the Liberty Bell, symbol of American justice and freedom for the oppressed—but not for the oppressors. Within the shadow of this Liberty Bell live three accused Nazi criminals. They are: Mykola Kowalczuk and Serge Kowalczuk, charged as members of a Ukrainian punitive unit that murdered Ukrainian and Polish Jews; and Wolodymir Osidach, accused of atrocities against Ukrainian Jews . . . .[4]

This marks the first time that two communities which have discovered Nazi criminals in their midsts, Philadelphia and Albany, have joined together to protest the presence of Nazi criminals in America. Our government became aware of the presence of these Nazi criminals some thirty years ago, but we are still faced with postponements and stalling, some of it seemingly deliberate. . . .

Beginning today, the National Jewish Community Relations Advisory Council, the umbrella group for Jewish community relations in America, is holding its annual plenary session at the Fairmont Hotel in Philadelphia. Although there has been initial action by NJCRAC and other major Jewish American organizations, not nearly enough emphasis has been placed on this scandalous issue. . . .

This evening at 7 P.M. on ABC television, you will have the opportunity to view in detail the issue of Nazi war criminals in America on "ABC News Closeup—Escape from Justice: Nazi War Criminals in America." For the first time ever, Americans will be shown actual documents implicating the CIA for having intervened on behalf of an alleged Nazi war criminal . . .

To encourage delegates to watch the program, Rabbi Silton arranged to place a television set in a small meeting room at the Fairmont Hotel, NJCRAC headquarters. He passed out fliers inviting delegates to join him for a "group viewing" of the special on Nazi war criminals. Few people joined him; it was dinner hour on the conference schedule.

Along with other delegates from Albany, he also distributed a revised proposition on unprosecuted Nazis living in the United States, which was approved and recommended by the Community Relations Committee (CRC) of the Greater Albany Jewish Federation, a constituent of NJCRAC. The purpose of the revision was to produce in the 1980–1981 Joint Program Plan booklet of NJCRAC a stronger statement than that issued in 1979–1980.

The Albany CRC recommendations stated:

We RECOMMEND that the Jewish community relations agencies locally and nationally should continue to press vigorously for the Justice Department's enforcement of the United States' law aimed at deportation and denaturalization of Nazis

living in the United States, and also should educate Jews and
non-Jews about the facts and moral implications of Nazi war
criminals living freely in our midst.

We RECOMMEND, in order to press for enforcement of
the law, that the Jewish community relations agencies initiate
or intensify the following programs and projects:

1. Monitoring proceedings and legal developments in
   those cities where trials are in progress, especially by
   attorneys.
2. As an integral part of this monitoring, irregular or in-
   competent conduct by judges or government attorneys
   should be reported to national agencies.
3. Where proceedings are not in open courtrooms, open
   hearings should be encouraged and legally requested.
4. A massive letter or postcard campaign to President
   Carter, registering frustration and concern with lack of
   concrete action.
5. Encourage better dissemination of public information
   on the issue by the Office of Special Investigations.
6. Set up special CRC (Community Relations Council) subcommittee on unprosecuted Nazi war criminals in local
   agencies, especially in cities where there are known [to
   be] alleged Nazi war criminals living.

We RECOMMEND, in order to educate Jews and non-Jews
about the facts and moral implications of the issue:

1. If witnesses against an alleged criminal come to a community from Israel (or Europe), they should be provided with hospitality, an opportunity to interact with
   the Jewish community, and where appropriate, opportunities to speak at Jewish and public schools. (They cannot discuss the hearing, but can discuss their background and life during the war.)
2. Public schools, Jewish schools, community leaders and
   clergy (Jewish and non-Jewish) should be encouraged to
   attend hearings.
3. Appropriate peaceful demonstrations.
4. Highlight the issue as part of Yom HaShoa [Holocaust
   Remembrance Day] programs, remembering Wiesenthal's warning that "If you forget the criminal, then
   you are forgetting the victim."
5. Keep the issue in the media, and media people informed about the issue.

6. Organize a rally in Washington on Yom HaShoah, to both serve as an education about the issue and as a protest that Nazi mass murderers and collaborators are still living freely among us.

When the 1980–1981 booklet came out, purportedly the result of "joint planning" by delegates at the January NJCRAC plenary, the recommendations on "Prosecution of Alleged Nazi War Criminals" were:

We recommend that Jewish community relations agencies: Continue their efforts, through the NJCRAC coordinating machinery, in jointly assessing the progress of the Office of Special Investigation [sic].

We recommend that Jewish community relations agencies: Jointly submit to the United States Supreme Court a friend of the court brief supporting the position of the United States Court of Appeals for the Fourth Circuit [in the case of Fedorenko].

We recommend that Jewish community relations agencies: Monitor, on the local level, in their judicial districts, the progress of these cases and other cases that may be pending.

Support efforts attempting to locate witnesses who can testify against alleged Nazi war criminals, and to cooperate with the Simon Wiesenthal Center for Holocaust Studies in their undertaking to compile a register of all Holocaust survivors in the Western hemisphere as a means of facilitating this search for witnesses.

Undertake educational programs on the significance of such prosecution 35 years after the Holocaust; and increase public awareness of the fact that nearly 250 additional Nazi war criminals may be residing in the United States.[5]

The only recommendation on this issue in the 1979–1980 Joint Program Plan booklet was: "We RECOMMEND that Jewish community relations agencies continue to monitor the use of money allocated to the Special Litigation Unit and the adequacy of its prosecution—and bring to public attention the progress and status of these legal proceedings." [6] While the 1980–81 recommendations neglected to incorporate many of the crucial Albany suggestions, they were an improvement over the previous year—the first time NJCRAC had ever addressed themselves to the issue in a Joint Program Plan booklet.

Rabbi Silton's rally, television viewing, and distribution of Albany's recommendations did not produce the results he had hoped, but they were positive additions to the NJCRAC plenary. As Bayer had feared, however, he also "did something" negative.

There were no workshops on Nazi war criminals, but Jacqueline Levine was scheduled to update delegates on the issue late Sunday afternoon. Because a preceding session ran overtime, the update was allotted only ten minutes and sparsely attended. Quickly reviewing the status of key cases and the OSI, Levine said that the NJCRAC subcommittee on Nazi war criminals had been extant for three years, and "from late 1978 to today" had met "at least six times in Washington and New York City."

A NJCRAC press release, dated Sunday, January 13, but obviously prepared earlier, said:

> Delegates to the plenary assembly of the National Jewish Community Relations Advisory Council (NJCRAC), which opens here Sunday, were briefed by Jacqueline Levine of West Orange, N.J. on a meeting with Mr. Civiletti and other Justice Dep't. officials on the current status of ex-Nazis living in the U.S.
>
> There is "growing anxiety" among American Jews because cases against alleged Nazi war criminals have dragged on for as long as 25 years, Mrs. Levine reported. She cited the cases of Andre [sic] Artukovic, Interior Minister of the Nazi puppet-state of Croati [sic] during World War II, and Valerian Trifa, a former leader of the pro-Nazi Iron Guard in Romania, now Bishop of the Romanian Church of America in Detroit. . . .

Frustrated and outraged by the scant attention to the topic, Silton approached Levine immediately after her update. In full view of the delegates and staff members present, he screamed at her for NJCRAC's negligence and finally told her she would end up in hell for her "sin." Visibly shaken by this personal attack, Levine left the room in tears. Since then, Rabbi Silton has refused to apologize, nor to recognize that he unfairly attacked a dedicated volunteer doing her best, blaming her for more than thirty years of negligence by the organized American Jewish community.

The Philadelphia incident marked the end of Rabbi Silton's attempts to use NJCRAC to seriously advocate justice for Nazi war criminals. He pursued the issue by himself, in more unorthodox ways, and NJCRAC's stance in their 1981–1982 Joint Program Plan was even less vigorous than the previous year's.

The 1981–1982 recommendations were:

> We recommend that Jewish community relations agencies urge continued adequate budgetary support for the Justice Department Office of Special Investigations.
>
> While commending the Justice Department on its assidu-ousness, we deem it advisable to continue to monitor its per-formance. On the local level, Jewish community relations agen-cies should monitor the progress of cases initiated in their respective judicial districts.
>
> Jewish community advocacy and support of vigorous pros-ecution of former Nazis may generate or exacerbate tensions between the Jewish community and ethnic or religious groups with which the accused are closely identified. Anti-Semitic agitators may be quick to exploit such situations to fan anti-Jewish feelings.
>
> We recommend that Jewish community relations agencies cultivate cooperative relationships with ethnic and religious groups concerned, with a view to minimizing tensions that may develop as a result of prosecutions of alleged former Nazis.
>
> The Simon Wiesenthal Center for Holocaust Studies contin-ues to work at compiling a register of Holocaust survivors in the West from among whom witnesses against accused former Nazis may be drawn.
>
> Jewish community relations agencies should cooperate in the search for such persons in their respective localities.
>
> Jewish community relations agencies should stress in their programs of interpretation that an estimated 250 Nazi war criminals are living in the United States and that the presence here of these perpetrators of crimes against humanity has long gone unchallenged.[7]

By this time, NJCRAC's recommendations were as con-cerned with the possible negative results of "advocacy and support of vigorous prosecution" as they were with seeking justice for Nazi war criminals. The practical and more potentially effective recommendations that the Greater Albany Jewish Federation suggested a year earlier were ignored.

Nevertheless, a full page is devoted to the issue, with most of the space used to describe the progress (or lack of it) in several important cases. The next year, the 1982–1983 Joint Program Plan relegated the issue to a "Continuing and Urgent" box, lumped together with "Constitutional Conventions" and "Holocaust." It covered the topic in five sentences, with no recommendations for action:

> Nazi War Criminals
> There is a continuing need to press the prosecution of Nazi war criminals living in the United States, both as a basic obligation and as a part of the ongoing campaign against anti-Semitism.
> For several years, the Office of Special Investigation [*sic*] of the Justice Department has been actively investigating and prosecuting such cases, after many years of neglect. In 1981, that Office undertook 13 cases in federal courts aimed at the denaturalization of alleged Nazi war criminals, and ten cases aimed at the deportation of alleged Nazi war criminals.
> The Jewish agencies and communities will continue to press this activity, and to cooperate with it in various ways. There will occasionally be the need, as in the past, to address the community relations problems attendant on tensions between the Jewish community and other ethnic groups, particularly the Ukrainians, resulting from such a trial.[8]

Again, concern about resultant tensions with other communities was stressed as much as the need to "press this activity."

At the 1983 NJCRAC annual plenary meeting, held in Cleveland in February, the subject of Nazi war criminals in America was never mentioned. When the executive director of the Greater Albany Jewish Federation pointed this out to Bayer, he was told the subject was only an "Albany issue."

Perhaps the impotence and ambivalence of NJCRAC's stance was best summed up by Bayer himself, in remarks during a *Reform Judaism* symposium:

I think the Jewish community could have been much more vigorous, so too the Christian community and the U.S. government which fought a war against Nazi Germany. But I do not think the Jewish community should be pointed out in particular for its lack of vigor. We are the victims. We were traumatized after World War II. We were languishing almost in a state of numbness. It was we who lost six million people. All of us accept responsibility for not having spoken out with a more vigorous voice, but I don't think that it's useful to go into those recriminations. What is important is that the present Justice Department continues to receive enough money, and excellent staffing to continue these investigations.[9]

Thirteen

The Other Major Jewish Organizations

Inaction, by nature, is not easy to document—especially when press releases promote the illusion of concern and action. Before the United States Congress made the issue "official" in 1974, the major American Jewish organizations largely ignored the presence here of Nazi war criminals. If the organizations were quietly "pulling strings" by talking with government officials, there is no public record of such activity. Dr. Joachim Prinz was national president of the American Jewish Congress (AJCongress) from 1958 to 1966, and chairman of the Conference of Presidents of Major American Jewish Organizations from 1965 to 1967. Although several knowledgeable people suggested him as an important source for information about the early involvement of these organizations, he told me in a phone conversation on November 21, 1982 that he had no recollection of discussion of the subject during his tenure.

Many of the dedicated individuals discussed in this book have charged that the major Jewish American organizations have done nothing on the issue, but this assessment is colored by emotion. Especially since 1974, there is evidence of at least lip service from some organizations and intermittent serious involvement from a few. But the issue has remained low priority, pursued with neither passion nor regularity. For virtually every major Jewish organization here, it is not unfair to say that more could and should have been done over the past thirty-eight years.

In addition to NJCRAC, each of the "big three" human/community relations organizations—Anti-Defamation League of B'nai B'rith (ADL), AJCongress, and American Jewish Committee (AJCommittee)—now has a staff "expert" on the subject. When Jacqueline Levine presented her update to NJCRAC on January 13, 1980 (see Chapter 12), she named the professionals on NJCRAC's subcommittee on unprosecuted Nazi war criminals: Abraham J. Bayer of NJCRAC, Elliot Welles of ADL, Phil Baum of AJCongress and David Geller of AJCommittee. "We all feel completely familiar with the material," she said. Bayer on that occasion described himself, the other three professionals and Mrs. Levine as "a carefully balanced group that is effective in pushing [the Justice Department]."

Former ADL general counsel Arnold Forster says that ADL issued press releases on Nazi war criminals early and often, but in the ADL library's subject index of press releases, "Nazi War Criminals" first appears in 1974. The chronological index for all press releases begins with 1971, and lists none for "Nazi War Criminals" until June, 1974. The Jewish Telegraphic Agency carried only one such release in the early 1960s, although Forster says many others were sent out (see Chapter 3). Much of ADL's work on Nazi war criminals, as on other issues, comes under their heading of "fact-finding," or gathering and filing away data.

In a June 1, 1980 interview in New York City, Abraham Foxman, associate national director of ADL, told me his organization has been involved in fact-finding about Nazi war criminals since 1949, when extradition-deportation proceedings began against Andrija Artukovic.[1] Whatever material ADL gathers at present "is put into the hands of the most capable agency that will use it, the Office of Special Investigations" (OSI). Before creation of the OSI, ADL information was turned over to the Justice Department and INS, he said.

"Speaking personally and as a survivor, Nazi war criminal work is a number one priority," Foxman added. "From the totality of Jewish continuity, however, it doesn't rank as number one. Number one is the survival of the Jewish people and the future." (Born in Baranowicze, Poland in 1940 and hidden on the "Aryan" side during the Holocaust, Foxman is among its youngest survivors. He emigrated to America with his parents in 1950.)

Asked about ADL's role in specific Nazi war criminal cases, Foxman said the organization had provided background and testimony for the Hermine Braunsteiner Ryan case and others, and had tried to find eyewitnesses. Speaking to some 300 ADL leaders at the 1980 meeting of the ADL National Commission, OSI Director Allan A. Ryan, Jr. said that from the time he became deputy director in December, 1979, he "can say of ADL that the men and organization behind them have been of substantial assistance to the office."

While Foxman said that ADL's involvement "goes way back" in terms of fact-finding, he added that its "full-time specialist," Elliot Welles, had been on staff for only three years. According to Foxman's time frame, ADL first hired this full-time staff person to deal with the issue in June, 1977.

Welles gave a different description of his employment by ADL. He said during an interview with me in his ADL office on June 30, 1981 that he had begun working with the organization three years earlier in June, 1978. He added that he did not work solely on Nazi war criminals for ADL, but also on civil rights matters. Although he had worked out of ADL headquarters for three years, he was funded until January, 1981 by an association of survivors of the Riga Ghetto. Before that date, ADL had provided office space, insurance and other benefits, but not salary. He was not actually "on staff" as a paid employee until six months after Foxman said he had been working full-time for three years for ADL. Nor was he working only on the Nazi war criminal issue.

A Vienna-born survivor of the Riga Ghetto, Stutthof and other concentration camps, Welles does not like to talk about his past or his work. He said he was first intrigued with the issue of Nazi war criminals in Austria and Germany after the war. He emigrated to the United States in 1949, at the age of twenty-three. Welles has a deep personal commitment to seeking justice for Nazi war criminals, and said he worked on the issue by himself before coming to ADL.

"It's like an obligation to me—a burning obligation to the victims," he said. "My soul will only rest when these murderers

are brought to justice. Germany has been dealing with the
problem for thirty-five years. INS had it for thirty-five years,
but did nothing with it. In the 1960s, I was all wrapped up
with the Nazi war criminal trials in Germany, but I didn't
know about the situation in the United States. Then we found
out about Maikovskis, Artukovic, Trifa, and I saw Chuck
Allen's book in 1963." Refusing to further discuss his involvement, he said, "As long as I live, this is my issue."
Because he had been gravely ill and suffers from numerous
chronic ailments as the result of his incarceration by the Nazis,
he seemed to imply that he didn't have much time left to
complete his work.

In Howard Blum's fictionalized *Wanted! The Search for Nazis
in America*, Welles is portrayed as Kurt Wasserman. His serious
involvement with the issue of Nazi war criminals in America
begins in the early 1970s, when he learns from an Israeli
friend (formerly from the Riga Ghetto) that accused Latvian
Nazi war criminal Boleslavs Maikovskis is alive and well in
Mineola, New York. Blum describes how Welles/Wasserman
was shipped with his mother from Vienna to the Riga Ghetto
in January, 1942. On February 5, 1942, the teenage Welles/
Wasserman's mother is taken away and murdered by the Nazis.
Blum writes that the order was signed by Maikovskis (who
was police chief in Rezekne, Latvia).

Dr. Gertrude Schneider, the Riga Ghetto survivor who
brought back from Latvia information on accused Nazi war
criminals Vilis Hazners and Maikovskis in 1971, is a friend
of Welles'. She said Welles was with her on the Chris Borgen
Channel 2 CBS-TV news program that year (see Chapter 1).
"But he kept his back to the camera," she told me. "He was
afraid someone from his East 80s [New York City] neighborhood, which is predominantly German, would recognize him
and seek revenge." Whether he does not want to dredge up
unbearable memories, feels secrecy aids his work, or has old
fears that still haunt him, Welles would not say more about
his activities in seeking justice for Nazi war criminals.

Aside from Welles' work, the most significant contribution
of ADL to the Nazi war criminal issue was probably their
joint filing, with AJCongress, of an *amici curiae* brief in the
denaturalization case of admitted Treblinka death camp guard

Feodor Fedorenko. Phil Baum, associate executive director of AJCongress, drafted the brief, which was also signed by ADL attorneys Forster and Jeffrey Sinensky on December 4, 1978. The "Motion to File a Brief Amici Curiae" section states: "Eight other national agencies associated with the National Jewish Community Relations Advisory Council (American Jewish Committee, Hadassah, Jewish Labor Committee, Jewish War Veterans of the U.S.A., Union of American Hebrew Congregations, Union of Orthodox Jewish Congregations of America, United Synagogue of America, Women's American ORT) as well as 102 local Jewish Community Relations Councils, have asked us to inform this Court that they share the concerns expressed in this brief." [2]

Ukrainian-born Fedorenko was accused of concealing his past Nazi activities when he entered the United States in 1949 and when he applied for citizenship in 1970. Despite eyewitness testimony from six Israeli survivors of Treblinka, U.S. District Court Judge Norman Roettger ruled on July 26, 1978, in Fort Lauderdale, Fla. that Fedorenko could remain a citizen. The trial judge ruled that INS had failed to prove Fedorenko guilty of having committed any atrocities, and that the defendant had lived an exemplary life in the United States.

ADL, AJCongress and NJCRAC all urged the Justice Department to appeal the July 26 ruling. During the fifteen-day trial, Roettger had questioned the credibility of the Israeli witnesses, suggesting some of them might have been coached. He had also held an impromptu press conference in the midst of the proceedings, at which he criticized the witnesses' credibility and discussed the case.

After Solicitor General Wade Hampton McCree, Jr. decided to appeal the district court ruling to the U.S. Court of Appeals for the Fifth Circuit in New Orleans, the *amici curiae* brief was filed. The most severe critics of the major Jewish organizations' failure to devote enough attention to the issue of Nazi war criminals commend these organizations for both the requests for appeal and the filing of the brief. If such pressure were applied more regularly, efforts to deport Nazi war criminals might be further along, they point out.

As for the organizations, they used the occasion for a self-serving round of credit-taking. AJCongress boasted in the April

20, 1979 *JTA Daily News Bulletin,* "The Department of Justice agreed to appeal the ruling in response to an 'urgent request' from the American Jewish Congress. Howard Squadron, president of the AJCongress, said he was 'deeply gratified' by the action. . . ." When the Supreme Court in January, 1981 upheld the court of appeals decision to revoke Fedorenko's citizenship, ADL and AJCongress reminded the Jewish community of their involvement in the case.[3]

On January 21, 1981, the Supreme Court, in a seven-to-two ruling, revoked Fedorenko's citizenship. He was ordered deported in February, 1983 by federal Immigration Judge Gordon Sacks. In March, 1983, Fedorenko filed an appeal with the Board of Immigration Appeals.

Unlike ADL's Welles, Baum of AJCongress and Geller of AJCommittee are not survivors. As his organization's associate executive director and legal advisor, fast-talking Baum deals with many issues packed into a crowded schedule. Nazi war criminals is a topic far from the top of his list.

Neither is the issue of high priority to Geller, whose AJCommittee title of Director of European Affairs covers responsibilities ranging far beyond Nazi war criminals in America. His letter to the editor appearing October 8, 1979 in *The New York Times* perpetuated the misinformation in Blum's book that Hermine Braunsteiner Ryan was deported.[4] (She was extradited to West Germany.)

Although many of the organizations affiliated with the Conference of Presidents of Major American Jewish Organizations have since 1974–1978 issued occasional press releases, resolutions, and other statements on the issue, only the Jewish War Veterans of the U.S.A. (JWV) made early public inquiries of the government.

Soon after Charles R. Allen, Jr.'s first article appeared in *Jewish Currents* in January, 1963, then JWV National Commander Morton London asked the attorney general why accused Nazi war criminal Gustav Hilger was in the United States. JWV also urged Senator Philip A. Hart, then chairman of a Special Senate Subcommittee on Refugees and Escapees, to seek legislation to prevent Nazi war criminals from entering the country. Both the national organization and the Department of New York of JWV have since then remained at the forefront in exposing the issue through articles, statements, conventions, and local meetings.

Two publications of the Union of American Hebrew Congregations (UAHC), *Reform Judaism* and *Keeping Posted,* did not begin coverage of the issue until 1980. They deserve recognition for their excellence in addressing the topic since that date under the editorship of Aron Hirt-Manheimer, himself a child of survivors who was born soon after World War II in a displaced persons camp in Germany.

The World Jewish Congress (WJC), an international Jewish organization that does not fall under the "umbrella" of the Conference of Presidents or NJCRAC, has probably been most active in concrete efforts to bring Nazi war criminals to justice. Bessy Pupko, the unlikely-looking Nazi hunter who currently directs this work for WJC, is less than five feet tall and more than eighty years old.

Since the end of World War II, Pupko has helped WJC to locate thousands of witnesses for trials of Nazi war criminals in West Germany, and in recent years, in the United States. Since 1973, she has headed these activities, working from a special division attached to the organization's New York City office. (WJC also has offices in Geneva, London, Tel Aviv, Jerusalem, Buenos Aires and Rome. Jewish communities in Communist countries are eligible for membership.)

In WJC's Park Avenue and 33rd Street office, Pupko is in charge of the glass-enclosed shelves which neatly hold files bearing the names of war criminals, concentration camps and ghettos. She spoke with me there on September 15, 1981. Her predecessors as head of the unit were Dr. Nehemiah Robinson, until his death in 1963, then Dr. Oscar Karbach, until his death in 1973.

It was Dr. Karbach who met with Tony DeVito and showed him the WJC list dated June, 1965 of fifty-nine alleged Nazi war criminals. DeVito's claim that the name Tscherim Soobzokov was on that list, as described in Howard Blum's *Wanted!,* was one reason Soobzokov sued Blum and others for libel. Pupko showed me the list on September 15, 1981, and Soobzokov's name is not on it (see Chapter 9).

When asked the source of her tireless devotion to her work, she told me, "It just grew naturally, like Topsy." At least part of her zeal must stem from the loss of most of her family in the Holocaust, including her parents, brother and a sister.

Pupko grew up in Vilna, Lithuania. During World War I, she and her family were refugees in Russia, and she studied there to be an engineer. When famine struck and the family returned to Vilna, she became a teacher of Jewish children. The language of instruction was Yiddish, and Pupko describes the school as "progressive—pedagogically and educationally." The major subjects she taught were mathematics, geography, and the natural sciences.

"Ever since I read as a child a book entitled *Abe Lincoln Who Freed the Black Slaves,* I was always thinking of going to the United States," she recalls. "America had a great attraction for me." When the political situation in Poland (of which Vilna was then part) became fascist under Pilsudski, Pupko decided it was time to leave. In 1936 she emigrated and joined a brother in the United States.

Pupko's first job here was as a teacher in Workmen's Circle schools. By 1942, she was a citizen and ready to help the United States win the war against the Nazis. "The Army needed cartographers, and I knew geography," she says. "I passed a civil service test and started working for the Army's map service in New York. I worked there until 1946.

"As the war progressed, I was cut off from my family in Europe, and I knew that most of them were in ghettos or camps. I learned later that only one sister, one sister-in-law, and one niece survived. I brought these three family members over here from Europe."

Pupko resigned from her civil service job in 1946 and began working in the New York office of the Institute of Jewish Affairs, WJC's research arm. After her personal losses in the Holocaust, she "wanted to work with Jewish people on Jewish problems," she says.

Pupko began her work with WJC as an English-to-Yiddish translator. "In the aftermath of the war, four staff people clipped anything about Jewish life remaining in Europe," she recalls. Along with other news concerning the situation of Jews throughout the world, she translated the proceedings of the Nuremberg trials. After the International Tribunal at Nuremberg, West Germany received the right to try Nazi war criminal cases. WJC began to seek out witnesses for the Central Agency for Prosecuting Nazi War Criminals, which was established in Ludwigsburg, West Germany. Because the Institute for Jewish Affairs had ties with so many Jewish communities, it could help locate witnesses and documentary materials, Pupko says.

"We don't make a lot of publicity," she explains. "We publicize the names of accused Nazi war criminals in the Yiddish press, not in the English press. The accused don't follow the Yiddish press, but witnesses often do, and that's how we locate them."

As examples, she mentions the cases of John Demjanjuk, accused of assisting in extermination of thousands of Jews at death camps at Sobibor and Treblinka, Poland; and Karl Linnas, accused of supervising and participating in the execution of prisoners at a concentration camp at Tartu, Estonia.

Pupko considers "useless" the tactics of organizations that advertise in Anglo-Jewish papers that all survivors from a specific ghetto or camp should register as possible witnesses. "You need to give the accused criminal's name in order to find witnesses," she says. "You need witnesses against a specific person, a specific act, not general witnesses."

Pupko said WJC released Demjanjuk's name to all of the Yiddish newspapers in the world, adding that he was also known as "Ivan the Terrible" at the camp. She received an answer from a witness living in Australia. (Cleveland resident Demjanjuk was ordered denaturalized in June, 1981, a decision upheld on appeal. His petition for Supreme Court review was denied on November 29, 1982. Deportation proceedings began in April, 1983, and one year later both his deportation and an extradition request by Israel were pending.)

In the Linnas case, Pupko began by seeking information from personal contacts at Kibbutz Lohamei Haghettaot (The Ghetto Fighters' Collective Settlement, in northern Israel). She says she learned from Estonian materials in the archives of the kibbutz that Linnas had been tried *in absentia* in the Soviet Union and condemned to death. (Linnas was ordered deported in May, 1983 and appealed his case to the Board of Immigration Appeals.) Pupko gave the information about both cases to the OSI, which has sent her letters thanking her for her help and "imaginative suggestions." [5]

Ironically, it was a "minor" Jewish American organization that ultimately catalyzed the leaders of some major Jewish American organizations to join a protest against Archbishop Valerian Trifa's position on the board of the National Council of Churches (NCC). On October 8, 1976, Wayne Perlmutter, then a seventeen year old college freshman, led a sit-in at the NCC convention at the Roosevelt Hotel in New York City. Acting on a tip from Dr. Charles Kremer and accompanied by Rabbi Avi Weiss of the Hebrew Institute of Riverdale, Perlmutter's Concerned Jewish Youth (CJY) group from New York City area high schools and colleges sat in until promised that NCC would consider in committee Trifa's status.

When there was no action from the NCC a week after the sit-in, on October 14 CJY took over NCC's Manhattan offices. Embarrassed by the surrounding publicity, the NCC agreed to hear evidence on Trifa from Perlmutter and other CJY members. A week later the activist youth group presented evidence to the NCC for twelve hours. According to *The New York Times*, "Warren Day, director of the council's news and information department, credited Concerned Jewish Youth for 'raising the consciousness' of the National Council." [6] During the week of Chanukah in December, 1976, Perlmutter led another demonstration outside NCC headquarters. Rabbi Alexander Schindler, then Chairman of the Conference of Presidents of Major American Jewish Organizations, and a few other national leaders joined this rally. Charles R. Allen, Jr., who spoke to the crowd of 600 from the top of a sound truck, today says this was his most stirring speech.

In January, 1977, CJY again took over the NCC's offices. Although the National Jewish Community Relations Advisory Council claimed credit in its October, 1978 report for Trifa's being asked to leave the NCC board, he was actually only temporarily suspended. CJY's public exposure of the Trifa-NCC connection probably played a much greater role in this temporary suspension than did NJCRAC's 1977 private meeting with the NCC (see Chapter 12).

Trifa was not CJY's first target. On Purim in the winter of 1976, they demonstrated in front of the Mineola home of

Maikovskis. After their activities at the NCC, in May, 1979, the group took over the offices of the Ford Motor Company in Manhattan, to protest the employment of Demjanjuk at the Ford plant in Cleveland. In June, 1979, Perlmutter moved from his Woodmere, Long Island home to Jerusalem, Israel.

Fourteen

Jim Gray
Chaser of Dreams

James Martin ("Jim") Gray's childhood as a devout Methodist in Rocky Mount, North Carolina is an unusual beginning for an obsessive seeker of justice for Nazi war criminals. But Gray's unique combination of brilliant mind, tempestuous personality and empathy with the underdog eventually led him to total commitment to this cause.

When Gray was only five years old in 1935, he surprised his mother by expressing a great desire to join the Methodist church. After a long discussion with the boy, his minister said he had never spoken with anyone of any age more ready for membership. Jim was taken into the church and became an avid Bible student. He remained an active Methodist until he joined the Navy.

His mother shared this and other memories in a March 18, 1980 letter to me. She recalls an incident when he was eleven: "I went to pick him up at a young people's church conference at Louisburg College, and the Bible teacher came out to meet me. She said she wanted to meet the mother of one so young knowing so much Bible."

When Gray started elementary school, he told his teacher: "I know everyone likes to play games, but I don't want to play games. I want to learn to read." After he had learned a few words, he would lie on the floor and go over the

James M. "Jim" Gray in uniform, October, 1959.

newspaper line by line, to see if he could find any of "his" words, his mother says.

Jim's intelligence did not always work to his advantage in school. By the time he was in high school, local education officials told his mother he had the highest I.Q. of anyone who had ever been a student there. But school bored him, he didn't bother to hand in homework, and he received poor grades. Because he had skipped second grade, he graduated at age sixteen.

Gray's childhood was not easy. When he was nine, his father deserted the family, leaving them penniless. "I regret it very much now, but I confided all my troubles in Jimmie," his mother told me. "He was so mature that I did not realize I was putting too much burden on him. His little brother, Harry, was only two at the time. Financially, we had some very rough years, but we had much love for each other and were very happy. Neither of the boys gave me any discipline problems, and I was a very strict parent—especially because I had to work and be away from them so much."

Gray took his first part-time job at age eleven, working on a laundry truck after school and on Saturdays. His mother took over her husband's sales job, and later became executive director of the Rocky Mount YWCA. She held this post for twenty-five years until retirement in 1975. While Gray was in the Air Force, his "home of record" was the YWCA, where his mother lived. "This circumstance on occasion produced problems on military records and orders," he later quipped.

Gray stayed in those quarters whenever he was home on leave, and was always interested in his mother's work. A friend later said that Jim's sense of social justice and his identification with the poor and oppressed may have come partly from his experiences at the YWCA. "He saw people from plain America there, and his mother as a saintly servant of human needs. This may be one reason he was critical of all forms of greed and harassment," the friend said.

After enrolling in East Carolina University in the fall of 1947, Gray wrote to his mother saying, "I am writing in the library. It is heavenly. If I lived to be 1,000, I could not read all the books, but I am trying." He was the first freshman to ever make the debating team, and had a straight-A average. But he lost interest in school before the end of the year, and refused to take his final exams.

Gray signed up with the Navy Reserve in the late spring of 1948, and did not return to college in the fall. Except for what he described as an "abortive effort" to return to East Carolina University for two months in 1950, he was an active duty reservist with the Naval Air Reserve Training Unit at the Naval Air Station in Norfolk, Virginia from May, 1948 until September, 1950. Until he was honorably discharged at his own request, he served as stationkeeper there. The day after his discharge, he enlisted in the Air Force.

During his nine years in the Air Force, Gray held a series of intelligence and communications positions. After basic training, he was posted to Security Service at Brooks Air Force Base in Texas, with the 6923rd Personnel Processing Squadron. He received eleven weeks of language training there, and then was sent to Army Language School at Monterey, California, for a special course in Russian. After returning to Brooks for traffic analysis training, he was posted to Fort Devens, Massachusetts, for instruction in cryptanalyis. From there, he was shipped to Chicksands Priory, Bedfordshire, England, for communications intelligence duties with the 10th Radio Squadron.

An airman first class, in September, 1953 Gray was transferred to the Office of Information Services, Central Air Materiel Area in Chateauroux, France. After serving for a year there as editor of the bi-lingual command weekly newspaper, he returned to the United States as a staff sergeant.

From October, 1954 until the end of 1956, Gray worked with the Advertising and Publicity Directorate of the 3502nd USAF Recruiting Group. He left for USAF Officer Candidate School (OCS) at Lackland Air Force Base, Texas in January, 1957, and was commissioned as a second lieutenant in July of that year. According to his mother, he had earlier qualified for OCS, but was never interested. It was only because he had fallen in love with the widow of a lieutenant colonel that he now opted for a commission. "A staff sergeant just couldn't marry a lieutenant colonel's widow," he told his mother.

Gray was next posted to Harlingen Air Force Base, Texas for navigation training. He then was involved in the production of target charts, work that required Top Secret clearance. In December, 1959, now a first lieutenant, he was honorably discharged at his own request. He never did marry the lieutenant colonel's widow.

At some point during his nine years in the Air Force, Gray learned of the existence of Nazi war criminals in America. When another airman first relayed this information to him, Gray called him a liar. During a heated discussion, Gray had been vigorously defending the United States as the best pos-

sible form of government. "If the United States is so won-
derful, then why is it harboring a Nazi war criminal like
Andrija Artukovic? " his cohort asked.

Gray "cussed him out" and insisted he was lying. Then,
typically, he thoroughly researched the subject. To his pro-
found surprise, he learned that Artukovic, former minister of
interior of Nazi-occupied Croatia, had been living peacefully
in Surfside, California since arriving as a "temporary visitor
for pleasure" on July 16, 1948 (see Chapters 3, 5).

When Gray returned to civilian life in 1959, his knowledge
of the Artukovic case lay dormant as he pursued his career
and other causes. The information simmered in his brilliant
mind, and burst forth some fifteen years later in a carefully-
orchestrated one-man public relations campaign.

Meanwhile, Gray attempted college again in 1960, this time
at Southern Louisiana University. He joined the campus Catholic Student Center, and soon left school to accompany a
group of priests and nuns on a trip to the Apostolic Vicarate
at Sisoguichi, Chihuahua.

"I became interested in their work among the Tarahumara
Indians, and assisted a Jesuit priest, Father Luis Verplancken,
in developing a brochure and a slide-tape presentation to
support fundraising efforts in this country," Jim said of the
trip. "I accompanied Father Verplancken upon his return to
Mexico with a large load of medicines and other materials
for the mission, and subsequently stayed several months with
his parents in Guadalajara, returning to this country upon the
expiration of my tourist card in November [1960]. During
this period, I supported myself as a freelance writer and
guide."

During the next ten years, Gray changed jobs an average
of once a year, usually working as a radio station news director.
He lived in Lake Charles, Shreveport and Alexandria, Louisiana; Weslaco, Texas; Chicago and Decatur, Illinois; Mount
Airy and Waynesville, North Carolina. He finally settled in
Asheville, North Carolina in October, 1970. He had married
in August, 1964, and always described his wife as "my red-
headed hillbilly." Their son was born in 1965.

It was in Asheville that Gray became interested in politics.
He worked in Asheville until 1977 at a variety of jobs: radio

station news director, public information officer for the city's Model Cities Program, and managing editor of the weekly newspaper, *Native Stone*. He also edited two monthly publications, *North Carolina AMVETS* and *The Labor Advocate,* and operated his own public relations business, Herald Communications.

Gray had more than a journalistic interest in AMVETS (an organization for American veterans of World War II, Korea and Vietnam) and *The Labor Advocate,* a newspaper for organized labor. He championed the causes of veterans' and workers' rights, serving as AMVETS district commander and encouraging a labor apprenticeship program in North Carolina.

While dedicating himself to these two areas of human rights, he also used them to expose an injustice that had seethed within him since his Air Force days: the existence of Nazi war criminals in America.

In June, 1974, Gray drafted for the North Carolina Department of AMVETS Annual Convention a "Resolution on U.S. Sanctuary for Accused War Criminals from World War II." The resolution said that a "recent report by the U.S. Immigration and Naturalization Service indicates that a minimum of seventy immigrants accused of having committed War Crimes in Nazi-controlled territory during World War II obtained post-war refuge in the United States."

Citing deaths, disappearances and two voluntary departures, the resolution said: "This still leave[s] a minimum of thirty-three accused War Criminals enjoying freedom and sanctuary in the United States—untried and unpunished because they have managed to avoid extradition and trial despite the fact that their true identity and whereabouts, as well as full details of the crimes of which they stand accused, are known to U.S. authorities."

Two clauses in the 1974 resolution best illustrate Gray's penetrating style:

> The blood of hundreds of thousands of murder victims whose only crime was their race, religion, or national origin cries out from the grave for justice and retribution. . . . our best assurance that the world never again experiences the insane

bloodbath and persecution of innocent victims which were the hallmark of the Nazi regime in World War II lies in bringing to the Bar of Justice all those who were responsible for such acts . . .

In the resolution, the North Carolina Department of AMVETS resolved to: ask the North Carolina congressional delegation to actively influence Congress to investigate the "circumstances that have produced privileged sanctuary and apparent immunity from extradition or prosecution for known War Criminals in the United States;" call upon Congress to influence the administration and appropriate federal agencies to find "underground" war criminals; and request that these agencies (including the Departments of State, Defense and Justice and the INS) investigate Nazi war criminal cases.

AMVETS also resolved to ask the National AMVETS Convention to adopt strong policy statement on the issue and to influence the federal government. Other veterans, church and civic organizations, and "all Americans interested in the administration of international justice and a final resolution of the issue of WORLD WAR II WAR CRIMES" were also called upon to support the North Carolina AMVETS position.

Reflecting his special interest in Artukovic, Gray dealt specifically with that case, stating "that because of its circumstances and notoriety, and because of the extreme gravity of the charges against him, particular emphasis and attention [should] be given to a final resolution of the case against ANDRIJA ARTUKOVIC, Minister of the Interior in the wartime Quisling government of the 'Free and Independent State of Croatia', who at last report was still enjoying privileged sanctuary in California despite a 'final' order for his deportation to his native Yugoslavia which has been outstanding and unenforced since his illegal 1948 entry into this country on a forged Irish passport was discovered in 1951;" and "that U.S. Military Authorities research their records and the Central Intelligence Agency check all its resources, in an attempt to finally substantiate or forever disprove allegations that this same ANDRIJA ARTUKOVIC, in his capacity as a ranking official of the USTASHA regime governing much of Yugoslavia during World War II, was responsible for the orders which sent 'dozens of captured American pilots' and other airmen to wartime firing squads in direct violation of the Geneva Convention and all accepted rules of civilized warfare.''

The passage of such a resolution in 1974 was of itself an accomplishment, but Gray did not stop there. After its adoption by AMVETS, Gray used his public relations skills to capitalize on the resolution's existence.

As editor of the *The Labor Advocate,* he reprinted the entire resolution in the June, 1974 issue of that publication. He wrote an accompanying editorial, stressing "AFL-CIO's traditional concern for human rights and international justice." He adroitly appealed to organized labor by including them among the victims of Nazi war criminals: "It is a matter of historical record that hundreds of thousands of ardent union activists—including both Communists and non-Communists— were victims of active persecution during World War II in countries under Nazi domination. Large numbers of them, whose only crime was promotion of workers' rights and resistance to Fascism, were exterminated in concentration camps," Gray wrote in the unsigned editorial. He "predicted" that "many of our union readers—particularly those who saw combat duty in Europe during World War II—will share [AMVETS'] concern."

Gray again singled out Artukovic, saying, "The AMVETS seem particularly concerned over the presence in this country of ANDRIJA ARTUKOVIC, who as Minister of the Interior for the wartime collaborationist government of Yugoslavia was responsible for a deliberate program of genocide and execution resulting in the deaths of several hundred thousand Jews, Gypsies, Serbs, and trade unionists, many of whom were killed in unusually barbaric manner . . . . Artukovic has somehow enlisted enough right-wing support to successfully avoid extradition for trial."

He then called for action:

If the revelation that we have large numbers of accused War Criminals living in our midst, enjoying freedom and sanctuary in the United States and apparently immune from prosecution for the crimes they stand accused of, disturbs our readers as much as it disturbed our brothers in the AMVETS, we suggest they do something about it.

As a first step, they might communicate their concern to their elected representatives in Washington. It might also prove productive if they were to solicit formal expressions of concern from their union local, their international union, their Central Labor Union, their churches, and any civic clubs or fraternal organizations to which they belong . . . .

The Labor Advocate strongly supports the intent and purpose of the AMVETS resolution. Those accused War Criminals now in this country against whom a strong case can be made should be delivered for trial and punishment; those against whom no strong evidence of probable guilt can be produced should be cleared and afforded permanent sanctuary, freed of any threat of deportation.

With the AMVETS resolution and *The Labor Advocate* editorial as "ammunition," Gray's next step was to write on June 27, 1974 to six federal agencies: Immigration and Naturalization Service, Federal Bureau of Investigation, Central Intelligence Agency, Department of Defense, Department of State, and Department of Justice. He wrote in his capacity as managing editor of *The Labor Advocate*, enclosed copies of the June issue, and requested information concerning each agency's "position, responsibility and involvement" in the question of Nazi war criminals in America. He received no replies.

During the next few years, Gray continued his one-man campaign against war criminals, while he ran his public relations business. "Jim always had to have a cause, and he went after it full blast," a good friend told me during a September 16, 1981 interview in Washington. "He didn't let anyone stand in his way. He had a hard time holding a job, because he told it like it was. A lot of people resented his intelligence. You either really liked him or literally despised him."

In 1976, Gray made a connection that ultimately gave him his best opportunity to use his innate political abilities to seek justice for Nazi war criminals. He was media-public relations counsel that year for the successful congressional campaign of Lamar Gudger (D-N.C.). By the early fall of 1977, he was working in Washington as special assistant to the freshman representative.

Wade Harrison, a young attorney who had worked on Gudger's staff with Gray, told me in a September 16, 1981 interview, "There was a tacit understanding in our office. Jim Gray came to Washington to work on the Nazi war criminal issue, and in return he handled certain political chores for Congressman Gudger. Jim used his position on Gudger's staff to impress people with the importance of the issue. He was a one-man organization, and made his own paper trail." (On at least one occasion in March, 1979, Gray wrote to Gudger on behalf of AMVETS, and to AMVETS on behalf of Gudger, regarding Nazi war criminals.)

Describing him as "a loyal friend who didn't give his friendship lightly," Harrison said he hated Gray when they first met. "He seemed cynical, but he had a realistic view of human nature and the political system. He was honest to a fault," Harrison recalls. "He was probably the most intelligent person I've ever met in Washington. He was terribly crude and cussed like a sailor, yet he had a tremendous vocabulary and was acquainted with the greatest literature. He had a dream—he wanted to be more than average and make a contribution to the world. He taught me a great lesson: Never be afraid to demand people's respect."

Congressman Gudger was a member of the House Judiciary Subcommittee that dealt with Nazi war criminals, during the years that former Representatives Joshua Eilberg and Elizabeth Holtzman led efforts to create a specific structure in the Justice Department for dealing with Nazi war criminal cases. Gray was behind Gudger's support for funding the new unit.

"Jim would either turn me off or turn me on. On this issue, he prompted me into action," Gudger told me on September 16, 1981. "He had a degree of genius, and a strange caustic personality. He had a great quality of empathy, and he was never neutral. He had an articulate, penetrating style of writing, and he could get attention because he wrote with passion. When he saw a conflict, he took sides. He had respect for American judicial commitment, and was offended when it didn't function. He was cynical in some ways, but felt we could do better. In Asheville, it looked like he had offended everyone who could help him. Pretty soon he couldn't utilize his talent there."

With Gudger's name and office backing his efforts, Gray intensified his campaign on the war criminal issue. In the congressman's name, he communicated with President Carter, Holtzman, the President's Commission on the Holocaust, CIA Director (Admiral) Stansfield Turner, the Department of Justice, Martin Mendelsohn, director of the Special Litigation Unit (SLU) on Nazi war criminals, and others.

On July 31, 1978, he resigned from Gudger's staff, in his words, "to undertake a special project for a client which seemed to hold future prospects for permanent employment under terms and conditions which appeared to make it worth any risk involved." When that "judgment proved faulty," Jim was back in Washington looking for a job. His relationship with Gudger was good and he "hung out" in his office on a consultant basis, but there was no permanent position available there for him. He continued to use his connection with Gudger to encourage the President's Commission on the Holocaust to take on the issue of Nazi war criminals, and to oversee the progress (or lack of it) in the SLU.

By this time, Gray was living alone in Washington in the rather seedy Allen Lee Hotel. When he had no money, the management let him stay without paying for his room. He sometimes took a turn at the switchboard during the night shift.

After the SLU was revamped into the Office of Special Investigations (OSI) in 1979, Gray applied for a position there. Rufus L. Edmisten, attorney general of North Carolina, wrote in a July 17, 1979 letter recommending Gray to Walter J. Rockler, head of the OSI: "Mr. Gray would be a superlative investigator, because I know of his personal interest in investigations for Nazi War Criminals. Jim is probably one of the greatest experts in the United States on this subject, and I am positive that he is the most well-informed individual on this subject in his home State of North Carolina."

With still no word on his prospects of a position with OSI, Gray was happy to learn on October 16, 1979, that his potential employer had that day filed a motion in U.S. Immigration Court, Los Angeles to reconsider and revoke the stay of deportation that had been granted to Artukovic in 1959. By the beginning of 1980, Gray finally received word he would soon be working in OSI. But this was not to be his fate.

At 9:31 P.M. on February 6, 1980, Jim Gray died suddenly of a heart attack at his hotel in Washington. He had just gone to his room, after telling the hotel clerk he was going to stay in and enjoy a good book—his greatest pleasure from the beginning to the end of his life. He was forty-nine years old.

On February 11, 1980, Congressman Gudger spoke of Gray (recorded in the *Congressional Record,* page E504, Vol. 126, No. 20). He said, "Jim had his critics, both here and back in North Carolina. We all do. But he had a special talent, a special energy, a special sense of humor which he often cloaked with brashness and pushiness. This profane pose too often was accepted for more than an image. Those of us who loved him knew better."

Gudger then read a poem of tribute written by Wade Harrison:

> Dream chaser.
> The elfin old man is dead.
> A diamond among stones; he masked his gentle
> brilliance with profane and scornful crudeness but not
> too well, for the twinkle rarely left his eye.
> Shallow people wearied him, the arrogantly
> powerful challenged him, the honest humbled him but the
> benevolent and strong made him happy.
> Dream chaser.
> His huge spirit has ascended to commune with the
> great souls he has known, but I know it will come back,
> like a thought, and touch those he revealed himself to.
> We will hear his gravelly voice when we are talking to
> somebody we do not like . . . and we will tell them the
> truth.
> Jim Gray is dead.

Fifteen _____

Charles R. Allen, Jr.
Takes the Lead Again

"What do you want to do, deport me? " was Charles R. Allen, Jr.'s response to a December, 1973 phone call from INS investigator John Weiss.

Weiss and his boss, Sam Zutty, were not seeking Allen's deportation; they wanted his help in setting up a special New York City task force to investigate and prosecute Nazi war criminals. Allen's mind was then on other matters. He was about to take off for some winter mountain climbing in Washington State.

Later the three met at Allen's attorney's office. When Allen offered to share his materials with INS in 1963, he had been told the Service was not interested. His investigations and writings were termed "communist-inspired." Ten years later he was more cautious, agreeing to speak with INS only in the presence of his lawyer.

Before the call from Weiss, Allen thought he was finished with the subject of Nazi war criminals. By 1968 the issue seemed dead, and that year Allen became worldwide director of public relations for CPC International, an international food processing corporation.

After his son graduated from college, he left CPC in 1975 and returned to his anti-fascist writing. He had planned to focus on theoretical aspects of fascism, such as the socioeconomic base of genocide, but was soon pulled back into the issue of Nazi war criminals in America.

Between 1974 and 1977, Allen uncovered major new cases: (1) Vladimir D. Samarin, accused of collaboration as a Nazi newspaper editor in Oriel, U.S.S.R., where he was responsible for anti-Semitic editorials urging genocide; a faculty member of Yale University until 1978; OSI filed a complaint against him in January, 1982; (2) Tscherim Soobzokov of Paterson, N.J., accused of membership in proscribed Nazi military units, including the *Waffen SS;* OSI filed a complaint against him in 1979 and withdrew the action in 1980; (3) Edgars Laipenieks of San Diego, Calif., accused of war crimes at the Central Prison in Riga, Latvia; OSI filed a deportation complaint against him in 1981; (4) Hubertus Strughold of San Antonio, Tex., a world-famous physiologist and the retired chief medical scientist for the U.S. Air Force, charged with complicit knowledge of experiments on human beings at Dachau concentration camp while director of the Nazi *Luftwaffe* [Air Force] Medical Research Center in Berlin.

From 1974 on, Allen has continued to research, write, lecture and consult on the issue of Nazi war criminals living in the U.S. In 1976, he was appointed to the board of contributing editors of *The Churchman,* the nation's oldest religious magazine, and he regularly contributes to such periodicals as *Reform Judaism, Martyrdom and Resistance, Jewish Currents* and *The Jewish Veteran.* At the same time, he has frequently written on the subject for the Associated Press, *The New York Times,* the Hearst newspapers, *The Los Angeles Times, The Miami News,* and *Newsday.* Between these short-term projects, he has since 1977 been writing what he describes as his "book of record" on the issue.

Allen focuses on governmental use of war criminals. By massive requests for documents available through the Freedom of Information Act, research of primary sources in archives, visits to Eastern and Western Europe, and interviews with alleged Nazi war criminals, he has often proved such utilization.

For the December, 1974 issue of *Jewish Currents,* Allen wrote "Hubertus Strughold, Nazi in USA." He had received Strughold's name from an INS investigator, but in September, 1974, INS removed it from their list of suspects.

Allen wrote: ". . . there are mysterious aspects in the Strug-hold matter which go to the very heart of the beginnings of America's Cold War strategies and tactics." [1] He cited a U.S. Army translation of a Nazi document which placed Strughold at a 1942 "scientific" conference. Fatal experiments performed on concentration camp inmates were discussed there.

"The first man in space wasn't an American astronaut or a Soviet cosmonaut," Allen says. "He was a Polish-Jewish baker at Dachau." Allen refers to the high-altitude experiments which radically altered air pressure until the Nazis' human guinea pigs died terrible deaths. Because Strughold was so prominent in both Nazi Germany and in the United States, and the OSI has not yet filed against him, this case still frustrates Allen.

Allen also wrote in *Jewish Currents,* "The Strange Case of V. D. Samarin: Nazi Collaborator at Yale" (November, 1976) and "Twisted Tales and Trails: Odyssey of a Nazi Collabo-rator" (on Soobzokov, December, 1977). The March, 1978 issue carried an exchange among Allen, Soobzokov's attorney, and the ADL.

When the General Accounting Office (GAO) issued its May 15, 1978 report, "Widespread Conspiracy to Obstruct Probes of Alleged Nazi War Criminals Not Supported by Available Evidence," an "unnamed journalist" was mentioned five times. This "unnamed journalist" is Allen, who said that the CIA, FBI, Defense Department and other agencies had close ties with alleged Nazi war criminals who entered the United States after World War II. He also said that he challenged the accuracy of the number of Nazi war criminals and collaborators that U.S. intelligence agencies admitted to the GAO were "utilized" over the last thirty years.

Shortly after the GAO report was published, Allen told me, "The GAO report indicates that my series of articles, later a small book entitled *Nazi War Criminals Among Us,* first forced this issue publicly onto the State and Justice Departments in 1963. The report further shows that my evidence of at least sixteen Nazi war criminals who I said were used by agencies of the government has since been borne out. The GAO learned that the Justice and State Departments deliberately rejected

my inquiries at the time, when I asked how many Nazi war
criminals were here and what they were being used for.

"The report serves the purpose of at least having made the
agencies admit that they 'utilized' Nazi war criminals and
collaborators. How, when, and whom, they don't say, and the
reason they don't say is that the CIA, FBI and other of the
ten major U.S. intelligence agencies won't tell them."

The GAO further found in its report that the same "unnamed journalist" was then using the figure of 254 for the
number of Nazi war criminals and collaborators living in the
U.S. This was only two more than INS's admission, in the
GAO report, of knowledge of 252.

Allen was called as a witness in July for House Subcommittee
on Immigration hearings on the GAO findings. He testified
at the July 19, 1978 hearing for two hours and twenty minutes.
Although his testimony was very detailed, careful and factual,
he was forced to comply with the House's ruling that no names
be used. Vigorously objecting to this regulation, he informed
the subcommittee that he would release names of Nazi war
criminals to the press after the hearing, and did so.

Allen's analysis indicated, he testified, that 149 accused Nazi
war criminals had been employed for the last thirty-three years
by thirteen government intelligence agencies, led by the State
Department, the FBI, the CIA, the Defense Intelligence Agency,
the Office of Naval Intelligence and the National Security
Administration. His testimony before the Eilberg subcommittee coincided with massively detailed requests he had made
of the thirteen government agencies under the FOIA and the
Privacy Act. These 149 alleged Nazi war criminals, according
to Allen, were collectively responsible for the genocide of 2.4
million people, mostly Jews, between 1939 and 1945.

"When I presented these figures in the hearing room, which
was crowded with close to a hundred people, there was a
visible stir and murmurs of shock," Allen said. "The subcommittee was perceptibly curious, but taken aback because the
figures exceeded the admissions by the CIA and the State
Department by quite a bit. Afterward when ABC-TV's 'Good
Morning America,' CBS and ABC Network radio expressed
skepticism at the numbers, my response was, 'In 1963, none

of you believed that one Nazi war criminal was alive in this country, let alone working for the government.' "

In addition to individual Nazi war criminals, Allen gave testimony about what he terms "transplanted" Nazi organizations from the World War II period which, he claims, have served as vehicles for Nazi war criminals. Among these organizations are the Rumanian Iron Guard, the Lithuanian Iron Wolf, the Latvian *Daugavis Vanagi* and the Yugoslavian *Ustashi.* Allen characterized them as "essentially Fifth Columnist and assassination bureaus." He said, "There have been chapters in the U.S. since World War II responsible for acts of violence, terrorism and anti-Semitic vandalism. There is also linkage with them to the American Far Right."

There are also Nazi war criminals who never lived in the U.S. but were used by U.S. intelligence agencies, mainly the CIA, in Europe, Latin America and North Africa, according to Allen's testimony. He quoted this information from West German and British sources and said that several hundred Nazis from the Third Reich, many of them well-known, were utilized.

"I also testified that I discovered another source for leads into the Nazi war criminal question, a source that the U.S. government has completely ignored," Allen said. "I am referring to the 680 U.S. citizens who paid dues to the Nazi Party in Germany between 1924 and 1942. Lists of the names, addresses and phone numbers of these members of the N.S.D.A.P.'s [Nazi Party's] *Auslandsorganisation* [out-of-the-country organization] were discovered by U.S. troops when Nazi Germany was defeated," he explained. "I checked out these lists and a spot check of nine U.S. cities revealed that at least thirty or forty per cent of them still survive," Allen testified. "Not one U.S. agency ever bothered to check out the connections with alleged Nazi war criminals living here."

Following Allen's testimony, he appeared on various radio and television programs. Allen said that Accuracy in Media, Inc. (AIM), which he described as an extreme right-wing group, tried unsuccessfully to prevent him from appearing on the ABC-TV "Good Morning America" show.

Several months later, Allen decided the real story would be told on television only if he did the telling. With a small grant

The author and Charles R. Allen, Jr. tape their three part television series, "From Hitler to Uncle Sam: How American Intelligence Used Accused Nazi War Criminals," 1979.

made through the Greater Albany Jewish Federation, he wrote and produced with me in the spring of 1979 three half-hour videotapes entitled "From Hitler to Uncle Sam: How American Intelligence Used Accused Nazi War Criminals." Actual documents pertaining to such use appeared on the screen as I interviewed Allen about some dozen key cases. (We had met in January, 1978, when Allen was invited by Rabbi Paul Silton to speak in Albany. See Chapter 17.)

Major American Jewish organizations and public television stations were approached as potential distributors, but both the title and material were too "hot" to handle. (The tapes have since been successfully used at schools, community meetings and teacher workshops.)

Although none of the national Jewish organizations would distribute the videotapes or publicize their existence, an incident at the national headquarters in New York City of the Anti-Defamation League of B'nai B'rith (ADL) is noteworthy.

I went there September 19, 1979 to show the videotapes to ADL's program department, and stopped in at the office of Justin Finger, national civil rights director, to ask an un-related question. By coincidence, Finger had on his desk a copy of my letter to ADL's New York State director, regarding a Nazi war criminal case. Finger and I briefly discussed the case, and he called in Elliot Welles, ADL's Nazi war criminal expert. I mentioned to them that I was at ADL headquarters to show the videotapes to their program department, and handed them informational fliers.

Finger saw Allen's name on the flier, and said, "Charles Allen! What are you doing mixed up with him? He hates Israel and he represents East Germany. ADL would never use any-thing that involves him." Finger indicated he would so rec-ommend to the program department.

I responded I was "mixed up" with Allen because he was the leading expert on Nazi war criminals in America, and that Welles had also worked with him. Finger asked Welles if he had ever discussed Israel with Allen, and Welles said they spoke only about Nazis and had a very good relationship on that subject.

I then pointed out that Allen does not "hate" Israel, and that he has spoken before and written for most of the major Jewish organizations in America. Finger said, "Not for ADL." Since Allen had done undercover work and ghost-written for ADL, and had appeared on an ADL-sponsored television pro-gram, Finger was wrong.[2]

Written defamation in the January 17, 1980 Washington *Jewish Week* followed the oral defamation of Allen by this high-level official of the Anti-Defamation League. Under the pseu-donym of "Melech ben Pesach," an article entitled "Selective Nazi Hunting" used innuendos, omissions and misinformation to allege that Allen had "Communist Party connections."[3]

When I asked editor-publisher Joseph Hochstein that month how he could print such a one-sided article without checking sources or speaking with Allen, he replied, "It is my under-standing that everything in here checked out as factual as-sertion, accurate and backed up by some source that is ac-ceptable. . . . I believed at the time the story was put together that it was compiled entirely of materials in the public domain. Therefore there was nothing I was aware of that required verification."

The article was not, however, "compiled entirely of materials in the public domain." What Hochstein called "factual" are on some points inaccuracies found originally only in Allen's FBI files, supposedly protected by the Privacy Act.

An example of the *Jewish Week*'s slant: mentioning a *Washington Post* article, "Melech ben Pesach" says that Allen "reappeared" there on October 24, 1976 in "a report entitled 'The Hunters and the Hunted.'" Had the *Jewish Week* writer or editors read this syndicated article written by Stephen Klaidman and carried by at least fourteen other newspapers (total paid circulation, 12 million), they would have learned that Allen was "the first writer to probe the pasts of alleged Nazis in the U.S. in 1962."

Hochstein admitted that he had never read either this *Post* article nor articles about Allen's 1978 testimony before the House Subcommittee on Immigration (as an expert on Nazi war criminals). Hochstein did not even know Allen had been called as such a witness. Nor was he aware of a major article written by Allen on the subject of Nazi war criminals, appearing in the September-October 1979 issue of *The Jewish Veteran* (the national publication of the Jewish War Veterans of the U.S.A.).

In discussing the *Jewish Week* article, James M. Gray (see Chapter 14) said, "Even if Allen were a card-carrying Communist, it wouldn't affect his work. And from the record, he hasn't been 'selective.' This is part of the anti-Soviet hysteria that is reacting to Soviet anti-Semitism. To go to this extreme is ridiculous. McCarthyism is not what the Jewish press should be indulging in."

The sordid smears of Allen as an individual are not the important issue. The real question is: why did a Jewish newspaper and an ADL official, ostensibly on the same side as Allen in the quest for justice for Nazi war criminals, choose to denigrate the work of a man who is said to have done more than anyone else to document and expose alleged Nazi criminals living in the U.S.? If bringing these criminals to justice were of deep moral concern to the Jews of the United States, why would the *Jewish Week* and Finger besmirch one of the few non-Jews who has dedicated himself to this end?

Gray was probably accurate when he put the blame on McCarthyism. Despite Allen's expertise on Nazi war criminals, his left-wing orientation has often frightened the conservative leaders of the American Jewish "establishment." In many cases, their fear of being labeled leftist, i.e. Communist, is stronger than their commitment to justice for Nazi war criminals.

"Some Jews call me a Communist and the Communists call me a Zionist apologist, but I'm neither," Allen says. "I'll continue to investigate, expose, write and speak out against any Nazi war criminal or collaborator, whenever and however I can. I'll work with any person or any group honestly committed to eradicating these vile subversions of our American democracy."

In addition to Allen's exposure of Nazi war criminals living here, his investigations have led to some tangential discoveries. On May 5, 1980, world-famous tennis pro Vitas Gerulaitis made an anti-Semitic remark at the West Side Tennis Club in Forest Hills, N.Y. In criticizing Jewish linesman Lee Gould, Gerulaitis said to news reporters, "That guy should be put into a crematorium and burned to death."

After Allen read this in the sports pages of the May 10 *New York Times* and *New York Post,* he told the Jewish Telegraphic Agency that Gerulaitis' grandfather, Stasys Cenkus, was an alleged Nazi war criminal. Cenkus was Lithuanian chief of the secret police, collaborating with the Nazi secret police in Lithuania, Allen said. Calling Cenkus one of the five top alleged Nazi war criminals living in America today, Allen told JTA he believes New York City newspapers never exposed the Cenkus case in order to protect the profitable market of professional tennis.[4]

Another newspaper story caught Allen's eye a year later, and he again exposed a Nazi war criminal connection. Yeshiva University in New York City had announced that its June 16, 1981 corporate dinner would honor prominent industrialist J. Peter Grace. There is documentation that Grace has both personally and as an executive utilized and interceded in behalf of convicted war criminal Otto Ambros, a director of the I.G. Farben Chemical Company during World War II now living in West Germany. Ambros has been a highly-paid consultant of W.R. Grace and Company, of which Grace is the chairman.

On May 21 Allen wrote a letter to Dr. Norman Lamm, president of Yeshiva University, expressing shock at the school's announcement of the award to Grace. Calling Yeshiva a "center of learning and scholarship" and "a living symbol of the intellectual, scientific and artistic gifts which the Jewish people have brought to all peoples," Allen protested the award to Grace. He said that "evidence shows indisputably" that Ambros was given a special visitor's visa at least four times at the behest of Grace. As a result of Allen's sending the letter to Dr. Lamm and his giving the story to JTA, Yeshiva University cancelled the dinner.[5]

Allen discovered in February, 1982 that another Nazi collaborator from West Germany had been invited here by two universities. Wolfgang Boetticher of the University of Gottingen, an expert on the music of Robert Schumann, was to participate in a Mendelssohn-Schumann Conference sponsored by Duke University and the University of North Carolina at Chapel Hill. Thirty-one members of the Columbia University Music Department in New York City had protested the inclusion of this musicologist, who had assisted Nazi war criminal Alfred Rosenberg (hanged at Nuremberg) in identifying Jews in the world of music.

After Allen helped to expose Boetticher's background and impending visit, the musicologist suddenly found he was unable to attend the conference. Had he attempted to do so, Allen was prepared to seek support to pressure the State Department to bar Boetticher's entry under the provisions of the Holtzman law (see Chapter 10).

More than ten years after INS called on him to help, and more than twenty years after his initial involvement, Allen is still trying to wrap up his Nazi war criminal work and focus on fascism from a more theoretical historic-analytic viewpoint. Meanwhile, the specific topic of Nazi war criminals in America grows ever larger as additional evidence comes to light.

When former Gestapo official Klaus Barbie was expelled to France from Bolivia in February, 1983, Allen was interviewed by newspapers, wire services, and radio news commentators from around the world. He discussed with them Barbie's utilization by American intelligence, and also wrote articles

on this subject for JTA and others. His three-part series in
JTA revealed:

> [Klaus Barbie] was aided in his escape from Europe in late
> 1949 and early 1950 by the Vatican, the U.S. Army's Counter
> Intelligence Corps (CIC) and the International Red Cross.
>
> This correspondent has pieced together from various doc-
> uments, including the State Department's, Barbie's movements
> since his first utilization by the CIC in 1947 until his expulsion
> from Bolivia 36 years later.
>
> Barbie took the so-called "monastery route," an underground
> railroad, so to speak, for scores of wanted Nazi war criminals.
> The route was known to the U.S. Embassy in Rome which did
> nothing to stem the flow of wanted war criminals from Europe,
> most of them originating in the American-occupied zone of
> Germany . . . .
>
> Further confirmation of the knowing role of the Vatican in
> the escape of Barbie—as well as scores if not hundreds of
> other SS genocidists—came in a hitherto "Top Secret" 35-
> page set of State Department documents which have come into
> my possession, largely by way of my Freedom of Information
> requests over the past five years. . . .[6]

Attorney General William French Smith at first ruled out
Justice Department action on Barbie, on the grounds that no
prosecution was likely to result and that his department was
not responsible for historical inquiries. After pressure from
Congress and journalistic exposés such as Allen's, Smith reversed his decision. On March 15, 1983, the Justice Department announced it would conduct a full investigation of the
alleged Barbie-U.S. government connection, headed by Allan
A. Ryan, Jr., director of the Office of Special Investigations.

The ADL (with the exception of Welles) generally ignored
or denigrated Allen's work on Nazi war criminals over the
years, especially his allegations of U.S. government utilization.
However, ADL national director Nathan Perlmutter said in
the March, 1983 *ADL Bulletin* that justice will not be complete
in the Barbie case until U.S. officials "open wide America's
closet doors and sweep them free of the Pentagon's and/or
State Department's dirty big secrets."

An article in the Rochester *Jewish Ledger* reported:

> Abraham H. Foxman, associate national director of the ADL,
> said the League will file a request under the Freedom of
> Information Act to compel disclosure of the facts surrounding
> the case of the "Butcher of Lyons" [Barbie] who evaded French
> justice and escaped to South America in 1951. . . .
> "We want the American government to make public infor-
> mation concerning allegations that this country, after World
> War II, protected Nazi war criminals, including Barbie, with
> false identities and new names, in return for their cooperation
> in providing intelligence on Soviet activities in Europe," Fox-
> man asserted.[7]

This is the most powerful public statement ADL has ever
made on the issue of Nazi war criminals' utilization, but
commendation of it is tempered by three facts: (1) private
citizen Allen had FOIA documentation years before ADL
requested it; (2) ADL's request was "safe," in that it followed
similar Congressional calls for action; and (3) the statement
refers to a Nazi war criminal now in France, not one living
in the United States.

In a December 21, 1983 press release, the ADL went so
far as to take credit for the discovery of "a second Klaus
Barbie case." Through FOIA requests, ADL had secured from
the U.S. Army Intelligence and Security Command at Ft.
Meade, MD. documentation on Robert Jan Verbelen, a former
Belgian Nazi war criminal now living in Austria.

Allen then obtained from Ft. Mead the documents that had
been released to ADL. In a three-part JTA series in January,
1984, he analyzed the Verbelen case in depth. "A claim in
the media that the Verbelen case is the second of its kind to
be uncovered since the Barbie matter is incorrect," he wrote.
"Specific CIC protective usage of major war criminals well
before the Barbie case broke has been documented on several
occasions." He cited as examples SS Lt. Col. Otto Skorzeny
and Dr. Walter Schreiber.[8]

Allen did, however make a Barbie-Verbelen connection.
Both were in the Nazi SD (*Sicherheitsdienst,* a security-intelli-
gence unit). Allen wrote:

> Verbelen's "chief task" against the Resistance necessarily had
> to bring him into an intimate working relationship with another

up and coming SD officer who also used the same SD methods, working out of the identical SD headquarters in Brussels as did Verbelen and eventually—while hiding from war crimes trials that condemned him to death as was the case with Verbelen—worked for the same employer, the Counter Intelligence Corps (CIC) of the U.S. Army.

Verbelen's fellow SD colleague in Belgium was none other than Klaus Barbie, according to evidence from both SS and U.S. Justice Department studies of Nazi sources.[9]

He ended his three-part series:

> Verbelen's murderous Nazi past, his connection during and after the Holocaust with Barbie, his employment by the CIC and his involvement with an American "third agency" raises the crucial question: Will the U.S. Justice Department make a full disclosure of this sordid chapter?
>
> The case of Robert Jean Verbelen is just beginning.[10]

Meanwhile, at the end of January, 1984, the Barbie-Vatican connection exploded into headlines around the world. On January 26, a *New York Times* article written by Ralph Blumenthal discussed allegations of Vatican involvement in the escape of Nazi war criminals, including Barbie. As the source for his information on Barbie, Blumenthal cited a 1947 report by Foreign Service officer Vincent LaVista, which "was obtained by a historian of the Holocaust, Charles R. Allen Jr. of Manhattan, who made it available to The New York Times." [11]

"I got an inkling of what was coming, when six different television crews from all over the world traipsed into my study that day," Allen told me. But that was just the beginning. During the next eleven days, Allen was interviewed about the alleged Vatican-Nazi war criminal links by international media that included: ABC-TV, NBC-TV, CBS-TV Network news, "Good Morning America" (ABC); television news from Italy, Holland, France, Great Britain, Canada, Spain, Portugal, Denmark, and the Soviet Union; and newspapers from most of these countries, plus Australia, Hungary, the German Democratic Republic, Yugoslavia and the People's Republic of China.

Allen says he specifically asked *The New York Times* to credit JTA with breaking the story in February, 1983, but *The Times* editors chose not to do so. To set the record straight, JTA editor Murray Zuckoff printed a special "Behind the Head-lines" box in the January 27, 1984 *JTA Daily News Bulletin:*

The New York Times apparently thought it had a "scoop" today in a story on its front page headlined "Vatican Is Re-ported To Have Furnished Aid to Fleeing Nazis." The Times cited as one source for this story "a declassified State Depart-ment report" date[d] 1947 "and never officially made public."

The fact of the matter is that this report and the role of the Vatican first appeared in a series of articles written by Charles Allen, Jr. in the February 16, 17 and 18, 1983 issues of the Jewish Telegraphic Agency Daily News Bulletin and reprinted at the time in numerous American Jewish newspapers across the country. Allen obtained the report under the Free-dom of Information Act.

The report, which until it was published in the JTA was a "Top Secret" 35-page set of State Department documents, was written by Vincent La Vista, an international lawyer who in 1947 was military attache to the American Embassy in Rome and, according to Allen, "already a skilled intelligence/dip-lomatic State Department officer." The report, dated May 14, 1947, titled "Illegal Emigration Movements In and Through Italy," became known as the "La Vista Report" in American intelligence circles.

The Times in today's story fails to mention the JTA series which first disclosed the existence and the contents of the La Vista Report. For a paper that claims to be a publication of record and contends on its masthead "All the News That's Fit to Print"—albeit almost a year late in this case—this omission hardly qualified its boasts.[12]

"The issue has been blown wide open, and is by no means closed," Allen told me. He anticipated that Vatican counter-reaction would be considerable, which it was. Allen's involve-ment in 1983–84 with the Barbie case was the latest chapter in an unfolding story that seems to have no end.

Allen says of his work, "My abiding purpose as a writer is constantly to raise our craft to, if not an art form, then the highest levels of social scientific inquiry—that is, to determine the truth of these questions to which we address ourselves."

Sixteen

Investigative Journalists at Their Best

While Charles R. Allen, Jr. is the ultimate example of an investigative journalist who has stuck to the Nazi war criminal issue "beyond the call of duty," several others have become more than routinely absorbed in it at various times.

"It was a question of pursuing justice with a small and with a large 'J' that became our prime concern," Charles Nicodemus of the *Chicago Sun-Times* says of his and William Clements' journalistic efforts to expose Nazi war criminals living in the Chicago area and elsewhere. "Justice was not being done by the Justice Department," he quips.

Nicodemus is Episcopalian; Clements, Irish-Catholic. Nothing in their backgrounds links them personally to the Holocaust. They began their Nazi war criminal investigations while working for the *Chicago Daily News* (which closed March 4, 1978). Asked how they got "hooked," Nicodemus told me in a March 30, 1983 telephone interview, "Investigative reporters have a predisposition for stories where it appears there are attempts at a coverup, or failure of the government to provide a course of action, with the result that justice is denied. Regarding Nazi war criminals, we had extensive contacts with [Rep. Elizabeth] Holtzman and [Rep. Joshua] Eilberg and Charles Allen, who all believed the government hadn't acted diligently. We became interested in seeing the war criminal suspect situation understood by the people and moved by the government as it should be.

"As for our special interest, the Chicago area has the biggest Lithuanian population in this country, a substantial Ukrainian population fed by *émigrés* after World War II, and the largest Polish population outside of Warsaw. We also have a substantial Jewish population. While pursuing the stories on their merit, we were aware that no other metropolitan area has as many suspected Nazi war criminals. This gave us substantial incentive to pursue the question. We became convinced the government hadn't diligently pursued it, and tried here to generate enough heat in enough ways to get the government to give the question the attention it deserved."

Nicodemus and Clements exposed three cases on which the government later filed: Frank Walus, Feodor Fedorenko, and Liudas Kairys. They were "scooped" by the Justice Department as they were completing their journalistic investigation of John Demjanjuk of Cleveland. As of this writing, the government has not filed against Stasys Cenkus of Howard Beach, N.Y., about whom the two journalists wrote in the fall of 1977.

Nicodemus learned of the issue from Jay Bushinsky, then the *Chicago Daily News* Tel Aviv correspondent. An American who has lived in Israel since the early 1960s, Bushinsky was foreign press liaison for the Israeli government during the Eichmann trial. There he met Gershon Lengsfelder, head of the Nazi war criminal section of the Israeli police force.

In the summer of 1976, Bushinsky learned from Lengsfelder that Israel was cooperating with the U.S. Immigration and Naturalization Service on the Nazi war criminal issue. Lengsfelder had received from INS a primary list of ninety-nine suspects, and other lists of over 200 names, with a request to help firm up allegations and find eyewitnesses. Bushinsky asked about Chicago names on these lists. There were five or six on the primary list; with others, the total was seventeen. In a September story, he reported this number of Chicago area suspects.

"The national desk bucked the story to the city desk, and the city desk bucked it to me," Nicodemus recalls. "They told me to brighten up the story and to make local phone calls, such as checking with INS. This ran on the front page in October, 1976.

"The next week I went to the city desk and said there was potential for follow-through. We hadn't used any names [of the seventeen suspects]. I said, 'Why don't we get the names from Bushinsky and see if we can track any down locally? And we can see if Bushinsky can find witnesses in Israel and talk to them. Putting together this story would be a unique contribution.' "

The city editor agreed, and Lengsfelder gave Bushinsky the names of witnesses, with the proviso the newspaper use pseudonyms for both suspects and witnesses (so that INS investigations would not be hampered). Nicodemus, Clements and Bushinsky then interviewed Walus and his accusers.

Calling Walus "Fritz Wulecki," their January 8, 1977 *Daily News* story was the first in print on him.[1] That month, the government filed charges against Walus (dropped in the fall of 1980).

Nicodemus says the government sped up its own investigations of Fedorenko and Demjanjuk, after learning he and Clements were working on those cases. The *Daily News* ran the Fedorenko story on August 13, 1977.[2] On August 15 the government filed for Fedorenko's denaturalization.

While completing these stories, Nicodemus and Clements heard through Bushinsky, from a source at Yad Vashem, that an article on Kairys had appeared in the Lithuanian newspaper *Tiesa.* "Almost as a lark, we wrote to Lithuania, asking the journalist there for certified documents of those shown in his newspaper," Nicodemus says. "We said we thought we could locate Kairys in Chicago, and asked for more information. This was November, 1977. To our surprise, in February, 1978, we got the documents we requested."

When the *Daily News* shut down in March, 1978, the two reporters moved to the *Sun-Times.* The Kairys story, their last investigation of an unfiled case, ran there on October 1, 1978.[3] (The government filed against him on August 13, 1980.) They have since written on other cases, already announced by the government. Clements died in August, 1983.

Ralph Blumenthal, investigative journalist for *The New York Times,* got involved in the issue of Nazi war criminals several years earlier than his Chicago colleagues. When he met Simon Wiesenthal at a 1972 cocktail party in New York City, the Nazi hunter told him he was in America for a series of lectures, and also here "about the bishop." After Blumenthal learned more about "the bishop" (Valerian Trifa), he spoke with his editors. "They said it was a good story, and I should chase it," he told me in a March 8, 1983 interview.

"I went to Jewish organizations and their libraries, and was surprised when in general their reaction was a big collective yawn. Everyone shrugged it off. But ADL did give me access to their library and a Rumanian translator. I found there the Rumanian press article about Trifa and his picture." (See also Chapters 4 and 8.)

In November, 1973, Trifa granted Blumenthal an interview at his Grass Lake, Michigan headquarters. "I called and told him I'd like to come out and talk with him. It was early, and he wasn't concerned," Blumenthal recalls. "I took along a photographer as a witness, and I taped the interview. I was greeted by one of Trifa's assistants, and then ushered into his presence. I put on the tape recorder and pulled out documents. 'Did you make this speech? Is this you in an Iron Guard uniform? ' I asked. He admitted both, and never complained about the article or denied saying what he said.[4]

"Then I became aware of a whole range of cases," Blumenthal continues. "Charles Allen made me aware of [Dr. Hubertus] Strughold, and of his presence at a 'conference' where experiments [on humans] were discussed (see Chapter 15). I was struck by the fact that someone from the armed services was interested, and an aide from the [Senator John] Stennis [D-Miss.] office—also [Rep. Henry] Gonzales of Texas— came to Strughold's aid. I couldn't get near Strughold; the military protected him. After Trifa, that's the story I'm proudest of. The whole American space program is based on these medical experiments of the Nazis, where people were put into vacuum chambers and the air removed."[5]

Blumenthal also looked into the Laipenieks, Maikovskis, Linnas and other cases. In January, 1984 he wrote a front page story on allegations of Vatican-Nazi war criminal connections (see Chapter 15).

"For the Linnas case, I went out to Greenlawn [Long Island]," he says. " [Linnas] answered the door. He talked to me about how the Communists were out to get him, but when I asked him about war crimes, he clammed up."

Blumenthal approaches his Nazi war criminal stories professionally, and says he is not "a zealot" nor "obsessed." "As an investigative reporter, I get a thrill out of exposing what needs to be exposed," he says. But he admits that his German-Jewish background makes this more than "just a story."

"My parents are from Germany," he says. "My mother was born in Poland/Czechoslovakia and my father outside of Berlin. They came to the United States from Germany after marrying in 1929. My mother's brother and other relatives perished, and my parents brought some family over. I grew up with this going on."

Born in November, 1941, Blumenthal was a young child at the time of World War II. "I read a lot of books on it in the late forties and fifties when it was fresh news," he recalls. "I had a chilling obsession to see pictures of bodies, victims of the Holocaust. Today I can't bear to look at these pictures."

Blumenthal went to City College in New York. During his second year there, he became editor of the college newspaper and was "bitten by the journalism bug." He has been at *The New York Times* since his graduation from Columbia School of Journalism.

During his junior year of college, Blumenthal spent the summer in West Germany. "I tried to look for places my father had lived, and was interested in discovering my roots," he says. "I visited concentration camps, and was shocked that none of the bus drivers knew where Dachau was. In 1968–69, I was stationed in Bonn as a *New York Times* correspondent. When I was assigned there, my editor asked me if I had any concerns. But I have positive vibes about Germany. I grew up in a German-culture household, with German language, food and music. I still like to hear and speak German."

Like Blumenthal, Herb Jaffe, investigative journalist for *The Star-Ledger* in Newark, N.J., was introduced to the subject of Nazi war criminals through a meeting with Wiesenthal. Jaffe discussed his stories with me in a March 22, 1983 telephone

The author's children, Daniel and Esther Wolk, meet Simon Wiesenthal in Albany, N.Y., November, 1979.

interview. He said that the Nazi hunter told him in 1977, "You've got some people here in New Jersey."

"He sort of inspired me," Jaffe says. "That's how I got to Chuck Allen—Wiesenthal suggested that I call him. I had always felt warmly toward the subject as a Jew, but never thought I would enter it as a journalist. But Wiesenthal said there were some alleged Nazi war criminals here in New Jersey, and he had quite a bit on [Tscherim] Soobzokov. Soobzokov was the most accessible because he was a public official; and because of his position, it was easiest to convince the newspaper to investigate him." (See also Chapter 9.)

After many months of investigation, Jaffe wrote a series of stories, the first running on page one of the March 5, 1978 *Star-Ledger*.[6] "I spent about one and a half years on Soobzokov, and also did a series of five or six articles on other alleged Nazi war criminals," he says. "You could stay on this subject forever; maybe I didn't stay long enough. But there came a period when there was nothing happening and nowhere to

go. There were changes at INS, and nothing was materializing."

Jaffe says his sense of history is one reason for his fascination
with Nazi war criminals. "I was a history major, and I'm a
history buff," he says. "Tracing the degeneration of twentieth
century Europe bothers me. Western Europe was the cultural
bastion of civilization, and it turned 180 degrees."

He is unaware of any personal losses in the Holocaust. "I'm
sure there are relatives I didn't know about who were murdered, like any other Jew," he says. "But besides this, I've
always had a distaste for everything that showed betrayal by
our government in accepting those who were our avowed
enemies, and who committed some of the most criminal acts
of all. If I were not Jewish, I'd still feel that way about [Nazi
war criminals] reaping benefits from us, after the philosophies
they subscribed to during World War II."

Jaffe was born in New Jersey, has always lived there (except
for time in the Army), and was at the *Star-Ledger* even during
college. He enjoys relating what Soobzokov told another *Star-
Ledger* reporter: "Soobzokov told her that he has documents
that prove that I'm a member of the KGB and I was out to
get him. Can you imagine? My grandfather was kicked from
Minsk to Pinsk by the Russians for being a Jew—and now
I'm a member of the KGB! "

Frank Dougherty of the *Philadelphia Daily News,* like Jaffe,
speaks of Nazi philosophy. "The philosophy that gave us Hitler
and the Nazis and the Holocaust is not dead. We can't kill
it, but we have to confront it," he told me in an April 6,
1983 interview. "The philosophy doesn't die with the death
of the evil deed-doers. The more you get into this, the more
you hear complaints that the Nazi war criminals are so old,
that the war was over forty years ago, that they'll be dead
soon. What people don't realize is the philosophy is not dead—
it's alive today."

Dougherty came to the *Daily News* right from high school
in 1961, starting as a copy boy and attending college at night.
He became involved with the Nazi war criminal issue in June,
1975, when he saw a story in the Philadelphia *Bulletin* about
a group of women survivors. The article said they were thinking about Hermine Braunsteiner Ryan, a supervisor of guards

at Ravensbruck, and wondering what had happened to her. It went on to talk about other alleged Nazi war criminals living here. One paragraph mentioned Vladimir Osidach, and said he lived in the Logan section of Philadelphia, a blue-collar neighborhood.

"I grew up in Philadelphia and I've been a reporter here since 1963, and I have never heard of this guy," Dougherty says. "The article said he was responsible for sending 14,000 Jews to death at Belzec. I went down to the library and couldn't find any clips on him. I found his name in the phone book.

"I went to my editor. At first the editor and I were skeptical, because the paragraph on the local name appeared only in the early edition. We figured it didn't pan out or they were working on it themselves."

This was the beginning of a two-and-a-half-year investigation of Osidach by Dougherty. "We found two Israeli citizens from Rawa-Ruska [the Ukraine], whom Osidach had arrested," Dougherty says. "The feds had said they would bring Osidach to trial if there were two witnesses. Another reporter was going to Israel. He had family there, originally from Poland. His Israeli cousin went with him to talk to the witnesses. The reporter brought back statements and photographs. I think the feds didn't want to open the case because Osidach was so sick, but they had said they needed two witnesses and they would do so.

"There was quite a bit of information on him from the Soviet Union," Dougherty continues. "We had payroll records and a photo of him from the Nazi police academy in Lvov."

Dougherty checked out Osidach's Logan neighborhood. Osidach was not in his house, which was "literally a stone's throw from the most Orthodox synagogue in Philadelphia." On Halloween, Dougherty even dressed up and went "trick-or-treating" at Osidach's son's nearby house.

In November, 1977, he tracked down Osidach at the Ukrainian National Association, a 200-acre retreat in Kerhonkson, N.Y. He had documented an investigative piece on Osidach, and now confronted him at this estate in the Catskill Mountains. Osidach's wife had obtained a job there as a domestic, which provided free room and board and an isolated hideout.

"I made Osidach the last person I was going to talk to," Dougherty says. "He talked to me, but he denied everything. His wife said they hid Jews in their cellar. She screamed at me. The owner of the association was a Sullivan County deputy sheriff. He pulled his badge on me. I was in a phone booth, talking with my editor and the paper's lawyer. She was screaming and banging on the door, trying to get in. I had my foot pressed against the door so she couldn't open it. It was a wild scene—it would have been funny if it were not so serious," Dougherty recalls.

The *Philadelphia Daily News* published the Osidach story in December, 1977, with photographs.[7] After his Osidach investigation, "War criminals sort of became my beat," Dougherty says. "So I also did the investigation of the Kowalchuk brothers. And I opened up another investigation on Arnold Trucis, but he died a month after it appeared."

"It started as a story, but it affected my life and thinking, the more I got into it," Dougherty says. "We grow up hearing numbers, and after a while the enormity of it washes over you. You see figures and statistics every day that are too big to hit you. Six million Jews—it's hard to see two or three who are suffering. One of the most frightening things to me is that some of the people doing the killing were the best and brightest that Germany had.

"The Gentile world has to be made aware the Holocaust was not a Jewish thing. The Jews were only the first to get it," he continues. "But who would have been next? It's a case of biding time. A lot of *goyim* say, 'Why are you bothering, an Irish Catholic like you?' People look at this as a Nazi-Jewish thing, but we are all interdependent. What happens to one group eventually has to affect others. Things don't happen in isolation," he says.

"All of this work on Nazi war criminals came about as a result of reading a single paragraph in 1975," he emphasizes. "It ages you in a sense, philosophically. It changes your thinking about the world."

Seventeen _____

Rabbi Paul B. Silton
Impatient for Justice

Before Rabbi Paul Silton masqueraded as an *SS* officer in November, 1979 (see Chapter 2), he had already more conservatively tackled the issue of Nazi war criminals. As the situation continued unresolved, his ideas were to become more radical.

In January, 1978, Silton had brought Charles R. Allen, Jr. to Albany for the first time. The rabbi had recently discovered the presence of Nazis here, but not much more. He had never heard of Allen, but had read Howard Blum's *Wanted! The Search For Nazis in America* (see Chapter 9). Only because Blum was unavailable (and recommended someone who subsequently suggested Allen) were Silton and the rest of the Albany community introduced to the foremost expert on the subject.

As the featured speaker for a teach-in for members of the Conservative movement's Leadership Training Fellowship, Allen spent most of the weekend with high school students from Temple Israel (Silton's Albany synagogue), Montreal, New Rochelle, and the Jewish Theological Seminary High School in New York City. He was interviewed by local media, taped a television program and spoke at a Sunday breakfast open to the public.

With this positive beginning, Silton attempted to spark, through Temple Israel, a national campaign. He announced the formation of an action committee, which circulated peti-

205

tions demanding that the United States government expedite pending deportation hearings. "I urge everyone to write immediately to his congressman and to the Immigration and Naturalization Service to voice his deep concern," the rabbi said at the time. During 1978 and 1979, he believed that informing the public and government officials was the best way to fight against the presence of Nazi war criminals.

On March 27, 1978, Silton arranged for a workshop on the subject for the national convention of the Rabbinical Assembly, the organization of Conservative rabbis to which he belongs. None of the rabbis present was stirred enough to join him in making the issue a top priority.

By the summer of that year, he had become more creative in his informational methods. In August, 1978, he used the day which commemorates the destruction of the Temple in Jerusalem (Jewish date, 9th of Av) to teach his campers at Temple Israel's Camp Givah a lesson on Nazi war criminals. Silton that day led a group of twenty campers and staff in a peaceful demonstration in front of the upstate New York (Washington County) home of alleged Nazi war criminal Vilis Hazners.

Rabbi Silton told me on that day, "I chose today because it is a day of mourning for past tragedies. We have to do something about the past, not just pray about it. This is the most significant *Tisha b'Av* [9th of Av] I have ever spent, reading *Echa* and *Kinot* [the *Book of Lamentations* and prayers on a similar theme] in front of Hazners' house and marching peacefully with signs that quote from the Psalms."

Although Silton was not expecting a confrontation (except perhaps from Hazners, who did not appear), he was met by a pro-Hazners contingent. Silton's group was challenged by several local residents and one man whose car bore Vermont license plates. They carried placards reading "Go Home, Jew Gestapo," "Jews Are A Vengeful People," and "Jews Are Hypocrites and Thieves—Remember Palestinians."

Hazners' defenders, led by a man identifying himself as John Christian, said that the charges against Hazners were false and Communist-inspired. Hazners was described by them as a "good and gentle man, incapable of atrocities." Christian said he spoke for the "Christian Defense League."

Another man, identifying himself as John, said that the media had only told one side of Hazners' story. He threatened to smash television equipment if he were filmed.

Silton's experience at the Hazners residence made him more determined than ever to see justice done. In November, 1978, Simon Wiesenthal and Rep. Elizabeth Holtzman were in the Albany area (separately) for speaking engagements. Silton used these opportunities to discuss with each of them the issue of Nazi war criminals here. Fired by the encounters, he became more obsessively committed to the cause. At around the same time, he was sent by INS to Miami to search for witnesses for the Hazners hearing, another reinforcing experience.

For a February, 1979 Leadership Training Fellowship teach-in, Silton brought to Albany Dr. Charles Kremer (see Chapter 4). The next month, the rabbi hosted Holtzman for a talk during Saturday morning services.

By May of that year, he was so frustrated by the lack of concrete action on the issue that he threatened to interrupt services at the National Cathedral in Washington, D.C., the culminating event of Holocaust Week activities, coordinated by the President's Commission on the Holocaust. To prevent the threat from becoming a reality, Dr. Michael Berenbaum, then deputy director of the President's Commission on the Holocaust, assured Silton he would be invited to meetings with high echelon U.S. officials to discuss the issue of Nazi war criminals in America. After meeting with Berenbaum, Silton said he was convinced that the church service was not the proper setting for his protest.

"Berenbaum assured me that there is a new and growing involvement and concern on the part of Jewish leadership, the Justice Department and the president on the issue of Nazi war criminals in this country," Rabbi Silton told me. "I had planned to say at the National Cathedral that we can no longer sin by failing to use our power, by further patience, by theological rationalization, by hesitating, by being over-cautious, by complacency, by conducting Holocaust memorial services that do not result in action. The greatest memorial that we can build to the 11 million victims, I was going to tell the congregants, is not to be found in words, not to be found in physical monuments, but in action."

The promised meetings were arranged for May 3, and I accompanied the rabbi to Washington. He said he planned to tell government leaders that Nazi war criminals should become a major concern of the National Holocaust Commission; that a committee of attorneys, rabbis and others should be funded to attend and monitor hearings, that such a committee should have the right to pressure for special trial attorneys to prosecute Nazi war criminals; and that this committee should be authorized to find witnesses to testify, by contacting all survivor groups, synagogues and Jewish organizations in the U.S. and abroad.

"The president of the United States and his advisers should be told," Rabbi Silton said, "that there is growing concern in the Jewish community and the growing possibility of mass protest if the government does nothing about the fact that hearings are now dragged out after thirty years of suppression of the issue."

Calling the experience "both enlightening and depressing," Silton later told me he believed the day was originally "orchestrated" to assure him that the government was acting expediently to bring Nazi war criminals to justice. "Frankly, I think our day in Washington was arranged so that I would see a positive situation and go home and shut up. However, I came home with information that proves the contrary," he said.

In addition to Berenbaum, Silton and I met with two presidential aides from the Domestic Policy Staff. The rabbi described as "flimsy" their excuses for President Carter's inaction regarding the West German statute of limitations for war criminals, and as "false" some of their "glowing" reports of the improvements in the Special Litigation Unit (SLU). We also met with Martin Mendelsohn during this last week of his directorship of the SLU (see Chapter 11). He revealed information about promised SLU funds and staff not materializing, and about the decision not to continue the Hazners hearing. The one upbeat note of the day was our introduction to Jim Gray (see Chapter 14).

In August, 1979, Silton again led a *Tisha b'Av* (9th of Av) demonstration at the Hazners home. With a group of eighteen college and high school students, he prayed from the Book

Rabbi Paul Silton leads Albany students in prayer in front of home of accused Nazi war criminal Vilis Hazners, on Tisha b'Av, August, 1979. (photo by author)

of Lamentations. Original prayers linking the destruction of European Jewry by the Nazis with the destruction of the ancient Temple in Jerusalem were also chanted. "As long as Hazners is here, this will be an annual event," I heard Silton pledge.

Demonstrators used toothbrushes to scrub the pavement, re-enacting eyewitness accounts that Hazners forced Jews to do likewise in the courtyard of the Riga police station, where he was a Latvian police chief under the Nazis. They also carried placards with photos of concentration camp victims and Biblical quotations. Hazners, then seventy-four, was not at home during the protest. (A neighbor said he had left for a doctor's appointment, but family members were in the house.)

A third demonstration at Hazners' home, organized by the rabbi on November 4, 1979, was nationally televised in January, 1980 on the ABC News closeup entitled "Escape from Justice: Nazi War Criminals in America." Some fifty members of the Jewish Students Coalition-Hillel organization at State

University of New York at Albany prayed, sang and carried placards. The demonstrators also carried a coffin to symbolize the victims of the Nazis.

When Silton learned in June, 1980 that the government had lost the Hazners case, he was furious and told me, "I would not be surprised, now that the voice of reason and the pursuit of justice are not successful, if I were to hear that the issue is dealt with in less popular ways—ways that might be most embarrassing to the pseudo-liberal leadership that heads American Jewry."

The rabbi became so consumed that he even hallucinated: "I was driving, and saw a *Chassid* in a van," he told me in June, 1980. "Suddenly I saw his face on a photograph of young *Chassidim* in Poland, being taunted by the Nazis. It was almost like a religious experience—the one scene came out of looking at the man in the van. To think that only forty years ago this whole culture flourished in Europe, and now there's not even a trace."

Admitting that "this thing is eating me up alive," the rabbi said, "I keep telling myself, 'Silton, give it up; what are you accomplishing?' " But he also complained to me that he was "a slave to my job, my family, when what I really want is to work on this issue."

So Rabbi Silton continued to pursue the issue as he went about his other duties. As the area's only *mohel* (ritual circumciser), he often traveled to remote corners of upstate New York. While talking with families and guests at these rites, and on other occasions, he sometimes got leads on alleged Nazis or potential witnesses. Grasping at any straw, he tracked them down in his rather unmethodical manner. At one point, he even paid a private detective for surveillance of Hazners. The result: loss of money, and no information.

Silton remembers that he always had a strong sense of justice, even as a young child in the Dorchester section of Boston. "I used to get mad at the kids for teasing a retarded boy in the neighborhood," he told me. "And I never wanted to run past a person who was limping, because I thought that would make him feel bad."

He says he first experienced anti-Semitism at the age of ten when two boys called him and his friends "dirty Jews," then began hitting them. "I punched them back. I was taught by my parents not to tolerate anti-Semitism," he recalls.

Silton's parents told me in an October 4, 1980 interview that he always had compassion for people, especially older Jewish men from Europe. At age fourteen, he regularly visited an old family friend at home, at a Jewish home for the aged, and at the Jewish Recuperative Center in Boston. His mother adds that he "becomes emotionally involved with everything," and that "he never learned to say 'no,'" to the point that he is "being used all around."

His father, a former Boston policeman, says that he is against the rabbi's war criminal-related activities. "He's dealing with the most dangerous criminals, and sticks out like a sore thumb. Where are all of the other rabbis? " his father asks.

Although Silton has no knowledge that any of his family perished in the Holocaust, his wife's mother is a survivor. "When I sit at my in-laws' table at Passover, I'm always aware of a picture on their wall," he told me. "It's a picture of my mother-in-law's mother, father and four children. Her parents and two of the children, twins, were murdered by the Nazis. When I looked at the picture after attending the Hazners hearing in 1977, I knew there were Nazi war criminals here. I'd look at the picture and say to myself, 'if people living in this country are responsible for the death of such families, these murderers have to be brought to justice.' "

In addition to family influence, Silton says his dedication to the issue of Nazi war criminals was fostered by some of his teachers at the Jewish Theological Seminary of America, especially the late Rabbi Abraham Joshua Heschel. "Rabbi Heschel marched with the Reverend Martin Luther King, Jr. and demonstrated on behalf of Soviet Jewry," Silton recalls. "This was religion at its highest. He used to say to us that he didn't want his grandchildren to come to his grave and spit on it and say, 'What did you do? ' My children already know I did something. It's important to me that my children know that I tried." (With the birth of twins in September, 1981, his children number seven.)

So Silton continues to act and to fantasize about drastic action. He has said that he sometimes feels like a biblical prophet of Israel when he speaks the truth and few in the

Jewish community care to listen. He describes as a "horrible experience" talking with other rabbis who are not as outraged as he. "I want to break down the tablets like Moses did," he says. "But on my tablets would be written all of the community Holocaust programs and discussions that don't accomplish anything.

"I don't like to feel helpless and let time take care of the Nazi situation. I think we have to act in the short time that we have on earth," the rabbi says. Sometimes he even talks of starting "some kind of vigilante group."

In February, 1983, Rabbi Silton realized that the American Gathering of Jewish Holocaust Survivors, to be held in Washington in April, would be a perfect setting for an informational panel on government utilization of Nazi war criminals. "Who could be a more receptive audience than thousands of survivors and their children, and what could be a better location than the Capital? " he asked friends.

Through Dr. Seymour Siegel, director of the U.S. Holocaust Memorial Council (and his former teacher at the Jewish Theological Seminary), Silton approached organizers of the gathering. With a promise of Siegel's "fullest cooperation," Silton and Charles R. Allen, Jr. met in New York with Sam Bloch, a survivor and a senior vice president of the steering committee. Bloch seemed sympathetic about the concept of such a panel (to include such experts as Allen, Holtzman and Allan A. Ryan, Jr. of the OSI). He said a final decision would be reached by a committee in a few days, and that the group would contact Silton before the week was out.

When the rabbi did not hear from any member of the committee for three weeks, on March 23 he called Norbert Wollheim (also a survivor), whom Bloch said was in charge. Wollheim told him there would be a panel on war criminals in general, with Ryan or his deputy presenting the topic of Nazi war criminals in America. The Nuremberg tribunals and other related topics would also be covered.

With the telephone conversation becoming increasingly heated on both sides, Silton tried to explain to Wollheim that Ryan, as a government employee, was not free to fully discuss utilization; Allen was the expert on this fact. Wollheim kept saying that Silton wanted to be a member of the panel, and

Silton kept saying that not he, but Allen, was the expert. I listened to their discussion, which ended with both men interrupting each other, as follows:

> Wollheim: I'm not interested in describing cases. We cannot bore our people. We want to tell people to be witnesses. We are interested in bringing to their attention what they as survivors can do. I'm not interested in a political hassle, the details of press coverage—only in how our people can help bring these people to justice.
>
> Silton: You're passing up an opportunity . . .
>
> Wollheim: Rabbi, we will take that responsibility. We are interested in certain other things—a statement involving Israel, getting together for certain purposes, to thank America for giving us this opportunity.
>
> Silton: During the Holocaust people in America gathered and there was no action . . .
>
> Wollheim: The purpose of the gathering is not to get even with mistakes made in this country . . .
>
> Silton: I can't think of anything more meaningful . . .
>
> Wollheim: The gathering will have neither time, nor is it the right place . . .
>
> Silton: Why are you afraid to ruffle feathers . . .
>
> Wollheim: We are not afraid. We have a certain line we are following . . .
>
> Silton: You're missing an opportunity . . .
>
> Wollheim: We can live with that. If I meet the *Rebonu Shel Olam* [God] in *Ha-olam Ha-ba* [the world to come] and I have to justify not doing what you want, I can live with that. We will mention the problem and tell our people how they can help. We are not interested in settling accounts in Washington. It is not a political rally. If you don't understand that, I'm sorry. It's not because we're afraid. But it's the wrong place. Details on Nazi war criminals will be boring. It cannot be done. Will you take it as a fact? Sam Bloch told me he made no commitment, and I believe him. He's been my friend for thirty years . . .

Silton: Then I'll do what I have to do . . .

With that, both men slammed down their phones, each convinced he was right and righteous. Both Silton and Allen swear that Bloch did make a commitment to them. Although Silton had experienced similar rebuffs from other Jewish organizations, he was incredulous that leaders of survivor groups could be so uninterested in presenting the real story of Nazi war criminals here. But Wollheim explained accurately the purposes of the gathering: thanking America and making a statement on Israel. Silton's proposal would serve neither.[1]

The rabbi was disillusioned, but as determined as ever to see justice done. His latest project was an April, 1984 conference, entitled "Justice in Our Time." Its purpose was to create a grass roots movement of concerned citizens, especially survivors, to prevail upon the government to take immediate action to deport Nazi war criminals. The Action Network for Holocaust Survivors and Friends, a new organization created to seek justice for Nazi war criminals in America, emerged from the April 27–29 Albany conference.

Silton's ultimate fantasy is to capture and spirit to Israel for trial a Nazi war criminal living here. He has "secret" plans, which he has already discussed with far too many people. Perhaps one day circumstances will be right for him to act on his plans. Meanwhile, he continues to direct the Temple Israel education programs, perform ritual circumcisions, earn a living for his large family, and dream about personally providing justice for at least one Nazi war criminal.

Eighteen

They Too Seek Justice

John Ranz is one of the few Holocaust survivors in America who have been activists on the issue of Nazi war criminals. Ranz believes that "we honor the Holocaust martyrs through deeds, not just talk." The founder and executive secretary of The Generation After and of The Survivors of Nazi Camps and Resistance Fighters, Ranz discussed his activities with me on March 15, 1983. He is more militant than leaders of other survivor groups here, and often scorns their activities.

Ranz's "deeds" have included New York City demonstrations against the West German statute of limitations for war crimes, and organization of picket lines in front of INS offices and at the site of the Maikovskis deportation hearing. He has also campaigned against the New York Catholic archdiocese's approval of a prayer in memory of Dr. Josef Tiso (hanged for war crimes in Slovakia).

Ranz has led his groups in fighting against anti-Semitism and neo-Nazism in America. In 1982 he brought a suit for criminal assault against two members of the Columbia Tenants Union, charging they had pushed him down a flight of stairs.

Ranz says of the Columbia Tenants Union that it is an "anti-Semitic organization on the Upper West Side [of Manhattan] that parades as a tenants union. Their main activity was instigating blacks against Jews and provoking physical violence in an area where there was always racial harmony between these two groups." (The Columbia Tenants Union has been expelled from the Metropolitan Council on Housing

215

for allegedly publishing anti-Semitic and racist articles in its newspaper, *Heights and Valley News.*[1])

Ranz and The Generation After have also targeted Lyndon LaRouche for action. Calling him "a powerful neo-Nazi operating in New York City," Ranz has led demonstrations in front of LaRouche's headquarters and sponsored meetings on "the LaRouche danger" at nearly all colleges in New York City. During the 1983 Democratic primary, Ranz protested the U.S. Senate candidacy of LaRouche-backed Mel Klenetzky.

"An anti-Semite is a potential Nazi, and a potential Nazi is a potential murderer," Ranz says. The Generation After, which claims some 500 to 600 members, publishes a newsletter and sponsors informational meetings on Nazi war criminals, neo-Nazis, and related issues. Half of the members, including Ranz's son Sheldon and daughter Shirley, are children of survivors. Unlike the children of others who have dedicated themselves to the Nazi war criminal issue, Ranz's are as committed as he.

Ranz has been an activist from youth. Reared in Lodz, Poland, he trained in Bendzin for life in Palestine. When the Nazis invaded Poland, he joined a kibbutz called "The Suicide Squad" and worked with the underground. One of his activities was collecting sworn affidavits of Nazi atrocities; these were secreted in a cellar.

On August 12, 1942, the Jewish community of Bendzin was herded into the football stadium to be either "selected" for labor camps or Auschwitz gas chambers, or temporarily spared. With other members of his "Suicide Squad," Ranz wore a fake militia arm band and pushed into the "free" group as many people as he could. Posing as a kitchen helper at the orphanage at which the Auschwitz "selectees" were awaiting transportation, he continued his rescue activities for three days and nights. When the Bendzin ghetto was surrounded on August 1, 1943, Ranz was taken to Auschwitz. He was liberated from Buchenwald in 1945.

He lived first in France and in Paris found and married Nitzah, his childhood sweetheart. She had passed as a Catholic orphan and served as an underground courier in Poland. They emigrated to America and settled in the Bronx in 1951. Of sixty-six close relatives, only he survived. Following in the tradition of his father, a Lodz needle trades union organizer, Ranz became a millinery worker in the Manhattan Gem Hat Company. He studied evenings at New York University.

"Our position is that the U.S. government has insulted, cheated and ironically abused the memory of six million Jews for the last thirty-five years, by harboring and protecting Nazi war criminals," Ranz told me. "If an individual would get punished for harboring them, why not the United States? It becomes more evident with the example of [Klaus] Barbie. The president of Bolivia did in one month more than the U.S. did in thirty-five years. I sent him a letter of congratulations for his humanitarian act [of expelling Barbie to France]."

Shirley Korman of Forest Hills, N.Y. told me her Nazi war criminal work is a part of her past that she doesn't want to talk about now. But from 1973 to the late 1970s, she was deeply involved. In the summer of 1973, Korman read in the newspaper that the INS was seeking the extradition of *SS* guard supervisor Hermine Braunsteiner Ryan. The stories about Ryan's atrocities enraged Korman into action.

As the Orthodox Jewish wife of a doctor and the mother of five children, the oldest then fifteen, on the surface Korman seemed a more likely candidate for president of her synagogue sisterhood than for chasing Nazis. When journalist Stephen Klaidman asked her in 1977 why she was so wrapped up in the issue, Korman told him:

> Sometime back I resolved that, if ever a situation arose where I could be productive in the apprehension of Nazis, I would. . . . Perhaps it was the Eichmann proceedings. I was conscious of the Holocaust. I'm a rather committed Jew. While I was fortunate in not losing any of my own family, the trauma was very deeply ingrained in my consciousness.[2]

Korman and another woman went to see Vincent Schiano, INS prosecutor for the Ryan case, and offered their help (see Chapter 9). She then searched out survivors of the camps where Ryan had been, and found some who eventually became witnesses.

Before long, the attractive and vivacious Korman realized this issue was virtually endless and consuming. She became involved in research, publicity and organizing demonstrations, often talking on her two phones at once. She met with Simon Wiesenthal in Vienna to learn what she could from him. She was no longer a model wife and mother, and has said the issue drastically altered her life.

In addition to her role in finding eyewitnesses against Ryan and others, Korman circulated a petition calling attention to the presence here of Nazi war criminals. Her aim was to bolster Elizabeth Holtzman's efforts to close an immigration law loophole that protected Nazi war criminals who came here after 1952 (see Chapter 10). Korman is said to have collected over 73,000 signatures, a formidable accomplishment.

Michael Hanusiak, neither a survivor nor a Jew, approaches the issue of Nazi war criminals from another perspective. He is the editor of the pro-Soviet *The Ukrainian News*, published weekly in New York City (with a monthly English edition). Although he was born in New Haven in 1913 and never visited the Ukraine until 1969, Hanusiak grew up with strong ethnic and cultural ties to his ancestral homeland.

"My father came here with the idea of making money and going back, but World War I started and the borders were sealed," Hanusiak told me in a July 23, 1981 interview in his office. "So he settled here, but he organized Ukrainian schools and cultural groups. He said we might return, and made me learn the language. My old man would grab me by the ear and say 'go' [learn]. I always dreamed of going to the land where my family had lived."

In 1973 Hanusiak wrote a small book entitled *Lest We Forget*, about Ukrainian Nazi war criminals. After a 1975 visit to the Ukraine, he published a second edition, a book of 188 pages. Included were photographs, documents and interviews with eyewitnesses. Unlike many Soviet accounts that downplay the Jewish experience, Hanusiak's book clearly portrays it. In his foreword, he says:

> For the first time we shall have the opportunity to see some original photographs of the actual participation of the Ukrainian police together with the Nazis and the SS. This should

again stir the reader and all of the American people to demand justice and a concerted action in the further exposé of those who contributed to the criminal atrocities against the Jewish nationals and the people of the Soviet union *[sic]* during the period from 1941–1945.

One of the photographs shows how an innocent Jewish family is being led into the woods.

Another photograph, which shows signs of being crumpled, shows how the Germans and the Ukrainian police working hand in hand are leading a Jewish family to be shot.[3]

"I became interested in Nazi war criminals in America from the point of view that the Ukraine was the area where the Nazis and their collaborators committed atrocities against Jews and also Ukrainians, Byelorussians and prisoners of war," Hanusiak told me in 1981. "The position of INS is to find out if [alleged Nazi war criminals] lied on their applications. In the Ukrainian-American and Jewish-American communities, there are those who take the position that these people lied because they didn't want to go back to the Soviet Union. Their political alliances are anti-Soviet.

"Many Ukrainian *émigrés* took over leadership here, in an anti-Soviet campaign. There are four Ukrainian fraternal organizations here. When the Nazi war criminal trials came, there were committees that fought the use of Soviet documents. They should say, 'We know there were [Ukrainian] people who committed atrocities, but let's not mar the whole community.' But they don't do that—they protect them."

Hanusiak, on the contrary, has given the Justice Department names of Ukrainians who are allegedly Nazi war criminals. He publishes stories on war criminal cases in *The Ukrainian News.* "I haven't heard from the Justice Department that my lists are Soviet propaganda," he says. "They've used them and ferreted out some Nazi war criminals." (According to Charles R. Allen, Jr., in the Fedorenko case, the U.S. Supreme Court officially authenticated the same documents given to the Justice Department by Hanusiak.)

Ben Bernstein is not a survivor, nor is he aware of losing any family to the Holocaust. He was born in Philadelphia in

1912, graduated from University of Pennsylvania Law School in 1937 and lives there today as a retired attorney.

Bernstein told me on December 12, 1982 that he learned in 1977 of the presence here of Nazi war criminals. That year he read Howard Blum's *Wanted! The Search for Nazis in America,* and attended lectures by Charles R. Allen, Jr. and Holocaust historian Nora Levin.

"My curiosity was aroused," he says. "Up until then, I was as ignorant as any other American Jew, or American in general." Bernstein's interest in the Holocaust was heightened. He read *The Destruction of the European Jews* by historian Raul Hilberg, and attended Temple University Holocaust seminars coordinated by Dr. Franklin Littell, Christian theologian-Holocaust expert.

"You could almost say this was a turning point in my retirement," he says. "I had retired in 1972 and was inactive in Jewish issues until this time. With the exception of my marriage, my involvement with the presence of Nazi war criminals here has had the greatest effect on me."

Since 1977, Bernstein has followed all of the Nazi war criminal cases and has been present at many. That fall the Albany, N.Y. deportation hearing of Vilis Hazners was his first. He has also traveled (at his own expense) to the trials of Feodor Fedorenko and Bohdan Koziy (Florida), Frank Walus (Chicago), John Demjanjuk (Cleveland), Karlis Detlavs (Baltimore), and Boleslavs Maikovskis (New York). In his home town, he observed the hearings of Wolodymir Osidach and Serge and Mykola Kowalchuk. He also went to New Orleans for the Fedorenko appeal.

Although he was a medical practice trial lawyer, Bernstein says he became interested in the Nazi war criminal cases from the viewpoint of the survival of the Jewish people. "My legal sensitivity was a secondary motivation," he says. "I have deeper insight into the trials than the average non-lawyer, but I got involved because I realized this was one of the milestones in the attempt to destroy the Jewish people. Every decision a judge wrote was a piece of history. If incorrect decisions were not appealed in time, we would have the irrevocable and unimpeachable rewriting of history. Most judges don't realize they are acting in the role of historians."

As an example, Bernstein cited the Fedorenko case, which the government won on appeal (see Chapter 13). "The national Jewish organizations became alive for the first time and pressured, and the case was appealed," he says. "The success of subsequent cases depends on the Fedorenko appeal, and that case was almost dead. Unless there is intense interest, the entire subject will go down the tubes. With the exception of the Fedorenko case, the national organizations have been lethargic and hardly maintained an interest in the area. To say that the issue is not on the priority list of major American Jewish organizations sums it up."

By late 1982, Bernstein was devoting less time to Nazi war criminals and more to the treatment of Israel by the media. "You can see Holocaust background in that," he told me in December of that year. "Without the background of the Holocaust, you can't appreciate what the media are doing to Israel today."

Seymour Kaplowitz, like Bernstein, was born in America. But his wife, Brenda, is a survivor of Auschwitz. She attributes his special interest in Nazi war criminals not only to her background, but to his immigrant parents' stories of escape from Russian pogroms. (Kaplowitz's own World War II experience was as a soldier in the Pacific Theater.)

In addition to his personal links, he was "always a fighter for what was right," she told me on March 27, 1983. "Whenever he saw that something was unfair to the Jews, he wrote to the government and encouraged others to write."

Kaplowitz and others in 1977 created the American Anti-Nazi Association of Greater Miami. Selma Harris, a founding member, told me in March, 1983 that she was inspired by a lecture by Anthony DeVito to create such a group. Garnering a list of interested people, including Kaplowitz, she invited them to an organizational meeting at Temple Israel, Miami, on November 13. Kaplowitz became president, and he and Rabbi Rubin Dobin published a mimeographed newsletter on Nazi war criminals and related issues.

Kaplowitz had moved to Florida in 1973. Before that, he taught dental laboratory technology in a New York City high school. In his speaker's biography, he described himself as "a

Seymour Kaplowitz in Florida with his wife Brenda, a survivor of Auschwitz.

political activist who strongly believes in the use of political action."

"Seymour took up the cause full-time," Isadore Hanken, his successor as president told me during March, 1983. "He gave it full blast, at all hours of the day and night." Among Kaplowitz's activities were monitoring and peacefully picketing the Fedorenko hearing, pressuring for an appeal of this case, speaking before other groups, and maintaining contacts with the West German Consulate in Miami and the U.S. government. Harris describes him as "running his feet off."

In November, 1979, Kaplowitz outlined his group's work on the Fedorenko case. In April and May, 1978, they printed and distributed circulars to encourage people to attend the hearing. His organization monitored the entire two week trial, averaging ten to twenty members present every day.

"In July, 1978, a verdict was given out that said in essence that Fedorenko was innocent and could retain his citizenship," Kaplowitz wrote in his outline. Calling this decision "a terrible miscarriage of justice," Kaplowitz went into action.

"If this decision were allowed to stand, it would protect all the hundreds and thousands of Nazi war criminals who have found a haven in this land," he stated. "We immediately approached some major [Jewish] organizations in this area, asking them to join with us in fighting this terrible decision." Kaplowitz's executive board was told "by people who never spent a minute in the courtroom" that there were valid reasons for Judge Norman Roettger's decision.

"Well, we decided to go it alone," Kaplowitz wrote. "We were determined to fight back. How? Firstly, by printing 5,000 appeal cards addressed to Attorney General Bell. Secondly, by sending over 125 letters with two attached *Miami Herald* editorials to selected congressmen and senators. . . . We sent out press releases. . . ." Kaplowitz said his organization also worked with Charles R. Allen, Jr., Justice Department Investigator William Crane, and Congressman William Lehman's office. "We organized a campaign of letters and mailgrams to Hon. Wade H. McCree, Jr., the Solicitor General, who finally approved the government appeal of the infamous decision," he said.[4]

A meeting held May 3, 1980 was the last at which Kaplowitz presided. Minutes indicate that he discussed the group's deep involvement in the Fedorenko case, and the importance of involving non-Jews in efforts to bring Nazi war criminals to justice. Upon Kaplowitz's sudden death soon afterward at the age of 61, Hanken took over. On November 23, 1980 the group decided to disband.[5]

Selma Harris may be speaking for many who seek justice for Nazi war criminals when she says, "It makes my blood boil—the tortures that others endured, and these people get away with it." She remembers that since the 1940s she has felt a certain amount of guilt. "I was in college in a free country, and what did I do? " she asks. While a member of Kaplowitz's group, she told his wife, Brenda, "Let *us* worry about it for a while. You've been through it."

Afterword _____

By the end of this century, Nazi war criminals will be a virtually extinct species. When there are no longer either Holocaust survivors to point fingers nor Nazi war criminals at whom to point, what will a detailed and objective history of the twentieth century say to future generations?

A thorough analytical examination of the impact of the many facets of the Holocaust on America and the American Jewish community is yet to be written: the role of the Jewish organizations during and after the war (including the Nazi war criminal question); U.S. immigration policies for Nazi collaborators and refugees; the State Department's role in tracking displaced persons attempting entrance to Palestine; Vatican-connected escape routes for Nazi war criminals; whether emphasis on the creation of Israel superseded rescue efforts by the Jewish Agency and others.

The U.S. government's knowing acceptance and utilization of Nazi war criminals and collaborators in the U.S. likewise needs thorough dissection. Some day the complete story of all these facets will be told in sordid detail. The valor of the individuals crying out today for justice for Nazi war criminals will then be fully recognized.

Although the Justice Department's Office of Special Investigations is now responsible for seeking out and prosecuting Nazi war criminals, public pressure and constant vigilance are as necessary as ever.

The untimely deaths of Jim Gray, Seymour Kaplowitz, and William Clements, the loss of influential positions by Reps. Elizabeth Holtzman and Joshua Eilberg, and the changing personal circumstances of everyone who has been deeply involved all point to this fact: the formidable task of seeking justice for Nazi war criminals cannot be left to a small corps of individuals, no matter how talented nor how dedicated.

As I was completing this book, a package arrived at my door. Sent by the widow of Seymour Kaplowitz and his colleagues in the now defunct American Anti-Nazi Association of Greater Miami, the package contained his files of correspondence, notes, speeches and clippings. It smelled of mildew and was moldy around the edges.

Notes

Chapter 1

[1] Simon Wiesenthal, interviewed by the author on "Heritage and Destiny," WTEN-TV (ABC), Albany, N.Y., taped November 17, 1978.

[2] This figure is based on Freedom of Information Act requests by Charles R. Allen, Jr.

[3] Lipschis was not an American citizen, but a citizen of West Germany (which, therefore, had to accept him). He did not contest the charges against him. These factors facilitated his swift deportation.
See Rochelle Saidel-Wolk, "Nazi War Criminal Deported by the U.S. is now in West Germany," *Jewish Telegraphic Agency Daily News Bulletin* 61 (May 2, 1983): 1 (hereafter cited as *JTA*).

[4] Rochelle Saidel-Wolk, "U.S. Official Says it Takes 8 Years to Complete Case Against Alleged Nazi War Criminal Who Is Citizen," *JTA* 58 (June 3, 1980): 4.

[5] Mike Wallace, "Nazi Connection" on "60 Minutes," CBS-TV, transcript of Vol. XIV, No. 33, final cut, May 16, 1982.

[6] Portions of Chapter 1 are based on Charles R. Allen, Jr. and Rochelle Saidel-Wolk, *Nazi War Criminals in America: Facts . . . Action*, (Albany, Charles R. Allen, Jr. Productions Inc., 1981) 1–5.

Chapter 2

[1] Immigration and Naturalization Service Show-Cause Order, file No. A10 305 336, Buffalo, N.Y., January 27, 1977.

[2] Avotins, Evian, Dzirkalis and Petersons, *Daugavas Vanagi: Where Are They?* (Latvia: 1963); Aklans and Siliabriedis, *Political Refugees Unmasked* (Latvia: 1965).

[3] Gertrude Schneider, *Journey Into Terror: Story of the Riga Ghetto* (New York: Ark House, 1980).

Chapter 3

[1] Milton Friedman, "The Nazis Come In," *The Nation* 174 (March 1, 1952): 200–201.

[2] "ADL Asks United States to Deport Nazi Slovak Collaborator," *JTA* 27 (June 23, 1960): 3.

[3] "Moscow Charges Two Americans with Aiding Nazis to Kill Jews," *JTA* 30 (December 11, 1963): 3.

[4] "Relationship Between Jewish Agency and J.T.A. Explained to Fulbright," *JTA* 30 (August 2, 1963): 4–5.

[5] Morris U. Schappes, "Issues and Events," *Jewish Currents* 16 (September, 1962): 34.

Chapter 4

[1] In addition to the awards to Wiesenthal and Dr. Kremer, secondary "Z'Chor" ("Remember") awards were presented to a group of individuals, mostly journalists, who had purportedly been active in seeking justice for Nazi war criminals in America. Several of the journalists who had been most deeply involved in the issue declined the award and refused to attend: author-journalist Charles R. Allen, Jr.; Ralph Blumenthal of *The New York Times;* Herb Jaffe of the Newark *Star-Ledger;* and Murray Zuckoff, editor of *JTA.* David Horowitz, then president of the United Nations Correspondents Association, was out of town and was surprised that his award was later sent to him.

A letter written to Dr. Kremer by Allen, and approved by the others who "boycotted" the event, sums up their objections to the dinner: "I do not engage in self-congratulatory benefits. If your group requires public support for its funding, that's one matter; to have your group do so by presenting awards to itself (via you) is quite another. . . .

"More importantly, the broader scope of the issue of Nazi war criminals and collaborators among us poses certain moral imperatives whose injunctions, in my view, must be taken seriously. They preclude, I feel, in general, anyone who was not a victim, a survivor, Fighter or Resistant of the Holocaust from gratuitous or patently self-aggrandizing 'honors'. . . ."

[2] Leigh White, "2,000 Jews Slain in Rumanian Terror; Eyewitness Tells Brutalities," *JTA* 8 (January 30, 1941): 1–2.

[3] Leigh White, "Several Hundred Christians Slain Trying to Defend Jews in Bucharest Pogrom," *JTA* 8 (January 31, 1941): 1–3.

[4] Hiley H. Ward, "Bishop Admits Past Pro-Fascist Ties," *The Detroit Free Press* (August 27, 1972): 1.

[5] Rochelle Saidel-Wolk, "Trifa Gets Time on Radio Free Europe," *JTA* 57 (May 8, 1979): 3.

[6] Joseph Polakoff, "Cooperation of Rumania in Trial of Trifa Questioned," *JTA* 57 (June 19, 1979): 4.

[7] Alan Hitsky, "Trifa Surrenders His Citizenship Papers to U.S. Officials; Action Halts Denaturalization Proceedings, Deportation Proceedings to Start," *JTA* 58 (August 27, 1980): 1.

[8] Robert Pear, "Bishop Accused in Death of Jews Relinquishes His U.S. Citizenship," *The New York Times* (August 27, 1980): 12.

⁹ Knowledgeable sources in Israel told me that Zamir would have broken protocol and discussed the case outside of his office if the Israeli government had wanted to accept Trifa. Speculations as to Israel's reluctance to do so included: setting a precedent to accept all future war criminals deported from the U.S.; the possibility of being unable to gather enough evidence to prove Trifa (or another war criminal) guilty; the expense and time involved for each trial; the psychological burden of the trial on survivors; and the moral issue of the possibility of invoking the death penalty.

A 1950 law enables Israel to prosecute Nazis for crimes against the Jewish people and humanity; it was applied only for the 1960 Eichmann trial. In reaction to the U.S. request to take Trifa, Gideon Hausner, prosecutor of Eichmann, said, "There can be no other response to the U.S. but to accept all Nazi criminals at all risks." Moshe Nissim, Israel's justice minister, said on May 31, 1983 that Israel had a historical obligation to bring every Nazi war criminal to justice, preferably in Israel.

See also Roberta Fahn Reisman, "Legal Experts Say Trial of Trifa Will Have Far-Reaching Consequences," *Buffalo Jewish Review*, (July 1, 1983): 1.

¹⁰ Dr. Charles Kremer, "No Punishment Fit For Trifa's Crimes," *The Jewish Press*, (August 26, 1983): 51. At this writing, Israel has made no final decision on the Trifa matter.

¹¹ Dr. Charles Kremer, interviewed by the author on "Heritage and Destiny," WTEN-TV (ABC), Albany, N.Y., taped February 24, 1979.

Chapter 5

¹ Charles R. Allen, Jr., *Nazi War Criminals Among Us*, (New York: *Jewish Currents*, 1963), 19–22.
² Ibid., 23.
³ Ibid., 14.
⁴ Ibid., 25–26.
⁵ Ibid., 18.
⁶ Ibid., 19–21.
⁷ Ibid., 19.
⁸ Ibid., 14.
⁹ Ibid., 17.
¹⁰ Ibid., 18.
¹¹ Ibid., 41.

Chapter 6

¹ "The Cry for Justice, An Editorial," in Charles R. Allen, Jr., *Nazi War Criminals Among Us* (New York: *Jewish Currents*, 1963), 41.
² All FOIA and Privacy Act documents cited in this chapter were obtained by Charles R. Allen, Jr., who made them available to the author. CIA

settlement to Allen is Stipulation of Settlement, Civil Action No. CV–81–2606 (Allen, Plaintiff against the U.S.A. and the CIA, Defendants).

Chapter 8

[1] Photo caption, *United Israel Bulletin* 28 (July, 1971): 1.

[2] David Horowitz, "Survivor of 1941 Pogrom Recounts Iron Guard Viorel Trifa's Murderous Assaults," *United Israel Bulletin* 29 (February, 1972): 1.

[3] Wolf Pasmanik, "Bulletin Exposés Led to the Reactivization of Case Against Pogromist Trifa," *United Israel Bulletin* 31 (Summer, 1974): 1.

[4] United States District Court, Southern District New York, Ferenc Koreh, Plaintiff, against Dean Milhovan, David Horowitz, Defendants, 77 Civ. 2613, (New York, N.Y.: September 21, 1979), pp. 3–4.

[5] Ibid., 5.

[6] Horowitz, *Thirty-three Candles* (New York, N.Y.: World Union Press, 1949), 154.

[7] Ibid., 350–351.

[8] Ibid., 501.

[9] Ibid., 96.

[10] Ibid., 432.

Chapter 9

[1] Howard Blum, *Wanted! The Search for Nazis in America* (New York: Quadrangle/The New York Times Book Co., 1977), 15.

[2] Ibid., 25.

[3] Ibid., 254.

[4] Ibid., 248.

[5] Ibid., 146.

[6] *The Congressional Record*, October 5, 1962, pp. 21483–21486, quoted in Charles R. Allen, Jr., *Nazi War Criminals Among Us* (New York: *Jewish Currents*, 1963), 23–26.

[7] U.S. Congress. House. Committee on the Judiciary. Subcommittee on Immigration, Citizenship, and International Law. *Alleged Nazi War Criminals: Hearings. Ninety-Fifth Congress, Second Session.* July 19, 20, 21, 1978. Part 2, Serial 39 (Washington, D.C.: U.S. Government Printing Office, 1979), 138.

[8] Ibid., 74.

[9] Ibid., 70.

[10] Ibid., 142.

[11] Ibid., 142–143. The memorandum, from Carl G. Burrows, assistant commissioner for investigations, to the New York regional INS office (dated September 30, 1971) stated, in part: "However, in view of the periodic and highly vocal interest in this case, it is requested the New York office review the evidence at hand and furnish a memorandum through your office setting forth what evidence is available to support any deportation

charge, and the manner in which such evidence might be used if deportation proceedings were authorized.

"Your comments on the recommendation of the District Director, New York, including whether the case should be assigned top priority, would be appreciated. Please ensure that no order to show cause is issued in this case prior to review by this office of the sufficiency of the evidence proposed to be used, and whether as a matter of policy a further attempt should be made to punish subject by deportation for the amassed offenses of which she was convicted in Europe."

[12] Ibid., 135.

[13] Blum, *Wanted!*, 18.

[14] Ibid., 81.

[15] U.S. Congress, *Alleged Nazi War Criminals: Hearings*, 136.

[16] Blum, *Wanted!*, 19–23.

[17] The list in question, entitled "Persons Now Living in the United States, [who] Allegedly Have Committed Crimes Against Humanity," is on file at the World Jewish Congress office in New York. Dated June, 1965 and marked "Not for Publication—Tentative List," it was compiled by Dr. Karbach and other WJC researchers. Sources given for the fifty-nine names listed are: *The Day-Morning Journal* (New York), *Folks-Sztyme* (Warsaw), *Forward* (New York), *Morning Freiheit* (New York), *Vochenblatt* (Toronto), *What Price Silence?* (second edition) by Chaim Suller (New York: 1964), and Jonah Rodinov of Riga, Latvia. I have seen the list, and the name Tscherim Soobzokov does NOT appear on it. (See Chapter 13.) Conspicuously absent from the sources was Charles R. Allen, Jr.'s *Nazi War Criminals Among Us*, which *The Day-Morning Journal*, *Folks-Sztyme*, and Chaim Suller, editor of *The Freiheit* and author of *What Price Silence?* openly acknowledged as their source.

Soobzokov's state and federal libel cases against Blum *et al.* were settled "to the satisfaction of all parties" by a sealed court order signed by U.S. District Judge Gerard Goettel (Southern Dist., N.Y.) on June 14, 1983, according to defense attorney Eugene Scheiman.

[18] U.S. Congress, *Alleged Nazi War Criminals: Hearings*, 69.

Chapter 10

[1] Rep. Elizabeth Holtzman, interviewed by the author on "Heritage and Destiny," WTEN-TV (ABC), Albany, N.Y., taped November 29, 1978.

[2] "Rep. Holtzman Attacks Immigration Service for Inaction on Nazi War Criminals," press release from office of Holtzman, Washington, D.C., dated April 3, 1974, 1.

[3] Memorandum from Rep. Holtzman to Leonard F. Chapman, Jr., INS commissioner, dated May 20, 1974: "INS has failed to contact directly the governments of the countries in which the various subjects are alleged to have committed war crimes to determine if there are outstanding warrants of arrest, requests for extradition, or documentary information

relating to any of the subjects. Nor is there any indication of attempts to find out if the West German government is interested in requesting the extradition of any subjects on the list. Almost all of the subjects are alleged to have committed crimes in areas which were under the administration of the German government. They are, thus, subject to extradition under our treaty with West Germany.

"There is no indication that INS has directly contacted any government or document sources in Israel, including: Yad Vashem; Archives of the Jewish Ghetto Fighters (Antok Zukerman); Mr. Lengsfelder, Head of Special Investigations Department for Nazi Crimes, Tel Aviv; Schaul Rosalio, Police Headquarters, Jerusalem; and Tuvya Friedman, Haifa Documentation Center.

"A few of these sources are being contacted unofficially through private U.S. citizens. This would not seem to be an adequate substitute for direct INS inquiries—especially because more than 10,000 Jews have immigrated to Israel from the Soviet Union in recent years. Some of these immigrants may have first-hand information, previously unavailable, about some of the individuals on the list.

"There is no indication from the status reports that INS has attempted to get in touch with the District Attorneys' offices in Stuttgart, Hamburg, Dortmund and Cologne, who have materials concerning war crimes committed in Byelorussia, Latvia, Southern Europe, and all concentration camps, respectively.

"Finally, there is no indication that INS has utilized the research facilities and sources of the YIVO Institute [Yidisher Visenshaftlikher Institut—Institute for Jewish Research], New York, or the numerous documents contained in the National Archives, including: International Military Tribunal, *Trial of the Major War Criminals* (Nuremberg, 1947–49), 42 volumes; Office of United States Counsel for Prosecution of Axis Criminality, *Nazi Conspiracy and Aggression* (Washington, D.C., 1946–48), 8 volumes & 2 supp.; Nuremberg Military Tribunals, *Trials of War Criminals* (Washington, D.C., 1947–49), 15 volumes; original documents in the Federal Records Center, Alexandria, Virginia; the Himmler files in the Manuscript Division of the Library of Congress; documents prepared by the United Nations War Crimes Commission."

[4] "Statement by Rep. Elizabeth Holtzman (D.-N.Y.) on Nazi War Criminal Investigation," press release from office of Holtzman, Washington, D.C., dated June 11, 1974, 1.

[5] Letter from Rep. Holtzman to Chapman, dated June 10, 1974, Washington, D.C., 7–8.

[6] "Nazi War Criminals, Chronology of Activities of the Subcommittee on Immigration, Citizenship, and International Law," (undated, with last entry May, 1982), Washington, D.C., 1.

[7] Letter from Rep. Holtzman to Secretary of State Henry Kissinger, dated May 20, 1975, Washington, D.C., which states: "I am writing to express my concern over the Department of State's continuing failure to

cooperate with the Immigration and Naturalization Service in its efforts to investigate alleged Nazi war criminals residing in the United States.

"I presume you are aware that the INS has been investigating allegations against several individuals—both citizens and residents of the United States—concerning participation in Nazi atrocities during World War II. A number of these persons are alleged to have committed atrocities in the U.S.S.R. or Eastern Europe. Accordingly, evidence against these persons—including eyewitness testimony—may be presently located there.

"Between January and August of 1974, the INS requested, on at least six separate occasions, that the State Department contact the Soviet Union and other foreign governments to obtain any eyewitness testimony or documents with respect to particular cases of alleged atrocities. In addition, Chairman Eilberg of the House Immigration Subcommittee made several similar requests during this period, two of which were addressed to you.

"It is my understanding that the State Department has still taken no action on these requests: as of last month, the INS had given the Department 'dossiers' on several alleged war criminals for 'presentation' to West Germany. I am informed that this presentation is 'preliminary' to contacting Eastern European governments. Sixteen months have elapsed since the INS made its first request of the State Department for contact with Eastern European governments. How much more time will it take to move this matter beyond the preliminary stage?

"I am at a loss to understand the State Department's reluctance to act in this matter. Surely the fear that witnesses who reside in Communist countries will give the Department biased statements or propaganda is not a valid reason. INS investigators are capable of evaluating the credibility of whatever material is obtained. Further, the use of any such materials would be limited by the 'due process' clause of the Constitution.

"We ought not to lose sight of the possibility that these materials, whatever the ultimate use to which they may be put, may contain important leads such as the names of witnesses located in Western European countries, Israel, or the United States. It is my understanding that West Germany—which certainly has a strong interest in protecting its nationals from baseless claims—avails itself of witnesses and documentary evidence from Eastern Europe and the U.S.S.R. in prosecuting alleged Nazi war criminals.

"In view of the foregoing, the State Department's failure to respond to the INS requests is utterly incomprehensible. In fact, the practice of contacting foreign governments only through the State Department has become a prescription for inaction. . . ."

[8] For a summary of the meeting, see: U.S. Congress. House. Committee on the Judiciary. Special Study Subcommittee. *Emigration of Soviet Jews: Report on its Trip to the Soviet Union, May 24–June 1, 1975, Ninety-Fourth Congress* (Washington, D.C.: U.S. Government Printing Office, May, 1976), 37.

[9] Letter from Holtzman to Kissinger, dated August 25, 1975, Washington, D.C.

[10] U.S. Congress. House. Committee on the Judiciary. Subcommittee on Immigration, Citizenship, and International Law. *Review of Immigration Problems: Hearings. Ninety-Fourth Congress, June 11, 12; December 10, 1975; and July 28, 1976, Serial 62* (Washington, D.C.: U.S. Government Printing Office, 1976), 62–63.

[11] "State Department to Ask Russians about Alleged Nazis," press release from office of Holtzman, dated January 30, 1976, Washington, D.C., 1–2.

[12] "Statement by Rep. Elizabeth Holtzman on Immigration Service Action Against Alleged Nazis in U.S.," press release from office of Holtzman, dated September 27, 1976.

[13] *Keeping Posted*, 26 (October, 1980): back cover. Document, photocopy of letter from CIA to Laipenieks, dated July 20, 1976, provided by Charles R. Allen, Jr. to accompany his article, "US Passport for Genocide."

[14] Letter from Holtzman and Eilberg to Chapman, attached to press release from office of Holtzman dated October 15, 1976, Washington, D.C.

[15] Letter from Chapman to Holtzman (undated), says, in part: "A careful review of all case files and records relating to the investigation by this Service of alleged Nazi war criminals revealed no evidence that there has been any request, written or oral, other than the aforementioned record checks, or any intervention of any kind by or in behalf of, any agency, Government or otherwise . . . . the only expression of interest by a Government agency was limited to the CIA request for a status report in the Leipenieks *[sic]* case."

[16] "Rep. Holtzman Charges INS Evasion on Government Role in Nazi Cases, Asks Congressional Investigation," press release from office of Holtzman, dated February 7, 1977, Washington, D.C., 2. Holtzman's February 7 letter, attached to the press release, said in part: "Your letter speaks of 'routine record checks' with 'several Government agencies' on each case, but does not elaborate any further on these checks. What agencies were involved? What did these record checks disclose? Did they reveal, for example, whether persons under investigation were employed or assisted by any of these agencies? I would note, in this connection, that it has been reported that the FBI testified in the Artukovic case. Is this true? If so, at whose request did the FBI testify and why did you not mention the matter in your letter? . . .

"Any failure by INS to respond candidly and completely on these matters can only continue to give credence to those who have accused the Service of covering up the full story of its Nazi war criminal investigations."

[17] "Rep. Holtzman Announces Immigration Service Task Force on Nazis," press release from office of Holtzman, dated July 26, 1977, Washington, D.C.

[18] "Nazi War Criminals, Chronology of Activities of Subcommittee on Immigration," (undated), 3.

[19] Comptroller General of the United States. *Report on Widespread Conspiracy to Obstruct Probes of Alleged Nazi War Criminals Not Supported by*

Available Evidence—Controversy May Continue (Washington, D.C.: U.S. General Accounting Office, May 15, 1978).

[20] "Rep. Holtzman Responds to GAO Report on Nazis in America," press release from office of Holtzman, dated May 17, 1978, Washington, D.C.

[21] Rep. Elizabeth Holtzman, interviewed by the author on "Heritage and Destiny," WTEN-TV (ABC), Albany, N.Y., taped November 29, 1978.

[22] "Holtzman Bill Authorizing Deportation of Nazi War Criminals Becomes Law," press release from office of Holtzman, dated November 2, 1978, Washington, D.C.

[23] "Justice Department Concessions on Nazi War Criminals Investigation Fail to Satisfy Holtzman," press release from office of Holtzman, dated March 15, 1979, Washington, D.C.

[24] John Corry, "The All-Star Race," *The New York Times Magazine* 129 (June 22, 1980): 18.

[25] *See also* Elizabeth Holtzman, "Examine U.S. Aid to Nazi Criminals," *The New York Times* (April 23, 1983): 23; Holtzman, interview by Walter Ruby, "U.S. Jews Have Right to Dissent from Israeli Policy," *Long Island Jewish World* (August 12, 1983); Holtzman, interview by Yaakov Rodan, "Liz: 'No Holds-Barred' Probe of U.S.-Nazi Ties," *The Jewish Press*, August 26, 1983, 42; "Ask Your Representative," hosted by Holtzman, WMCA Radio, New York, September 25, 1983.

Chapter 11

[1] Fredric U. Dicker, "Deportation Cases Bungled," Albany *Times-Union* (November 4, 1977): 1.

[2] Dicker, "Extradite Hazners, Bonn Asked," Albany *Times-Union* (March 9, 1978): 1.

[3] Charles R. Allen, Jr., "Nazi War Criminals in the United States," *The Jewish Veteran* 34 (September-October, 1979): 12.

[4] Rochelle Saidel-Wolk, "Nazi Hunter Being Replaced," *JTA* 58 (January 7, 1980): 4.

[5] Ibid.

[6] George Weinstein, Commander, Department of New York Jewish War Veterans, letter to Attorney General Benjamin Civiletti (January 25, 1980). Files of author.

[7] "Why Was Mendelsohn Removed?" *Jewish Journal* 10 (January 11, 1980): 14.

[8] Jack Anderson, "Nazi Hunter Victim of Infighting," *The Washington Post* (January 9, 1980): B15.

[9] Wolf Blitzer, "Israel is Key in U.S. Nazi Hunt," *Jewish Journal* 10 (January 11, 1980): 8, reprinted from *The Jerusalem Post.*

[10] Joseph Polakoff, "U.S. Nazi Hunter Gets New Post," *JTA* 58 (August 13, 1980): 4.

[11] Allan A. Ryan, Jr., "The Search for Nazi War Criminals: Why Now? ", Text of remarks at ADL First Amendment Freedoms Award event, Indianapolis, Ind. (April 1, 1981): 8–9, 13, 14, 15.

[12] Ryan, interviewed by Herbert Kaplow on "Unprosecuted and Unpunished? War Criminals in the U.S.," Directions, ABC News, (ABC-TV), New York, April 18, 1982.

[13] Allen, "Special Analysis Report on Barbie: How Complete Is It? ", JTA 61 (August 24, 1983): 1.

[14] Ryan, "Forty Years and Four Years: The Prosecution of Nazi War Criminals in America," Text of remarks to ADL, Washington, D.C. (June 12, 1983): 11–12.

Chapter 12

[1] "Report of the Conference of Presidents of Major American Jewish Organizations" for year ending March 31, 1978 (New York).

The thirty-seven constituent members of the Conference of Presidents of Major American Jewish Organizations are:

American Israel Public Affairs Committee
American Jewish Congress
American Mizrachi Women
American Zionist Federation
Anti-Defamation League of B'nai B'rith
ARZA-Association of Reform Zionists of America
B'nai B'rith
B'nai B'rith Women
Bnai Zion
Central Conference of American Rabbis
Emunah Women of America
Hadassah
Herut Zionists of America
Jewish Labor Committee
Jewish National Fund
Jewish Reconstructionist Foundation
Jewish War Veterans of the U.S.A.
Labor Zionist Alliance
Mizrachi-Hapoel Hamizrachi
National Committee for Labor Israel, Inc.

National Council of Jewish Women
National Council of Young Israel
National Federation of Temple Sisterhoods
National Jewish Community Relations Advisory Council
National Jewish Welfare Board
North American Jewish Youth Council
Pioneer Women
Rabbinical Assembly
Rabbinical Council of America
Union of American Hebrew Congregations
Union of Orthodox Jewish Congregations of America
United Synagogue of America
Women's American ORT
Women's League for Conservative Judaism
Workmen's Circle
World Zionist Organization-American Section, Inc.
Zionist Organization of America

The Council of Jewish Federations has observer status.

[2] Joint Program Plan, National Jewish Community Relations Advisory Council, 1979–1980, 30 (Hereafter cited as NJCRAC).

[3] Nora Levin, "Tolerating the Nazis Among Us," *Sh'ma* 9 (December 8, 1978): 17.

[4] Sergei Kowalchuk's denaturalization trial was held in Philadelphia on October 19–28 and December 11, 1981. Post-trial arguments were heard on January 18, 1982. On July 1 1983, he was ordered denaturalized. As of this writing, the case is on appeal. On March 17, 1981 the U.S. District Court for Eastern Pennsylvania ordered that the citizenship of Woladimir Osidach be revoked. The defendant filed a notice of appeal, but died on May 26, 1981 before the appeal was heard. The appeal was then dismissed on grounds of mootness, July 21, 1981. Citing the death of the key witness, OSI moved to dismiss the complaint against Mykola Kowalchuk, June 5, 1981.

[5] Joint Program Plan, NJCRAC, 1980–1981: 30.

[6] Joint Program Plan, NJCRAC, 1979–1980: 30.

[7] Joint Program Plan, NJCRAC, 1981–1982: 19.

[8] Joint Program Plan, NJCRAC, 1982–1983: 49.

[9] Abraham J. Bayer, "Escape from Justice: Nazi War Criminals in the US" symposium, moderated by Aron Hirt-Manheimer, *Reform Judaism* 9 (November 1980): 9.

Chapter 13

[1] Charges were first made in 1948, but the deportation proceeding was filed May 9, 1951.

[2] Motion for Leave to File Joint *Amicus Curiae* Brief and Joint *Amicus Curiae* Brief of the American Jewish Congress and the Anti-Defamation League of B'nai B'rith, United States Court of Appeals for the Fifth Circuit, Docket No. 78–2879, New York, N.Y., December 4, 1978.

[3] "Decision on Fedorenko Hailed," *JTA* 59 (January 23, 1981): 2.

[4] David Geller, "As One Nazi War-Crime Suspect's U.S. Trial Approaches," letter to the editor, *The New York Times* (October 8, 1979): 18.

[5] At this writing, the Demjanjuk and Linnas cases were unresolved.

[6] George Dugan, "Church Council Group Will Consider Charges Against Archbishop Trifa," *The New York Times* (October 22, 1976): 28.

Chapter 15

[1] Charles R. Allen, Jr., "Hubertus Strughold, Nazi in USA," *Jewish Currents* 28 (September, 1974): 6.

[2] Ben Epstein and Arnold Forster in *A Measure of Freedom* (New York: Doubleday, 1951) incorporated Allen's writing and investigation.

On January 9, 1978, Allen was interviewed on "Heritage and Destiny" (WTEN-TV, ABC, Albany, N.Y.), produced by the author for the Anti-

Defamation League of B'nai B'rith and the Greater Albany Jewish Federation.

[3] Melech ben Pesach [pseud.], "Selective Nazi Hunting," (Washington) *The Jewish Week* (January 17, 1980): 30.

[4] Rochelle Saidel-Wolk, "A Top Ex-Nazi Living in N.Y.C.," *JTA* 58 (May 30, 1980): 3.

[5] Saidel-Wolk, "Yeshiva U. Says it Cancelled Dinner Honoring U.S. Businessman Who Aided Convicted War Criminal," *JTA* 59 (June 2, 1981): 3.

[6] Allen, "Barbie's Escape from Europe Was Arranged by the Vatican, the CIC and the International Red Cross," *JTA* 61 (February 16, 1983): 1.

[7] "ADL Wants U.S.-Barbie Probe," (Rochester, N.Y.) *The Jewish Ledger* (March 17, 1983): 7.

[8] Allen, "The Verbelen Case" (Part One of a Three Part Series), *JTA* 62 (January 24, 1984): 1.

[9] Allen, "The Verbelen Case" (Part Two of a Three Part Series), *JTA* 62 (January 25, 1984): 1.

[10] Allen, "The Verbelen Case" (Part Three of a Three Part Series), *JTA* 62 (January 26, 1984): 1.

[11] Ralph Blumenthal, "Vatican Is Reported To Have Furnished Aid to Fleeing Nazis," *The New York Times* 133 (January 26, 1984): 1.

[12] Murray Zuckoff (not bylined), "Behind the Headlines, The New York Times—A Year Late," *JTA* 62 (January 27, 1984): 2.

Chapter 16

[1] Charles Nicodemus, "Nazi Jew Killer Living on SW Side? ", *Chicago Daily News* (January 8, 1977): 3.

[2] Charles Nicodemus, William Clements and Jay Bushinsky, "Nazi Death Suspect in Miami," *Chicago Daily News* (August 13, 1977): 1.

[3] Charles Nicodemus and William Clements, "Nazi Guard Traced to Chicago," *Chicago Sun-Times* (October 1, 1978): 8.

[4] Ralph Blumenthal, "Bishop Under Inquiry on Atrocity Link," *The New York Times* (December 26, 1973): 1.

[5] Blumenthal, "Drive on Nazi Suspects a Year Later: No Legal Steps Have Been Taken," *The New York Times* (November 23, 1974): 48.

[6] Herb Jaffe, "Jerseyan in Nazi Collaborator Probe," *The Star-Ledger* (March 5, 1978): 1.

Other Jaffe articles on Soobzokov in *The Star-Ledger* on March 6, 8, 12 and April 9, 10, 11, 12, 13, 1978.

[7] Frank Dougherty, "Nazi Crime Suspects Find Home in U.S.," *Philadelphia Daily News* (December 8, 1977): 3.

Chapter 17

[1] A panel entitled "Nazi War Crimes and Punishment" was presented at the American Gathering on April 12, 1983. Participants were: Neal Sher, acting director of OSI; Benjamin Ferencz, prosecutor, Nuremberg trials; Professor Henry Friedlander, Brooklyn College; Elizabeth Holtzman; French Nazi hunter Serge Klarsfeld; and Abraham J. Bayer, who heads the Nazi war criminal effort of the National Jewish Community Relations Advisory Council (see Chapter 12). Norbert Wollheim was chairman.

Chapter 18

[1] Guy Hawtin, "5 Tenant Activists Sued Over Fraud and Anti-Semitism," *New York Post* (December 10, 1982, Wall Street Extra): 20.

[2] Stephen Klaidman, "The Nazi Hunters," *Present Tense* 4 (Winter 1977): 22.

[3] Michael Hanusiak, *Lest We Forget* (New York: Commercial Printers, 1975): 2.

[4] Seymour Kaplowitz, typed notes for speech given by him November 19, 1979 to a Florida Hadassah chapter; given to the author by Brenda Kaplowitz, Selma Harris and Seymour Hanken.

[5] In 1982, Rabbi Rubin Dobin began publishing a newsletter for the Miami Beach-based American Anti-Nazi Association, of which he is chairman.

According to the March/April 1983 Newsletter: "The American Anti-Nazi Association is a national ad-hoc organization that is dedicated to informing the public about the ever-present dangers of neo-Nazism and the spread of Hitlerite hate propaganda anywhere in the world." This is not the same organization as Kaplowitz's, nor does this issue of the newsletter cover Nazi war criminals in America.

Index _____